Rape on the Public Agenda

Rape on the Public Agenda

Feminism and the Politics of Sexual Assault

Maria Bevacqua

Northeastern University Press
Boston

Northeastern University Press

Copyright 2000 Maria Bevacqua

Library of Congress Cataloging-in-Publication Data
Bevacqua, Maria, 1968–
    Rape on the public agenda : feminism and the politics of sexual assault / by Maria Bevacqua.
        p. cm.
    Includes bibliographical references and index.
    ISBN 1-55553-447-3 (cloth : alk. paper)—
    ISBN 1-55553-446-5 (pbk. : alk. paper)
        1. Rape—United States. 2. Feminism—United States.
    3. Feminists—United States—Political activity. 4. Anti-rape movement—United States. I. Title.
    HV6561 .B49 2000
    364.15′32′0973—dc21   00-020542

Designed by Graciela Galup

Composed in Granjon by Coghill Composition Co., Richmond, Virginia.
Printed and bound by Edwards Brothers, Inc., Lillington, North Carolina.
The paper is EB Natural, an acid-free stock.

MANUFACTURED IN THE UNITED STATES OF AMERICA
04   03   02   01   00   5 4 3 2 1

Contents

Figures and Tables

Abbreviations

BARCC	Boston Area Rape Crisis Center
BAWAR	Bay Area Women Against Rape
CETA	Comprehensive Employment and Training Act
D.C. RCC	Washington, D.C., Rape Crisis Center
DOJ	United States Department of Justice
ERA	Equal Rights Amendment
FAAR	Feminist Alliance Against Rape
FBI	Federal Bureau of Investigation
HEW	United States Department of Health, Education, and Welfare
LEAA	Law Enforcement Assistance Administration
MWTFR	Michigan Women's Task Force on Rape
NBFO	National Black Feminist Organization
NCASA	National Coalition Against Sexual Assault
NCPCR	National Center for the Prevention and Control of Rape
NCVS	National Crime Victimization Survey
NIMH	National Institute of Mental Health
NOW	National Organization for Women
NOWRTF	National Organization for Women Rape Task Force
NYRF	New York Radical Feminists
NYWAR	New York Women Against Rape
RCC	Rape Crisis Center
TBN	Take Back the Night
UCR	*Uniform Crime Reports*
VAWA	Violence Against Women Act
VOCA	Victims of Crime Act

Acknowledgments

THIS PROJECT would not have been possible without the material and collegial assistance of several individuals and institutions. Emory University's Institute for Women's Studies and Graduate School of Arts and Sciences provided financial support and a scholarly atmosphere amenable to the advancement of women's studies and its scholars. Special thanks go to Lee Ann Lloyd and Linda Calloway of the Institute for Women's Studies. The office space provided by Woodruff Library at Emory enabled me to pursue my investigations and writing in relative peace. The Department of Women's Studies and the College of Social and Behavioral Sciences at Minnesota State University have been extremely supportive of this project. I thank Cathryn Bailey, Susan Coultrap-McQuin, Penny Herickhoff, and Carol Perkins for providing advice and assistance during the final stages of its completion. I also appreciate the research advice of Sandy Roe, John Boiney, and Jim Lynch. I am grateful to Terri Teleen of Northeastern University Press for believing in this project from the start and providing feedback, advice, and gentle nudging. John Weingartner, Ann Twombly, Jill Bahcall, and the staff of Northeastern University Press have been very supportive. I also appreciate the work of the readers who reviewed my manuscript in part and in full, including Cynthia Veldhuisen, Sharon Van Natta, Janice Hibbs, Chelsea Hibbard, Sonia Tetlow, and Liz O'Sullivan. Their helpful comments only improved the project; any errors that remain are my own.

Many thanks to the Arthur and Elizabeth Schlesinger Library on the History of Women in America, at Radcliffe College for a grant that aided me in using their vast collections, a resource that benefited my research immeasurably. A women's studies grant from the Rare Book, Manuscript, and Special Collections Library of Duke University also helped me to develop my database. Betty Furdon of the Cambridge Women's Center enriched my store of facts by opening the center's Women's Movement Archives to me and providing cheerful assistance. I also thank Marisa Figueiredo and the Redstockings Women's Liberation Archive for their help. Many thanks to Lee and Tony Pettit for their generosity.

I am pleased to express my gratitude to John Bevacqua, Liz and Tom Gualtieri-Reed, Irene Caldararo, Michele Olszewski, Julia Motherway, and Carla Rees, all of whom sheltered and nurtured me on various research excursions and proved steadfast friends over the years. Diane Bell, who was among those who helped me realize that it's good to be a feminist, and who introduced me to the field of women's studies, has been a wonderful mentor for many years. Members of my dissertation committee—Karen O'Connor, Beverly Guy-Sheftall, and Regina Werum—have imparted much wisdom and lent much assistance.

Numerous friends deserve special acknowledgment for helping me through this project with good humor. I thank Kim Springer, Maria Cimitile, Cat and Susan Tanner, Kirsten Rambo, John Drabinski, Mary Alma Durrett, the staff of DeKalb Rape Crisis Center, the North American Neighborhood Alliance, and the Sunday Brunch Club for sharing so much. Tim Haas, whose company, insight, and organizational skills helped me get through graduate school and life in general, has been a wonderful comrade and friend for many years. Tim's reading of the whole book in manuscript was also immensely valuable. Deborah Ivie helped me in more ways than I can count. Jane Kalbfleisch has been there with me through trying days and joyful ones. Colleen Valentine deserves special thanks for persevering during the most stressful period of manuscript preparation. And Shulie and SashaCat have taught by example the importance of eating, sleeping, and playing.

My heartfelt gratitude goes to Karen O'Connor for her patience, her prodding, and the immense help and encouragement she has provided me. When she agreed to become my dissertation advisor, Karen told me that her role was to serve as "a cross between your mother and Attila the Hun." Her prescience on that score is testament to her expertise and wisdom. Karen's involvement in every step of the academic process has gone far beyond the call of duty and is much appreciated.

Diodata and Anthony Bevacqua, my parents, have provided unwavering support to me in all my endeavors. Their love, steadfastness, and belief in my abilities have nourished me all my life. My brothers, John and Tony, provided support, cheer, and goodwill from long distances.

Finally, my gratitude goes out to the hundreds of feminists and activists who initiated and sustained the anti-rape movement that is the subject of this book. These pioneers dared to politicize the personal, stop blaming women for causing rape, and take active steps toward the ultimate, still unfulfilled, goal of putting an end to rape. I am amazed both at how much they have accomplished and at how little has changed. My particular gratitude goes to all of them who helped me by providing interviews, papers, and advice: Loretta Ross, Beverly Harris Elliott, Denise Snyder, Libby Bouvier, Betsy Warrior, Susan Schechter, Pat Groot, Nkenge Toure, Gloria Dialectic, Susan Brownmiller, Laurie McLaughlin, Mary Beth Carter, Kathryn Geller Myers, Debbie Levenstein, and Nikki Craft. Liz O'Sullivan, who belongs to the foregoing list, has been a most helpful giver of advice, sharer of ideas, and interviewee. This diverse movement, I firmly believe, has transformed the experience of rape in our society, has raised public consciousness about rape, and has helped lift the veil of guilt, shame, and silence that long shrouded victims of sexual assault. I thank all the activists of the future who take up this legacy and carry on the struggle.

Rape on the Public Agenda

An Introduction to Anti-Rape Politics

FEW RESEARCHERS DENY that the women's movement, particularly the second wave of feminist activism that arose in the mid-1960s, has had a significant impact on the American social and political landscape. Advances in women's reproductive freedom, more equitable workplace participation, access to credit, enhanced opportunities for education, and greater political participation have come about largely because of the mobilization of the women's movement in the second half of the twentieth century. In addition to politicizing specific issues, feminism has emerged as an ideology with serious implications for all aspects of American society. Indeed, Myra Marx Ferree and Patricia Yancey Martin (1995, 3) have observed, "The very centrality of feminism to American social and political debates . . . suggests that the women's movement has successfully called into question many taken-for-granted ideas about male dominance and institutionalized privilege based on gender." Other scholars have gone on to criticize the mainstream women's movement for failing to embrace the issues considered most pressing to poor women and women of color (e.g., hooks 1984; Davis 1991; Guy-Sheftall 1995). And it was during the mobilization of the second half of the twentieth century that the issue of rape arrived on the feminist agenda as a major problem facing women, one rooted in male dominance and reinforced by existing laws, attitudes, and behaviors.

My purpose here is to examine the history, growth, and impact of the feminist anti-rape movement, in the tradition of other movement histories that account for the development of political approaches to social issues and social problems (Ruzek 1978; Schechter 1982; Nelson 1984; Pleck 1987; Dobash and Dobash 1992). The book begins by locating the roots of rape consciousness in the women's movement, traces the development of an anti-rape ideology on the feminist agenda, describes the later advance of the rape issue onto the public agenda, and investigates the various manifestations of anti-rape politics. This study tracks the issue of rape from the earliest expressions of feminist consciousness to the rise of public consciousness, from guerrilla actions targeting individual rapists to the growth of the rape crisis center response, from legal reform to the take back the night campaign, from rousing polemic to feminist theory. From its roots in second-wave feminism, the anti-rape movement has generated an ideology, a body of literature, and a tremendous amount of organizing around the issue of sexual violence, all of which have been insufficiently documented.[1] My objective is to fill this void in women's studies scholarship, shedding light not only on the evolution of the feminist response to the rape issue, but also on the importance of this issue to the women's movement as a whole.

Several questions have guided my research, questions I attempt to answer across these chapters: How and when did feminists first articulate the experience of rape as a women's issue? What were some of the sources of this rape consciousness? Did various feminists, for example, liberal, radical, and black feminists (not mutually exclusive categories), identify the problem differently? How was the issue of rape articulated on the feminist agenda? What were posed as possible solutions to the problem—education, legal reform, separatism, or self-defense training, for example? What goals did the anti-rape activists articulate and achieve? When and how did the issue of rape move from the feminist agenda to the wider public policy agenda? What was the political context that made policy makers generally receptive to anti-rape goals? When did certain categories—date rape, wife rape, and acquaintance rape—emerge, and what difference did they make? What was the impact of the anti-rape movement on American political and social life?

The centrality of rape to women's lives—and the degree to which it can be considered a social problem—has been demonstrated in various studies of the incidence and prevalence of rape.[2] One major source of rape statistics is the Federal Bureau of Investigation's (FBI's) *Uniform Crime Reports* (*UCR*), which measure the rates of all crimes reported to the police annually. In 1997, the FBI recorded 96,122 rapes (70 per

100,000 females). Because many persons who have been raped reveal their victimization to no one, especially not to law enforcement officers, these rates are widely considered to reflect only a fraction of actual rapes perpetrated in the United States each year. As early as 1973, the FBI acknowledged that rape is "probably one of the most underreported crimes" (U.S. Department of Justice 1973, 15). Even the Department of Justice (DOJ) recognizes the limitations of its own statistics.

In an attempt to account for unreported crimes, the National Crime Victimization Survey (NCVS) of the Bureau of Justice Statistics (BJS), again under the auspices of the DOJ, polls households and individuals on their victimization experiences. The NCVS estimates that 172,400 rapes (160 per 100,000 females) took place in 1993, more than twice the *UCR* number. Despite this higher incidence, the NCVS has found rape to be a relatively rare crime, a finding inconsistent with studies conducted by other researchers. The methodology of the survey has received much criticism (Estrich 1987; Koss 1992, 1993).[3]

Setting out to rectify the discrepancy and uncover more accurate figures, other researchers have conducted studies using methods that reflect a more feminist understanding of rape than does the DOJ. In the sociologist Diana Russell's (1984) study, 22 percent of women questioned reported being the victim of an attempted or completed rape.[4] Significantly, according to her findings only 11 percent of rapists were strangers to the women they attacked, and only 10 percent of victims reported the rape. In a study initiated by *Ms.* magazine, funded by the National Institute of Mental Health (NIMH), and led by the psychologist Mary Koss, one in four college women (27 percent) reported having experienced rape or attempted rape since the age of fourteen (Koss 1988). Finally, in a study by Gail Elizabeth Wyatt (1992), 20 percent of white women and 25 percent of African American women reported to interviewers that they had been victims of rape or attempted rape in their lifetimes, approximately one-half of which were perpetrated by acquaintances or intimates.[5] Unlike the *UCR* and NCVS incidence figures mentioned above, the Russell, Koss, and Wyatt studies document rape prevalence. Their data suggest that sexual assault directly affects a significant proportion of American girls and women.

Feminists (e.g., Griffin 1971; Brownmiller 1975) have also asserted that rape is a source of fear for all women, whether as individuals they have been victimized by it or not. One study to determine the level of women's fear of rape, conducted by Margaret Gordon and Stephanie Riger, found that one-third of those questioned reported that physical harm was their most common worry, and that "rape is what they fear most" (1989, 20). Moreover, research into the likelihood of sexual aggression among "normal" college men has found that 28 percent indicated the likelihood of using force or rape in the sexual behavior (Briere and Malamuth 1983). The body of rape research, then, has established the widespread incidence and prevalence of rape and the scope of women's fear of it. The findings also give some indication that, based on men's attitudes, this fear is well founded.

In spite of the sobering statistics demonstrating the seriousness of the problem, an alarming amount of distortion and misinformation about the anti-rape movement has been circulating for quite some time. In *The Second Stage* (1981), for example, Betty Friedan opines that sexual politics, or the politicization of women's personal lives, had taken over the women's movement by 1980. In her view, feminism's concern with sexuality, and with holding men accountable for sexual violence, has diverted and sapped the movement's energy: "Obsession with rape, even offering Band-Aids to its victims, is a kind of wallowing in that victim-state, that impotent rage, that sterile polarization. Like the aping of machismo or obsessive careerism, it dissipates our own well-springs of generative power" (Friedan 1981, 257). Exactly how or why a single issue could garner so much movement attention, to the overall detriment of women, is unexplained. Because her approach reduces a rich, complex movement to a "bedroom war," and further reduces women's serious grievances about rape to so much wallowing, Friedan fails to account for the tremendous amount of activism, lobbying, and theorizing that has marked the anti-rape movement.

Among post-structuralist feminists, the degree of misinformation on the campaign against rape is more subtle and less disdainful than Friedan's. The theorist Sharon Marcus explains that feminist antirape literature, activism, and policy development on rape in the United States during the last two decades have increasingly concentrated on police procedures and legal definitions of rape. This focus can produce a sense of futility: rape itself seems to be taken for granted as an occurrence and only postrape events offer possible occasions for intervention.

... Attempts to stop rape through legal deterrence fundamentally choose to *persuade men* not to rape. (1992, 388; emphasis in original)

As an alternative, Marcus proposes that efforts at rape prevention emphasize self-defense strategies for women, which would halt the progress of individual rapes rather than simply react to completed acts. This well-intentioned account ignores the many ways that the anti-rape movement has placed preventive strategies on its agenda; for example, youth education programs and self-defense and assertiveness training for women are nearly universal among rape crisis centers. One of the goals of this book is to replace such good-faith misunderstandings as Friedan's and Marcus's with an accurate historical account.

As the mass media have given more attention to the rape issue in recent years, a backlash of sorts has developed. For example, Katie Roiphe argues that feminists have gone too far in convincing women of their victimization, creating a "rape hype" that equates a "bad night" with sexual assault. She questions rape statistics such as those reported by Russell (1984), Koss (1988), and Wyatt (1992), and relies on anecdotal evidence to dispute them: if one in four women is raped, surely she would know some of them, says Roiphe (1993, 27). To her way of thinking, college women either are brazen liars or have been hopelessly brainwashed by the anti-rape movement. Either they invent stories by reconstructing non-rape events into rapes, or they are too uninformed to know the difference between consent and nonconsent—hence the inflated numbers of women who claim to have experienced rape. Echoing Friedan, Roiphe maintains that "rape crisis feminists" are guilty of wallowing in women's victim status, an accusation echoed in similar claims by Neil Gilbert (1991), Camille Paglia

(1992), and Christina Hoff Sommers (1994).[6] Given the scope and potential impact of this backlash, I seek here to provide a thorough, complex history of the campaign against rape that corrects such misrepresentations.

Focusing on the meanings of terms used in popular discussion of sexual violence has been a valuable contribution of the anti-rape movement. In this book, I borrow Susan Estrich's (1987, 8) definition of *rape,* which itself is based on the common-law definition: "A man commits rape when he engages in intercourse . . . with a woman . . . by force or threat of force; against her will and without her consent." I consider different types of rape and sexual assault in the context of our evolving societal understanding of rape, but the concept of forced sexual activity is central, regardless of the gender of the victim and perpetrator. I use the terms *rape* and *sexual assault* interchangeably, although *rape* predominates. The phrase *anti-rape movement* refers to the wide constellation of actions, activities, activists, organizations, and writings that have focused on eliminating, attenuating, preventing, or responding to rape. The phrase *rape consciousness* denotes an understanding of rape as an issue affecting and limiting women. I use both *victim* and *survivor* to refer to a person who has experienced a sexual assault, although *victim* predominates. Finally, unless otherwise indicated, the term *women's movement* refers to the second wave of feminism, which began in the mid-1960s.[7]

Of particular import to this study is the issue of how rape is both typical and atypical among feminist concerns. Many items on the feminist agenda are easily identifiable as controversial subjects that will remain contentious even as gains are made in the name of such issues. For instance, from the time abortion became a public issue, the division between its pro-life opponents and pro-choice proponents was clearly defined (O'Connor 1996). Likewise, Jane Mansbridge (1986) explains that when the equal rights amendment (ERA) was discussed as an abstract issue of individual rights, it enjoyed relatively strong support among the populace. But when the discussion turned to the impact— or, rather, the imagined impact—of the ERA, support declined sharply. Positions on these and other feminist issues are clearly marked.

Rape, though, appears to be beyond argument: who would come out as being sympathetic toward this crime, or against a woman's right not to be raped?

Thus, I am mindful that the term *anti-rape* implies the existence of some equal and opposite and explicitly *pro-rape* force. To the contrary, however, the act has long been criminalized in law codes and treated in the psychological literature as antisocial behavior. While few people would express favorable sentiments toward rape, the movement against rape sought to uproot societal attitudes that fostered what feminists have termed rape culture (Buchwald, Fletcher, and Roth 1993). In "rape culture," sexual assault is tolerated, violent and sexual images are intertwined, women are blamed for being raped, sexist attitudes prevail, and male sexual privilege goes unquestioned. This description surely applies to the United States at the dawn of the twenty-first century, and it was even more apt in the years before the beginning of the anti-rape movement. At that time, sexist and racist attitudes created an environment in which rape's seriousness was routinely dismissed, victims were disbelieved or blamed for bringing on their own assaults, and poor men and men of color were considered more likely to be rapists than other men. An excerpt from an investigative interview illustrates the treatment of a rape victim in the late 1960s by law enforcement and medical personnel and exemplifies popular attitudes toward rape:

Ms. White: [The police] were skeptical.

Interviewer: How do you know?

Ms. White: Their cross-questioning. They repeatedly asked, "What were you doing on the highway? Why were you out at eleven-thirty? Why would you let him in your car? Don't you know better than that? You look like a mature grown woman who should certainly know the facts of life," and "What were you doing out alone?"

... I asked to see a doctor. ... I felt as though I was safe at last, and yet I was met with such hostility, such skepticism. ...

. . . The interrogation never stopped, day and night. . . .

Interviewer: You were interrogated by some of the law enforcement people or by the [hospital] staff or by both?

Ms. White: By both. The first staff member who saw me was a psychiatrist. His first words were, "Haven't you really been rushing towards this very thing all your life?" He knew nothing about me, nothing!

. . . But the psychiatrist said, "You know, things don't just *happen.* You *make* them happen."

Interviewer: This was prior to having listened to the details of your story?

Ms. White: That's right. (Russell 1975, 224–25; emphasis in original)

Accounts of similar treatment of rape victims by police, prosecutors, and hospital staff were legion in the small-group discussions and writings of the early years of the anti-rape movement. Ms. White's narrative recounts the "rape myths" that this movement sought to dispel, including the beliefs that women's behavior brings on rape (going out at night unescorted, for example) and that they secretly crave rape. Victims who reported having been attacked saw their credibility questioned and their lives and actions scrutinized much more than those of perpetrators. Even criminal law, as practiced, embodied an ethos of distrust of women's claims (Estrich 1987). Moreover, prior to the anti-rape movement, the non-stranger rapes—wife rape, acquaintance rape, and date rape—were rarely perceived as rape at all, a situation that has been challenged but is little changed even today. In the face of entrenched hostility toward victims, especially those whose attackers were known to them, the anti-rape movement took on the challenge of developing a new, pro-woman understanding of rape.

Because this campaign can be traced to feminist activism, my book is rooted in the women's movement in the United States. Susan Brownmiller's *Against Our Will* was the first widely read volume to address rape, but consciousness of sexual assault as an experience shared by many women of many backgrounds existed well before its publication in 1975. For example, African American activists in the anti-lynching movement of the early 1900s expressed a political understanding of the rape of black women by white men. Later, radical feminist consciousness-raising groups provided the context in which the elevation of rape consciousness led to concerted political efforts to address the problem. As such groups attempted to reveal to women the commonality of their oppression, and to politicize their personal experiences, rape came to be understood as an issue with ramifications reaching further than individuals' private lives. Activists sought to transform societal attitudes on rape, its victims, and its perpetrators, using the truths revealed in survivors' own stories to reconceptualize this problem. What followed this raising of rape consciousness in feminist circles was a national campaign that challenged popular assumptions about sexual assault even as it brought the issue of rape to a variety of public forums—police departments, hospitals, universities, and state legislatures, among others—that had never before confronted the issue in so serious a way.

This book also attempts to make sense of the public and legislative responses to the issue of rape and examines the national political context in which they occurred. Sources indicate that the historical connection between rape and the construction of race in the United States has been a decisive element in the framing of the rape issue, particularly as the contemporary discourse has virtually ignored the historical use of fraudulent rape charges in the lynching of black men. This history has constructed the African American man as the quintessential rapist and the African American woman as sexually available and therefore unrapeable. Moreover, the receptivity of policy makers and the wider polity to newly raised rape consciousness was enhanced by a growing attention to crime as a major issue on the public policy agenda in the 1970s. This trend is marked by white, middle-class fears of minority and lower-class criminality. It was through the lens of law and order that policy makers viewed the question of rape as a simple matter, and tough rape policies, albeit couched in race-neutral terms, were seen as necessary protections for the nation's women from black criminality. This framing of the issue, again, ignored black women's experience of rape. The importance of race and class to policy makers' response to the anti-rape movement cannot be ignored.

An explanation of this book's interdisciplinarity, method, and organization is useful here. My project is informed by a women's studies perspective, approaching its subject matter through a variety of disciplines and placing the lives and activities of women at the center of inquiry (Sapiro 1994). As feminist scholarship, it attempts to "rethink the structural changes necessary to meet the needs of actual women" (Richardson and Taylor 1993, 1), meaning that it recounts and assesses actual phenomena and works to effect positive change for women. At the heart of my thesis lies the assertion that feminists were indeed effective in their efforts to address the rape issue because they were able to make significant, lasting changes in public policy and public consciousness. On few other issues was the women's movement able to garner as much widespread public ideological support as it did with rape. I maintain that, overall, the anti-rape movement has achieved public goods for women, and I seek to advance this movement by contributing a more accurate and thorough history of it. As a member of this movement—a rape crisis advocate, a feminist teacher and writer, and a woman living in a rape culture—I have a personal and political stake in this goal.[8]

A wide range of secondary and theoretical sources served as the interpretive tools for developing this chronicle. Historical analysis reveals those special characteristics of rape activism that helped to single it out for relative success among women's issues, so the literature of women's history has proven indispensable (Evans 1979; Giddings 1984; Echols 1989; Davis 1991). Because social science scholarship has helped me to understand the emergence and dynamics of social movements and public policy, this project is also guided by the literature of social movements and interest groups (Freeman 1975; Gamson 1975; Garner 1977; McGlen and O'Connor 1983; Costain 1992; Staggenborg 1995) and of public policy (Murphy 1973; Boneparth 1982; Anderson 1994; Gelb and Palley 1996; O'Connor 1996; Conway, Ahern, and Steuernagel 1999). My book, in turn, contributes to and advances each of these areas.

I use a feminist, multiple-methods approach to account for the variety and complexity of sources and issues involved in the anti-rape movement. As the feminist sociologist Shulamit Reinharz (1992, 197) notes, "By combining methods, feminist researchers are particularly able to illuminate previously unexamined or misunderstood experiences." This approach permits a depth of understanding and insight that any single method, such as interview alone, would not yield. Here, I combine content analysis of primary source materials with in-depth interviews of key players in the anti-rape movement.[9]

First, archival investigation reveals the history of the development of rape consciousness and makes it possible to examine various anti-rape projects. Because many groups and individuals were part of a vast communications network on which the incipient anti-rape movement relied, written documentation helps to establish the connections between the women's movement and the anti-rape movement. For this, I found the manuscript collections held at Radcliffe's Arthur and Elizabeth Schlesinger Library on the History of Women in America to be immensely useful. There I examined the personal papers of eight individuals and the organizational papers of three groups (National Organization for Women [NOW], Women's Anti-Rape Group [WARG], and New York Women Against Rape [NYWAR]). The Women's Movement Archives held at the Cambridge Women's Center, containing records of such organizations as Cambridge Women Against Rape, Female Liberation, Cell 16, Bread and Roses, and the center itself, supplied substantial archival data. The Rare Book, Manuscript, and Special Collections Library of Duke University gave me access to the records of the Atlanta Lesbian Feminist Alliance. I collected further data from the Redstockings Women's Liberation Archive in New York City and the Pennsylvania Coalition Against Rape. In addition, I reviewed select privately held papers of Elizabethann O'Sullivan and, to a lesser extent, Nikki Craft and Susan Brownmiller.[10] O'Sullivan's personal archive holds the records of the founding of the D.C. Rape Crisis Center, in which she took part. This proved to be a particularly fortuitous discovery for me, because the D.C. center was the first one ever established and it had thought these papers lost. In total, I went through approximately sixty-five cartons of papers of various kinds. These collections have provided a rich documentary base.

Print media provided another bountiful source of information on the anti-rape movement. I reviewed twenty-three feminist periodicals and newsletters, ranging from 1967 to the present, for their rape-related content. Among these, I studied those issues dating from the early years of the women's movement most carefully to account for the development of rape consciousness within it. Most of these are held in bound volumes and on microfilm at the Schlesinger Library, the New York Public Library, and Emory University's Woodruff Library. Additionally, I investigated with particular care the available issues (twenty-nine in all) of two periodicals dealing specifically with rape, the *Feminist Alliance Against Rape Newsletter* and its successor, *Aegis.* An assortment of rape-themed secondary literature from the 1970s—including Horos (1974), Csida and Csida (1974), Medea and Thompson (1974), Brownmiller (1975), and Russell (1975)—has proved to be another source of information on political and theoretical developments from the first five years of the anti-rape movement. To track the coverage of the issue and the anti-rape movement in the popular press, I reviewed seven newspapers, including the *New York Times, Washington Post,* and *Los Angeles Times,* for the years covered in my study. Moreover, dozens of hours of NEXIS searches, involving such topics as news articles containing the terms *feminist* and *rape,* provided a broader, national base of information on the mass media since the late 1970s.

To establish the public policy context for the anti-rape movement, I investigated the pertinent government documents, including bills introduced in and passed by Congress, publications of executive agencies, and Supreme Court decisions and amicus briefs. I reviewed these materials both in hard copy at the Government Documents Center of the Woodruff Library, Emory University, and through LEXIS.

To complement the documentary data, I spoke with thirteen organizers, writers, and activists of the movement. Oral interviews provide experiential insight into individual and collective activities, motivations, and decisions, and thus uniquely supplement the written record. I structured these interviews informally and conducted them both in person and by telephone. My questions focused on personal involvement in the women's and anti-rape movements, other political affiliations, organizational structure, sources of funding, and internal controversies, but interviewees took much leeway in guiding our talks in areas they deemed worthy of comment. Interviews lasted between forty-five minutes and two hours. I conducted follow-up interviews with four informants. I recorded all significant information from every source, print and oral, in an "anti-rape time line" (excerpted in Appendix 1), which served as the main database for my project. Together, these sources add up to a complex chronicle of this movement.

This book is organized into five chapters. Chapter 1 traces the historical development of the issue of rape on the feminist agenda, guided by historical and social-movement literature. While activists at the turn of the twentieth century developed a political analysis that subtly included rape, a feminist politics of rape developed through the consciousness-raising sessions of second-wave feminism. Anti-rape activists borrowed from the organizational base of the existing women's movement and drew upon the networks of communication built into it. With an elevated consciousness of rape as a women's issue, and following several critical mobilizing events, they had placed rape squarely on the feminist agenda by 1970. This chapter investigates the contexts that made this possible. It also considers the widespread perception that women of color took very little interest in anti-rape organizing in the 1970s and locates evidence to the contrary. Significantly, the chapter traces the evolving ideology of rape, consistent with existing feminist theoretical frameworks, that defined this act as the ultimate expression of male dominance over women—as violence they face merely for being female. The early goal of the feminist anti-rape movement was nothing short of "an end to rape as we know it," a goal that has not yet been realized. The articulation of a feminist politics of rape came to take on social-movement proportions in its own right, though still within the wider context of feminism. Thus, in this chapter

I conceptualize the campaign against rape as a self-reliant social movement within a larger social-movement framework.

Chapter 2 investigates the major strategies of the anti-rape campaign, going into greater detail to explore the varieties of anti-rape organizing in practice. The two major concerns of the movement, setting up rape crisis centers and reforming rape law, are examined closely in the larger feminist context. This chapter reads the various strategies, especially those involving rape law reform and crisis centers, as related trends within a wider movement context and sheds light upon how diverse feminist anti-rape activists cooperated to effect their desired changes. Finally, the chapter explores the meanings of such designations as "liberal," "radical," and "reformist," locating the ways in which various groups of feminists coalesced around the rape issue.

Chapter 3 examines the historical development of rape as an item on the public agenda and as a policy issue between 1973 and 1980, using the interpretive tools of policy studies and interest groups. It considers how feminists translated rape from their own agenda to the public one in a relatively short time, and investigates the political context in which these changes took place. This exploration reveals that anti-rape activists used the various new skills gained from their struggles for abortion rights, passage of the ERA, and other legislative activity, to make rape a public policy issue. What resulted was unprecedented local, state, and federal legislative and budgetary attention to the issue and the development of programs to respond to and educate the public about rape. This chapter goes on to explore the growth of a tough-on-crime legislative agenda, which posited minority criminality as the primary threat to American life, and its implications for rape policy. The terms and meanings of co-optation, by which the radical edge of anti-rape politics was dulled to accommodate a more professional, institutional approach, are also of central concern.

Chapter 4 presents the policy developments on the issue of rape from 1980 to the present. As Chapter 3 explored the ways it moved from the feminist to the systemic and institutional agendas, this chapter looks at how rape remained on the public agenda by investigating media coverage and legislative developments. Issues considered here include the development of a rape typology, by which the generic term *rape* came to be replaced by more specific terms such as *marital, date,* and *acquaintance rape* in popular understanding and usage. The chapter then traces the growing involvement of university students in anti-rape organizing and reviews policy initiatives, including the Violence Against Women Act of 1994. Lastly, it considers recent tensions and developments in anti-rape organizing, specifically the phenomenon known as the "sex wars" and the rise of an anti–anti-rape backlash.

Finally, Chapter 5 finds that feminist anti-rape efforts can be termed successful for having elevated public consciousness about the issue, won passage of pro-victim legislation, and established victim-support programs. But in terms of feminists' initial framing of the issue—positing rape as a tool used by men to ultimately buttress white male dominance—the successes in the public policy arena have been but small steps toward the ultimate goal of eliminating the problem of rape.

Over the past thirty years, rape has been a central issue in feminist theory, politics, and organizing. As a concern first articulated by feminists, its importance has diminished very little since the years when it was first raised. But the evolution of the anti-rape movement has transformed women's lives significantly: it has changed the public response to rape victims and altered how our society views this crime. The campaign against rape—the "model of the women's movement at its most effective" (Davis 1991, 314)—deserves a history and analysis of its own. In this book I seek to give it one.

I

HISTORICAL DEVELOPMENT:
RAPE ON THE FEMINIST AGENDA

THE ISSUE OF RAPE is of course not unique to the late twentieth century. Four thousand years ago, the Code of Hammurabi provided penalties for the rape of virgins, daughters, and wives as violations of a man's property. The Jewish and Christian Scriptures contain stories and parables about rape, such as that of Bathsheba by King David. Historians have established the existence, if not pervasiveness, of sexual violence against women in various parts of the world through the ages (Lindemann 1984; Clark 1987; Sanday 1996). Just as long and tenacious is the history of blaming women for being raped: Lynn Henderson (1992, 135) traces this tendency at least as far back as the Middle Ages.

In spite of rape's presence in Western history, it did not become a subject of political commentary in the United States until the nineteenth century. Although the rape of slave women by white masters and overseers in the slave states was well known, it was hushed up (Davis 1983; Giddings 1984; White 1985; Jones 1985). The early advocates of women's rights and woman suffrage viewed rape as an example of women's lack of autonomy. Ida B. Wells and other black women activists understood the connection between lynching of black men (and some women) by whites and the rape of black women by white men. But widespread, action-oriented feminist opposition to rape did not appear until the second wave of the women's movement in the United States.[1] The feminist consciousness in place in the late 1960s allowed movement women to analyze the role that rape plays in perpetuating male dominance, abetted by the passivity and fear instilled in women through socialization.

In this chapter, I review the historical evidence of anti-rape activity in the United States during the nineteenth and early twentieth centuries, and then trace the history of second-wave feminist politicizing of the rape issue beginning around 1970. Specifically, I attempt to uncover the events and political climate that gave rise to the first contemporary articulation of rape as a women's issue of political dimensions, using the lens of social-movement theory through which to view the rise of an anti-rape movement. I address three primary questions: How did rape arrive on the feminist agenda? How did activists frame the issue? How was this newly raised rape consciousness disseminated among feminists? This chapter sets the stage for the development of political strategies by the women's movement that would carry the issue from the narrow radical feminist agenda to the wider public policy arena.

Historical Roots of Rape Consciousness

In the middle of the nineteenth century, the movement to address gender inequality in the United States got under way when middle-class white women working in the struggle to abolish slavery began to problematize their virtual exclusion from the public sphere and their total lack of legal and political identity (DuBois 1978; McGlen and O'Connor 1983). Although violence against women was not the subject of direct feminist action at that time, members of the women's rights and woman suffrage movements did occasionally and covertly allude to the issues of rape, women's autonomy, and women's sexuality. For example, upon his marriage to the suffragist Lucy Stone in 1855, Henry Blackwell refused his legal right to "custody of the wife's person" (Blackwell 1930, 166–68), which some have interpreted as a promise not to "attempt to impose the dictates of his sexual desires upon his wife" (Davis 1983, 207). Women's rights advocates of the time understood that the marriage contract effectively made the wife the legal sexual servant of her husband, a component of what came to be labeled marital rape in the 1970s.

The case of Hester Vaughan in 1868 embroiled the women's rights advocates Elizabeth Cady Stanton and Susan B. Anthony in a controversy involving sexual coercion and infanticide. In an effort to unite the women's rights movement with the concerns of working-class

women, the suffragist leaders had formed the Working Women's Association, which operated out of the office of their newspaper, the *Revolution*.[2] Hester Vaughan was an English immigrant employed as a
domestic servant in Philadelphia; her employer "seduced" and then
fired her, leaving her impoverished (Stanton 1868, 312). She became
ill, gave birth, and was found in her room three days later with her
dead infant. Vaughan was later convicted and sentenced to death for
infanticide. Stanton, Anthony, and their associates in the Working
Women's Association took up her cause, circulating petitions, organizing a protest rally, and publicly requesting that the governor of Pennsylvania pardon and release Vaughan. "Is it not terrible," they asked,
"that this victim of a man's craven lust should be thus foully dealt
with, while her seducer walks the earth free and unmolested?" (*Revolution* 1868, 357). The governor ultimately agreed to the pardon. This
case gave the suffragists an opportunity to investigate and politicize the
sexual vulnerability of working women, the double standard that held
only Vaughan responsible for the pregnancy and the infant's death,
and the political powerlessness of women (DuBois 1978, 146–47). The
conclusion of the case, however, marked the end of the organized outcry against these injustices by Stanton and Anthony.

Later, the *Revolution* printed a letter to the editor supporting the
death penalty for rapists. The letter writer comments that the crime
seems to "excite no comment unless accompanied by the murder of the
victim. . . . We must not suffer this country to become a place unsafe
for a woman to be alone in; we must force men to guard us against
such a state of things by stringent legislation" (quoted in Papachristou
1976, 62). She goes on to suggest a petition drive to lobby state legislatures to make rape a capital crime. Although the message is couched
in the language of protectionism and advances an extremely harsh penalty not embraced by anti-rape activists in the late twentieth century,
this letter demonstrates a consciousness of rape as a problem rooted in
women's position and women's rights.

Furthermore, according to the historians John D'Emilio and Estelle
Freedman (1988), opposition to both coercive and repressive sexuality
formed the nexus of the free love movement promoted by Victoria

Woodhull, Ezra Heywood, and others in the 1870s. Infanticide was at issue again when *Woodhull and Claflin's Weekly* (1874, 8) printed an editorial denouncing this "great crime," but arguing that the problem is rooted in women's lack of sexual autonomy: "As things are we believe that woman's social and sexual rights are usurped . . . , that she has neither the power to choose the mate she would like, or the time, and that alas too frequently even her good-will is not asked previous to the procreative act. It is for these reasons we object to 'marriage.' " Woodhull and Claflin refer to the injustice of men's unquestioned sexual access to their wives' bodies; it would be a century before marital rape as a concept would arrive on the public agenda.

A decade later, in 1886, the free love advocate Moses Harmon, publisher of the journal *Lucifer, the Light Bearer* (which became the *American Journal of Eugenics* in 1907), was prosecuted and imprisoned under the Comstock anti-obscenity law for printing a letter condemning, again, marital rape (D'Emilio and Freedman 1988, 164–66). The free love advocates' opposition to marriage as an institution, promotion of uncensored sexual expression, and belief in equality and sexual freedom for women led to their denunciation of rape as antithetical to each of these. Several ideas espoused by free lovers came into wider acceptance in the early years of the twentieth century, but they did not lead to specific politicization of, and organizing around, the issues of rape or marital rape.

The first outcry against sexual assault as a systematic abuse of women came in response to the rule of "lynch law in America" in the years following the emancipation of slaves. It was through her investigation and reporting of the violent, extralegal lynchings that were taking place throughout the South and in parts of the North that Ida B. Wells articulated in 1892 a political understanding of sexual assault. The ostensible reason for this frequent resort to mob violence was to protect white women from rape by animalistic black men. Wells discovered, though, that rape charges were not even made, let alone proven, in over two-thirds of all lynchings. She observed that there had been rapes in some of the cases, but went on to point out that black women had endured this crime from white men far more than white women had ever endured it from black men. "Very scant notice is taken of the matter when this is the condition of affairs. What becomes a crime deserving capital punishment when the tables are turned is a matter of small moment when the negro woman is the accusing party" (Wells-Barnett 1995 [1900], 74). Wells stated bluntly that "the rape of helpless Negro girls, which began in slavery days, still continues without reproof from the church, state or press" (quoted in Giddings 1984, 31).

She based these claims on ample evidence. Throughout her writing career, Wells sought to debunk the myth of the black rapist and to expose the rapes of black women by white men, although frequently in veiled terms. She cited specific cases that testified to the difficulty of convicting white men for the rape of black girls or women and the lenient treatment of those few who were so convicted in the late nineteenth century. For example, in Baltimore in 1891 "three white ruffians assaulted a Miss Camphor, a young Afro-American girl, while [she was] out walking with a young man of her own race. They held her escort and outraged [raped] the girl. . . . The case went to the courts, an Afro-American lawyer defended the men, and they were acquitted" (Wells-Barnett 1969 [1892], 11). What is most remarkable about this account is that there was a trial at all. So, while the supposed defense of "their" women's honor drove hordes of white men into a murderous frenzy in which due process of law was not even a consideration, the rape of black women was minimized, denied, or completely ignored.

Other black clubwomen made similar observations. In a speech to white women at the World Columbian Exposition in 1893, Fannie Barrier Williams, an activist and one of the only black members of the Chicago Women's Club, stated clearly that black women's "morals" were in constant danger and in need of protection. She intended a thinly disguised indictment of the impunity with which white men could rape black women (Giddings 1984, 86). In 1892 the writer and educator Anna Julia Cooper noted black mothers' desperation to protect their daughters' bodies from sexual abuse by white men (Giddings 1984, 87).

The sexual violation Wells, Williams, Cooper, and others denounced was closely connected to the systematic rape of black women decades earlier under slavery. White men's access to their bodies went largely unquestioned by the dominant culture of the Old South. Scholars have documented the historical construction of black women's sexuality as lustful and lewd, which led to the controlling image of the Jezebel.[3] This presumption of lasciviousness, historians find, probably had its origin in European men's first travels to Africa, where they mistook women's semi-nudity in tropical climates for promiscuity (White 1985, 29; Omolade 1995, 362). Furthermore, under slavery, black women were never afforded the same privacy as were white women, so, again, the slaves' more frequently glimpsed semi-nudity was assumed to proclaim their sexual laxity (White 1985, 31–33). In the late nineteenth century, the myth of black women's promiscuity was firmly established in the popular imagination and in scholarship (Morton 1991, 28–29).

Given this construction of black women's bodies and sexuality, the pattern of assault on female slaves was at once explained and excused. Jacqueline Jones (1985, 37) acknowledges that the statistical prevalence of rape among female slaves is impossible to establish with any precision, but historians have found substantial evidence of such abuse in the slave narratives dictated and written before and after 1865 by both men and women (Lerner 1972, 46, 149–50; Blassingame 1972, 83; Jones 1985, 20, 28, 37–38; Evans 1989, 109–10). In his 1917 book, *A Social History of the American Family,* the historian Arthur Calhoun explains that the masters' "right of rape" and the emphasis placed on breeding new slaves "debauched" slave women (quoted in Morton 1991, 30). Nearly all their extant narratives refer to having been raped, or threatened with it (Hine 1989, 912; Brent 1973 [1861]).

Deborah Gray White (1985, 152–53) finds evidence that slave men's rape of slave women was tolerated by the social order, so men of both races enjoyed access to black women's bodies. Anna Julia Cooper (1988 [1892]) notes that her mother, as a slave, endured the shame of bearing her master's child, and that this kind of shame continued past slavery for women who had been sexually abused (in Giddings 1984, 87). Of course, sexual assaults by masters were not legally considered rape:

since the slave was property, the criminal label never even applied. Evidence both of female slaves' resistance to sexual abuse (Omolade 1985, 365–69) and of acquiescence to sexual relationships with masters has also been unearthed (D'Emilio and Freedman 1988, 101–2).

Following emancipation, black women continued to experience assault and rape by white men (Lerner 1972, 155–59, 163–64). When fierce racism proliferated in the South during and after Reconstruction, white men used rape to terrorize the whole black population, rendering it nearly powerless to resist or retaliate lest further white violence result (Lerner 1972, 171–72; Hall 1983, 331–35; D'Emilio and Freedman 1988, 105). In 1892, Anna Julia Cooper commented that white women did not encounter "such snares and traps as betray the unprotected, untrained colored girl of the South, whose only crime and dire destruction often is her unconscious and marvelous beauty" (Cooper 1988 [1892], 32). Thus, in the late nineteenth century black women possessed an understanding of rape as connected to racism, sexism, and economic oppression, albeit one couched in the protectionist terms of the day.

Echoing the ideas of Ida B. Wells's anti-lynching campaign, the historian Jacqueline Jones connects the post-emancipation sexual violation of black women to the phenomenon of lynching: "White men considered free and uninhibited access to black women as their prerogative and at the same time declared taboo any sexual activity between black men and white women" (Jones 1985, 149). Furthermore, the labor performed by black women often put them at greater peril of sexual assault by white male overseers as wage earners on postbellum plantations and by white male heads of household as domestic servants. Anti-miscegenation laws codified the taboo against interracial sex.[4] Allegations of sexual activity between black men and white women— whether the charges were founded or not, whether the sex was consensual or nonconsensual—justified lynching. So when Wells and other black women politicized lynching, they also called up this history of rape condoned under slavery, and rape ignored following emancipation.

African American women's understanding of the connections between racism, violence, and sexuality prompted an organized, if covert, response. According to the historian Darlene Clark Hine, the black clubwomen's movement was initiated in part by Ida B. Wells's own speaking tour to call attention to lynching. Because they made connections between sexual violation and demeaning sexual stereotypes, Hine argues that the clubwomen's actions to reverse the negative sexual images of black women can be seen as acts of resistance to sexual assault (1989, 918). The clubwoman Fannie Barrier Williams spoke publicly, in shrouded terms, of African American women's need to be free from threats of white men's sexual violence (Giddings 1984, 86). Even black women's struggle for the right to vote can be seen as resistance to their damaged sexual image, says Hine. Nannie Helen Burroughs argued that with the ballot the black woman would have a weapon with which to defend her virtue in court (Hine 1989, 918).[5]

Best documented among overt and covert responses to sexual assault among African American women in the late nineteenth and early twentieth centuries is the offensive they mounted against the immediate problem of lynching. As the historian Gerda Lerner has observed (1972, 193), the campaign to end these extrajudicial executions attacked two elements of the same myth: that of "the black rapist of white women" and that of the "bad black woman," both of which were "designed to apologize for and facilitate the continued exploitation of black men and women." A vocal "race woman," Ida B. Wells focused most of her writing career on calling attention to the problem of lynching and pressing for its end.

Wells's prediction that such mob justice would end when Southern white women decided it would end proved accurate. In 1930, Jessie Daniel Ames formed the Association of Southern Women for the Prevention of Lynching (ASWPL) in part to resist the insult of white men's supposed chivalrous attitudes toward white women (Hall 1983, 338). Ames's all-white group had the support of black clubwomen, who understood the connection between lynching violence and sexual violence for black women. By 1935, the ASWPL had thirty-five thousand members. The group lobbied state legislatures, wrote letters to newspaper editors to denounce lynching and raise public consciousness, and even marshaled volunteers to confront violent lynch mobs (Grant 1975, 137–38). The ASWPL and other political organizations fought for legislation to end lynching until the mid-1950s. In spite of their best efforts, none of the two hundred anti-lynching bills introduced in Congress ever passed (Grant 1975, 168).

In 1948 *Adam's Rib,* a collection of essays by Ruth Herschberger, a feminist writer and poet, posed the question, Is rape a myth? Herschberger laid much of the groundwork for the 1970s' feminist conceptualization of rape as a problem rooted in male dominance. She attributes sexual assault to the cultural construction of male and female sexuality as diametrically opposed, one aggressive, the other passive. Furthermore, Herschberger posits, probably for the first time anywhere in print, "Rape is a form of violence involving the personal humiliation of the victim" (1948, 19), one in which men "virtually encourage various members of their sex" to participate (1948, 21). The equation of rape with violence and not sex, popularly attributed to Susan Brownmiller's 1975 book, *Against Our Will,* thus first found expression as early as 1948. In analyzing the mechanics of rape, and in linking it to a gendered power structure, Herschberger was ahead of her time. It would take another twenty years and the rebirth of interest in women's role in society for activists to claim her work as feminist (Medea and Thompson 1974, 15).

Conceptualizing the Anti-Rape Movement

Conditions of the late 1960s set the stage for a campaign against rape to emerge as a social movement out of the larger women's movement. The political scientists Nancy E. McGlen and Karen O'Connor explain that the goal of most social movements is to attain some public good (1983, 5). They postulate that a social movement arises when various factors are in place: an organizational base, a network of communication among potential organizers, shared consciousness of a common oppression, and a critical mobilizing event or events (1983, 4–16). In addition, according to Claire Fulenwider (1980, 16–17), such movements seek to effect ideological change among individuals and within society, coupled with structural change.

The relationship between the anti-rape and women's movements raises an interesting question about how social movements develop: is the effort against rape simply a faction or element of the women's movement, or can it be considered a social movement unto itself? Few authors have examined the emergence of "spin-off" movements at any length. For example, the sociologist Barbara Ryan, in a study of the U.S. women's movement, found that many socialist women chose to join feminist caucuses within larger socialist organizations, forming "a movement within a movement" that lacked autonomy (Ryan 1992, 71). Ryan does not explore the broader implications of this development, nor is this finding an example of single-issue organizing, as the campaign against rape was.

For her part, Jo Freeman (1995) refers to single-issue movements as "submovements," finding that once the older and younger branches merged in the mid-1970s, younger-branch feminists chose to remain active in single-issue spin-offs that were forming. In similar fashion, the sociologists Myra Ferree and Beth Hess (1985) review the wide range of feminist organizations that have emerged since the inception of the women's movement. However, they do not investigate the extent to which such groups are simply expressions of feminist ideology or are independent and self-sufficient. Overall, the role of single-issue, or spin-off, movements has yet to be explored in breadth or depth.

I suggest that the effort against rape can be read as a social movement within a social movement. It resembles the civil rights and other independent social movements, but it was never divorced from the wider context of feminism and must be analyzed in that light. The first anti-rape activism took place within the women's movement (or, more specifically, within the women's liberation movement), and the first anti-rape activists were already involved to varying degrees in feminist politics. Hence, the campaign against rape relied on the women's movement for its existence and its strength. The remainder of this chapter investigates the organizational base of the anti-rape effort in second-wave feminism, the existing communications networks that the women's movement provided, the centrality of shared consciousness in the emergence of the campaign against rape, the anti-rape movement's critical mobilizing events, and the feminist ideology of rape that has emerged from the movement.

The impact of mobilizing events, combined with the evidence of popular support for changes in the ideology of rape, led feminist activists in 1971 to declare that "the next major focus of the women's movement [is] rape and protection against it" (Sheehy 1971, 26). Throughout the 1970s, ideological developments would blend with the dominant tough-on-crime, law-and-order climate to achieve support for various anti-rape projects and reforms from lawmakers and other governmental officials. In later chapters, I will examine the receptivity of the political process to the changes proposed by the anti-rape movement and the impact of the movement on public policy.

The Organizational Base of the Anti-Rape Movement

From its earliest years, contemporary U.S. feminism took various forms, with liberal and radical branches emerging nearly simultaneously. It is a matter of little dispute that the anti-rape movement of the late twentieth century took place in the context of the second wave of feminist activity. Speaking for feminists and anti-rape activists, Susan Griffin (1986, 27) observes, "The issue of rape was in no way ever separate from the question of the whole liberation of women as we had been defined by patriarchy, and we did not see it as separate." Second-wave feminism gave rise to public awareness of sexual assault as a women's issue and to the anti-rape movement. A short history of the origins and ideology of that movement will help set the stage for a deeper understanding of its roots.[6]

In the late 1960s, the women's movement was quite polarized: while radical women saw the reform of a sexist, racist, capitalist system as pointless and counterrevolutionary, the liberal branch pursued legal and economic equality with men within the status quo. Radical feminists sought to understand the relationship between men and women in political instead of personal terms and to use the personal as the basis for politics. They viewed sex, not race or class, as the primary source of oppression, unlike black radicals and New Leftists, respectively. It was in the context of the activism and theorizing of younger, radical women that the articulation of rape as a serious, pervasive, political problem would take shape.

Radical Feminist Movement

White women involved in the radical protest movements of the 1960s began to realize over time that their assigned tasks often involved no more than typing and making coffee, traditional feminine jobs that merely replicated "women's work" outside the movement and were hardly revolutionary.[7] Many of those working to dismantle hierarchy and create participatory democracy realized that these values did not extend into the realm of male-female relations within the movement, where women's subordination and men's dominance were widely upheld as natural. Discontented women broke off from the male-dominated New Left and were soon joined by others previously uninvolved with radical movements; together, they formed the radical (or "women's liberation") branch of the women's movement (Freeman 1975, 57; Evans 1979; Echols 1989).

For several years thereafter, the radical branch practiced a feminist politics distinct from that of the liberal branch. Although there was no single dogma to which all radical feminists subscribed, they generally posited that the liberation of all women would be achieved only by eradicating male supremacy and its institutions: marriage, the family, and religion, among others. In a related camp were the "politicos," radical women who denounced the sexism of the New Left but whose primary political energies remained within it.[8] Instead of forming a national organization to pursue their political goals, the younger feminists organized in small groups with regional bases, such as the New York Radical Women (NYRW), Boston's Cell 16, and DC Women's Liberation (DCWL). These groups were ideologically opposed to traditional notions of leadership and centralized structure, which some have interpreted as undermining the organizations' ability to achieve their objectives (Joreen 1973).

Anti-Rape Movement and Radical Feminism

Rape arrived on the feminist agenda in 1970 in the context of radical feminist consciousness-raising groups. Several aspects of radical feminist politics and theory of the time created conditions favorable to an articulation of rape as a women's issue. First, a central feature of the small women's liberation groups was consciousness-raising (C-R), the strategy credited with providing the critical context in which women talked about sensitive, even painful experiences openly. In this environment, rape was discussed candidly and nonjudgmentally, and participants in the movement came to understand rape as a common women's experience with political implications. (I will discuss the importance of C-R in developing rape consciousness later in this chapter.)

Second, radical feminists' willingness to flout convention and raise sensitive issues in public made them well suited to breaking the taboo surrounding rape. Whereas the older, women's rights branch of the movement focused on maintaining a respectable image to avoid negative publicity (NOW even went so far as to purge lesbian members [Davis 1991, 262–64]), respectability and societal approval meant very little to the radicals. For example, Anne Koedt's 1970 essay, "The Myth of the Vaginal Orgasm," now widely anthologized as a feminist classic, focused attention not only on female sexuality, but on the clitoris, the center of women's sexual pleasure (Koedt 1973). Koedt indicts heterosexual intercourse as not pleasurable to women because it does not directly stimulate the clitoris. For radicals, discussing such volatile subjects was part and parcel both of the immediate goal of politicizing the personal and of the larger project of eliminating male supremacy in all its forms. This and other articles, such as Sidney Abbott and Barbara Love's "Is Women's Liberation a Lesbian Plot?" (1971) and Ellen Strong's "The Hooker" (1970), demonstrate the inclination of the younger branch of the movement to analyze, politicize, and publicize the most personal and potentially offensive issues in women's lives.

Third, the radical feminists were apt to engage in unfeminine behavior to bring attention to an issue. The sociologist Jessie Bernard (1971, 38) points out that women's liberationists, unlike members of the liberal branch, "used tactics as incompatible with the feminine gender role (and hence with the greatest shock value) as they could devise." The historian Alice Echols captures this phenomenon succinctly: radical women "dar[ed] to be bad" (Echols 1989). This sense of daring was a substantial prerequisite for analyzing the taboo subject of rape and helped to lay the groundwork for the anti-rape movement.

Finally, accepting the radical feminist aphorism "The personal is political" created the conditions by which the younger-branch women found politics in even those aspects of their lives that they believed to be embarrassing, shameful, and quintessentially private. Their analysis of male dominance as a total system called into question all the components of that system, such as work, family, reproduction, and marriage, and the ways these components reinforced women's subordination (Firestone 1970; Morgan 1970; Millett 1970). Through this exploration of what were traditionally thought to be personal matters, radical women would come to understand rape as a political problem that functions to keep women subordinate to men, not a personal problem for which individual women should feel shame or guilt. The insights gained through this process of politicization formed the backbone of the feminist anti-rape ideology that developed alongside the anti-rape movement.

Radical feminism was localized, with pockets of organizers in numerous cities and college towns across the country, and the activists of the anti-rape movement came from various local women's movement groups. The Boston area women's liberation group Cell 16 made the practice of martial arts for self-defense against male violence one of its trademark strategies as early as 1969. This group was well known for its militant feminist stance and promotion of martial arts training for women. Cell 16's stringent focus on such training and on celibacy for women earned it a reputation as "the quintessential radical women's liberation group" (Echols 1989, 158). One of its members, Betsy Warrior, crafted a poster that became quite popular in anti-rape circles: a woman fights off a would-be rapist with a kick to the groin and a punch to the face. The text reads, "Disarm rapists: Smash sexism." Warrior notes that women in the Cambridge group were promoting self-defense and female autonomy as feminist strategies, but they were not singling out rape from women's other experiences (telephone interview, 26 June 1996). In spite of Cell 16's pioneering work in self-defense, Women Against Rape, operating out of the Cambridge Women's

Center, was not formed until 1972. WAR, which included the activist Libby Bouvier, went on to become the Boston Area Rape Crisis Center (BARCC).

Elsewhere, the New York Radical Feminists (NYRF) took up the topic of rape for consciousness-raising in the fall of 1970 and made it their centerpiece issue. Susan Brownmiller, a longtime activist and author of *Against Our Will* (1975), explains that she first became interested in the issue of rape during her involvement in an NYRF consciousness-raising group called West Village 1 in the fall of 1970 (Brownmiller 1975, xiii). She recalls that before the issue was raised there, occasional references to rape had already been made in radical literature: Eldridge Cleaver (1968) and Shulamith Firestone (1970), for example, referred to rape in their famous books, and feminist periodicals around the country made occasional mention of it (Susan Brownmiller, telephone interview, 2 September 1996). But before 1970, there had been no feminist analysis of the reality of sexual assault in women's lives.

Brownmiller explains that she first came to view rape as a significant issue when Diane Crothers, a member of her C-R group, brought a feminist periodical from another state to a meeting. It contained a first-person account by a woman who, hired as a stripper for a bachelor party, was gang-raped by the groom and his friends. Later, members of a local feminist group leafleted cars at the man's wedding with flyers reading, "John R. is a rapist." Crothers suggested that rape was an issue West Village 1 should discuss. That evening, three women in the C-R group described their harrowing experiences of rape or attempted rape. Before this meeting, Brownmiller had held the "typical liberal-left position: that rape was a false accusation by a white woman against a black man down South. . . . The perpetrator was always somehow a white woman"; the fact that her friends and C-R peers were now revealing their experiences made her rethink her views (Susan Brownmiller, telephone interview, 2 September 1996).

In addition to the NYRF consciousness-raising sessions, and the 1971 speak-out on rape and rape conference, New York's Women's Anti-Rape Group (WARG) was founded at an open meeting of women interested in rape organizing, held at the New York Women's Liberation Center in October 1971 (Women's Anti-Rape Group records). This group was the forerunner of the rape counseling collective New York Women Against Rape (NYWAR), which went on to create the city's first feminist rape crisis center (NYWAR records). Marion Sawyer, Maz Troppe, Carolyn Ward, Dodie Glass, and Eileen Fitzgerald were the five WARG members who founded NYWAR. Another New York group, The Feminists, gathered in protest at the trial of a sixteen-year-old confessed rapist, Hector Medina, in September 1971. Members leafleted outside the courtroom, then went inside to witness the sentencing of Medina. Two protesters, Michaela Griffo of the Radical Lesbians and Lyn Vincent of The Feminists, were arrested for disturbing the hearing (Price 1971). It is unclear whether this action led to further organizing around rape by The Feminists, the Radical Lesbians, or individual members of the organizations. But it is clear that after the fall of 1970 rape consciousness had been elevated among New York women's liberationists.

Elsewhere in the country, a group of activist women at the Crenshaw Women's Center in Los Angeles formed an anti-rape squad when one of the center women was raped while hitchhiking. The squad went on to create the rape hotline after the Crenshaw Center closed in 1972 (Matthews 1994, 20–21). In Santa Monica, the Westside Women's Center began C-R on rape in 1971 and formed the Venice Anti-Rape Squad that same year (Matthews 1994, 22–23). Lee Abrams became active in organizing Berkeley's Bay Area Women Against Rape (BAWAR) in 1971, after her daughter was raped at Berkeley High School (Csida and Csida 1974, 149). In Washington, D.C., the beginning of a rape crisis center project in 1972 grew out of the founding meeting for an area women's center (Elizabethann O'Sullivan, personal interview, 8 June 1995). Seattle Rape Relief, also formed in 1972, was the result of a speak-out on rape held at the University of Washington (Csida and Csida 1974, 157). The Chicago group Women Against Rape came into being after a rape conference held at the Loop YWCA. Beginning with C-R groups in 1970, then, groups of radical women were at the forefront of politicizing rape, and they made up the primary organizational base for the anti-rape movement.

Liberal Feminist Movement

A number of events are credited with giving rise to the liberal (or older or women's rights) branch of the women's movement: first, the 1963 Report of the President's Commission on the Status of Women called attention to widespread gender discrimination in the United States; second, the publication of Betty Friedan's *Feminine Mystique,* also in that year, first articulated the problem of middle-class women's lack of fulfilling roles and responsibilities; third, again in 1963, the Equal Pay Act prohibited pay discrepancies based on sex in most jobs; and finally, Title VII of the Civil Rights Act of 1964 included sex as a prohibited form of workplace discrimination (a provision that the Equal Employment Opportunity Commission [EEOC] failed to enforce when it began its work in 1965). All of these events called attention to women's unequal status in American society. Furthermore, the presence of a thriving civil rights movement in the 1950s and 1960s helped to highlight inequities in political representation, employment, and education in the United States. In fact, the main organization of the liberal branch of the women's movement explicitly set out to follow the model of one of the oldest civil rights organizations, the National Association for the Advancement of Colored People (NAACP).

In 1966, Betty Friedan, Kathryn (Kay) Clarenbach, Pauli Murray, and other politically active women formed the National Organization for Women (NOW) "to take action to bring women into full participation in the mainstream of American society now, exercising all the privileges and responsibilities thereof in truly equal partnership with men," according to the group's Statement of Purpose. To this end, its goals stressed legal, educational, and economic equality between the sexes. For NOW and other liberal feminist organizations, the U.S. liberal tradition provided the main ideological guidance: women should be granted equal access to the resources and responsibilities of society. One of its first actions was to urge the EEOC to enforce the sex discrimination prohibition contained in Title VII. From its founding, the structure of NOW was centralized, bureaucratized, and democratic. It remains the most prominent and active women's organization in the United States.

Other older-branch groups began to emerge shortly after the establishment of NOW, among them the Women's Equity Action League (WEAL) and the National Women's Political Caucus (NWPC). WEAL was formed in 1968 when several NOW members, concerned over the organization's controversial pro-choice stance on abortion, broke off to start a more conservative group (O'Connor 1980, 94). The NWPC was formed in 1971 by Shirley Chisholm, Betty Friedan, Gloria Steinem, and Bella Abzug to increase the number of women elected to public office and to advance women's issues. While the older-branch organizations often diverged from each other quite sharply and experienced internal conflict over highly contested issues such as abortion and the ERA, the various adherents of liberal feminism have sought to level the playing field on which women and men participate in American society.

Anti-Rape Movement and Liberal Feminism

The older branch of feminism provided part of the organizational base of the anti-rape movement, but only after women's liberationists had been politicizing rape for at least two years. For example, the Women's Legal Defense Fund, a "clearinghouse for D.C. attorneys with feminist concerns" (O'Connor 1980, 102), issued a press release calling for the revision of rape laws in December 1972, well after rape consciousness had begun to be raised in radical women's groups. In 1973 rape became an organizing issue for liberal feminists.

NOW made no mention of rape in its 1966 Statement of Purpose or in its Bill of Rights, adopted in 1967. Furthermore, the personal papers of the group's first president, Betty Friedan, show complete silence on the issue during her tenure (Friedan papers). In 1970 and 1971, the years when radical feminists were discussing rape in personal and political terms in C-R sessions, NOW quietly passed Resolution 115, favoring more serious treatment of the crime and its victims by law enforcement, at its national conference on 20 March 1971.[9] Although fifteen of the organization's chapters, including NOW–Northern Virginia, were investigating rape laws and devising anti-rape strategies at that time (Largen 1976, 70), few or no NOW resources were dedicated to rape until 19 February 1973, when the national conference passed by acclamation Resolution 148, creating the NOW Rape Task Force (NOWRTF). It was charged with examining existing rape statutes, proposing a model rape law to recommend to state legislatures, researching treatment of rape victims, investigating sound self-defense tactics, and looking into the possibilities of coalition with other anti-rape groups "for exchange of resources and support" (NOW records).[10]

The chapter and task force structure of NOW allowed for substantial local autonomy and issue selection among members. Mary Ann Largen of NOW–Northern Virginia, the first national NOWRTF coordinator, encouraged chapters interested in working on the rape issue to survey their local needs and demands. She developed a questionnaire for conducting such projects, advising NOWRTF members through the November 1973 *Rape Task Force Newsletter* to interview hospital personnel, police, and prosecutors on the handling of rape cases (NOW records). Largen encouraged the chapters to pursue whatever rape-related reforms seemed most necessary in their locales, whether that meant launching an effort at law reform, a rape crisis center project, or a community rape task force. Thus, the chapter structure of NOW allowed for considerable grassroots anti-rape work.

The task force drew from existing NOW resources and communications networks even as it created new links with other emerging anti-rape groups, from both the older and younger branches of the women's movement. The NOWRTF presented its model rape law as Resolution 20 at the 1974 national conference in Houston and saw it passed. The conference also held two rape workshops (NOW records). The task force proved to be a crucial national conduit for anti-rape projects with a law reform or public policy focus. Within two years of its formation, over two hundred NOW chapters were involved in anti-rape organizing (Largen 1976, 70).

It is noteworthy that NOW did not officially take up rape as an organizing issue until after the Supreme Court's 22 January 1973 abortion decision in *Roe v. Wade*. Earlier, liberal feminist organizations had focused most of their attention on enforcing Title VII, passing the ERA, and liberalizing abortion laws. The *Roe* decision freed up some of these resources to permit NOW to work on other issues, including rape. Moreover, the equal rights amendment had already been submitted to the states by Congress when NOW took up the question of rape on the national level. The experience of organizing around abortion and the ERA created a network of seasoned activists who possessed a sophisticated understanding of the governmental process necessary to pursue the liberal feminists' anti-rape goals, most importantly law reform. NOW's embrace of the rape issue also took place as the group was becoming somewhat radicalized (Flammang 1997, 83). However, in 1978, when the organization declared a state of emergency to push for ratification of the ERA and committed all of its resources to that cause, it suspended NOWRTF and all national task force organizing. Rape, then, was not a priority on the liberal feminist agenda for at least six years into that branch of the movement's existence, and it took a backseat to another major issue when that became necessary.

Black Feminist Critique

Since the 1970s, feminist critics have pointed out that mainly white, middle-class women made up what is commonly thought of as the "women's movement," and that its agenda reflected this homogeneity (Cade 1970; hooks 1981; Moraga and Anzaldúa 1981; Davis 1983; Guy-Sheftall 1995). Flora Davis (1991, 358) notes that except for a few token women in leadership positions NOW's membership through the 1970s and beyond was predominantly white and middle class. Likewise, Alice Echols (1989) demonstrates that women's liberationists usually emphasized female commonality at the expense of class and racial differences. For example, the slogan "Sisterhood is powerful" was coined by Kathie Amatniek (who later changed her name to Sarachild) in 1968 to encourage women to form bonds based on their common oppression—womanhood—and to overlook differences that proved challenging, such as those based on class and racial experience. Echols further notes that in some cases women of color were explicitly excluded from movement activities. For instance, one group of white radical women organizers specifically chose not to invite radical black women to a national conference, fearing opposition or ridicule from those who were not identified with women's liberation (Echols 1989, 105–7, 369–77). By making such decisions, activists and writers in the women's movement overlooked the ways gender, race, class, and sexuality mediate each other within a superstructure that is at once sexist, racist, classist, and heterosexist (Lorde 1984; hooks 1984; Collins 1991). As in other social-movement groups, the politics of identity created the potential for both schism and coalition in the women's movement.

While most predominantly white feminist groups usually made some attempt to include women of color throughout the 1970s, they failed to draw them in large numbers (Echols 1989, 291–93). During the period of greatest radical feminist activity, women's liberationists believed, often accurately, that most black women activists preferred working exclusively within the black liberation movement, while liberal feminists seemed largely preoccupied with the concerns of middle-class white women (Echols 1989). Although women of color, among them Aileen Hernandez, Florynce Kennedy, Pauli Murray, Shirley Chisholm, Michele Wallace, and Cellestine Ware, did assume important roles in the mostly white feminist organizations, many other black women worked as organizers on a par with men in the black liberation struggles of the 1950s and 1960s (King 1987; Crawford, Rouse, and Woods 1993; Barnett 1995). Books such as Toni Cade's *Black Woman* and Michele Wallace's *Black Macho and the Myth of the Superwoman* raised the issue of sexism within the black community and among revolutionary black men.[11] According to one researcher, polls have indicated that black women have been as supportive of feminist goals as white women, or even more so (Giddings 1984, 345). Organizations focusing on black women's issues began to emerge in the early 1970s, notably the National Black Feminist Organization (NBFO) in 1973 and its spin-off, the Combahee River Collective, in 1975. Beverly Guy-Sheftall (1995) calls attention to African American women's two centuries of politicizing class, race, and gender through speeches, organizing, action, and theory.

Women of Color and the Anti-Rape Movement

The involvement of women of color in the campaign against rape has been the matter of some debate. As a social movement within the context of feminism, the campaign appeared to match the demographics of the larger women's movement. The beginnings of the anti-rape effort in Washington, D.C., typified this phenomenon. According to Elizabethann O'Sullivan, the first members of the D.C. Rape Crisis Center (D.C. RCC), founded in 1972, were white women in their twenties and thirties (personal interview, 8 June 1995). Initially, the center's clientele matched this demographic, in spite of Washington's majority–African American population. The collective openly expressed the desire to attract black and working-class women in its founding minutes of 28 May 1972 (O'Sullivan papers). This "whiteness" becomes even more significant in light of the fact that, also according to O'Sullivan, the majority of those who used the center's services fit a demographic description similar to that of the women in the collective. In the more liberal pockets of anti-rape organizing, the NOWRTF newsletter, published by Mary Ann Largen, sought advice from local RTFs on how to reach out to minority women (NOW papers). O'Sullivan notes that the racially charged nature of the rape issue, together with the long, volunteer hours required of movement personnel, probably discouraged women of color from participating during the early years of organizing (personal communication).

This seeming lack of interest had more to do with the framing of the rape issue by white feminists than with apathy on the part of women of color, according to Angela Y. Davis. She contends that "the failure of the anti-rape movement of the early 1970s to develop an analysis of rape that acknowledged the social conditions that foster sexual violence as well as the centrality of racism in determining those social conditions, resulted in the initial reluctance of Black, Latina, and Native American women to involve themselves in that movement" (1990, 45). In Davis's view, campaigners against rape failed to understand the still powerful memory of how fraudulent rape charges had been used against black men in recent U.S. history, as well as the brutality associated with such charges: "thousands of terroristic lynchings have been justified by the conjuring up of the myth of the Black rapist," says Davis (1990, 44). The myopia of the mostly white anti-rape activists, then, prevented them from understanding the deep interconnections between rape charges and racism in U.S. history.

According to Davis, women of color distrusted anti-rape organizers on at least two grounds: the belief that majority-white women's groups did not address black women's issues, and the fear that the regulation of rape, particularly by a criminal justice system that they perceived to be racist, would disproportionately target black men, despite the fact that the vast majority of rapes are intraracial (Davis 1990, 43). Nancy Matthews (1989) notes that the bilingual East Los Angeles Rape Hotline was founded in 1976 by Latinas for the Spanish-speaking community. But it was not until the 1980s that the anti-rape effort in Los Angeles, greatly aided by increased state funding for rape crisis services, approached real diversity in its own makeup and that of the population it serves.

Some African American activists reject the view that women of color did not become involved in the campaign against rape. According to the activist Loretta Ross, the anti-rape movement in Washington, D.C., was a space where women of color flourished in their feminist initiatives. Ross describes the D.C. RCC as a hub of organizing for black women in the late 1970s. The center was able to attract their attention and that of Latinas by expanding its focus from an exclusive concern with rape to issues of poverty and racism as they related to rape. The rape crisis center group was also committed to politicizing other areas of abuse, such as domestic violence and sexual harassment. The majority-white board of the D.C. RCC, according to Ross, was genuinely interested in developing black feminist leadership in the organization. The increasing availability of funds for staff positions in the mid-1970s created this opportunity for diversity, O'Sullivan observes (personal communication). Most important, Ross asserts that the problem was not uninvolvement on black women's part but a lack of documentation of their participation. She explains that women of color did not sit idly by and wait for white women to invite them into the movement, but took the initiative and organized around the rape issue on their own and in conjunction with other groups. Criticisms that black women were not involved erase their experience and present a distorted view of anti-rape organizing (Loretta Ross, personal interview, 16 October 1995).

Others have amplified Ross's contention that black feminists were involved in the effort against rape. Nkenge Toure, who worked in various capacities with D.C. RCC from 1975 to 1988, explains that women of color, with the help of "politically minded" founders of the organization, made that group a safe space that encouraged black feminist organizing. Toure and others took the lead in shaping a center that could meet the needs of communities of color. The appointment of black women to staff positions was important, she notes, but the center became inclusive because women of color took information about rape and about the center to the grass roots and made that information relevant. She agrees with Loretta Ross that women in the Washington area forged an activist network organizing around various feminist issues. Finally, Toure asserts that the D.C. RCC's focus on women of color began to diminish during the late 1980s (telephone interview, 9 January 1997).[12]

African American women became involved in anti-rape work in New York City as well. For example, according to Essie Green Williams, an organizer of the National Black Feminist Organization, the first NBFO conference in 1973 held a workshop to explore political perspectives and women's experiences of rape. Williams notes that feminists of color needed to investigate and define the rape issue for themselves before any coalition with mostly white groups was possible, even though they experienced continual pressure from black liberation organizations to ignore the white women's movement (Connell and Wilson 1974, 243–46). This suggests an important aspect of grassroots activism: a movement that addresses the needs of a community from within that community will gain more legitimacy than one that approaches it from the outside (Dubrow et al. 1986, 8).

Williams's explanation for why black women should become involved in the anti-rape movement captures the sense of divided loyalties (to gender and to race) that African American feminists have expressed: "At the same time that the black woman does not want to be another foot on the black man's head, she is trying to point out that a lot of the interactions that go on between black men and black women are very oppressive. It's a very difficult situation to deal with" (quoted in Connell and Wilson 1974, 245). The sexual nature of the rape issue only complicated the loyalty problem.

Alliances among the NBFO, NYRF, NYWAR, and the Women's Anti-Rape Coalition resulted in close collaboration and in co-sponsorship of events, such as the August 1974 speak-out on rape and sexual abuse (Brownmiller papers). Thus, while black women were justifiably wary about involving themselves in a movement dominated by white women, who might not make any effort to address specific issues of concern to them, they did participate in forging an anti-rape politics that was accountable to African Americans and to people of color generally.

Rape, then, having arrived on the radical feminist agenda by 1970 and on the liberal feminist agenda by 1972, had by 1973 also become a cause for feminists of color. It is clear that the radical branch of the women's movement first took up the issue and first broke the taboo against the open discussion of this "new" issue. In consciousness-raising sessions, speak-outs, and the newly formed anti-rape projects, victims told their stories and, perhaps for the first time, refused to blame themselves for their own rapes. Women came to realize that this experience, which they had previously interpreted as simply a personal issue, instead had political roots because it was common. They began to analyze the problem of rape in all its legal and political complexity. Later, liberal organizations took up the issue and brought their own focus to anti-rape organizing, and black feminists began to develop a political perspective on rape based on their own experiences. As these groups were defining the issue and investigating the parameters of the problem, the feminist anti-rape agenda burst onto the movement scene. Rape was now being discussed, debated, and theorized as never before.

Communications Networks

Both the formal organizations of the women's rights branch and the small, grassroots groups of the radical branch of the second wave of the women's movement created a communications network for anti-rape activists just as they provided an organizational base on which the movement drew. Jo Freeman (1975, 62) explains the importance of a "preexisting communications network which was . . . cooptable to the ideas of the new movement" to the formation of a social movement. By "cooptable" Freeman denotes the potential of a communications network to be receptive to the new ideas of the incipient movement (1975, 68).[13]

As a movement within feminism, the anti-rape effort similarly relied on existing networks that connected like-minded individuals and groups. The features of such networks included a number of thriving journals and newspapers and an organized cadre of activists and feminists who were linked by shared movement activity such as frequent meetings to raise consciousness, define strategy, and plan actions. This network comprised younger- and older-branch women already familiar with such terms as *power, sexism, male chauvinism,* and *oppression;* therefore, in Jo Freeman's sense of the word, it proved co-optable. The network was also able to mobilize resources on which the new movement could draw. By 1974, when the Feminist Alliance Against Rape (FAAR) was founded, the anti-rape movement had developed its own communications network and no longer depended on the organizations and groups of second-wave feminism for such networks.

Radical Feminist Communications Networks

The journals and newspapers of women's liberation proved an important conduit for disseminating ideas, including rape consciousness, among the younger branch. According to the journalist Anne Mather (1974, 82), between March 1968 and August 1973 more than 560 feminist periodicals were being published in the United States. The mainstream and underground journals and papers that circulated among feminists included *Everywoman* (Los Angeles), *Second Wave* (Cambridge), *No More Fun and Games* (Cambridge), *It Ain't Me, Babe* (Bay Area, California), *Big Mama Rag* (Denver), *Woman's World* (New York), *Off Our Backs* (D.C.), *Turn of the Screwed* (Dallas), *Women: A Journal of Liberation* (Baltimore), *Rat* (New York), and *Notes from the First (Second,* and *Third) Year* (New York). These publications served as both a bulletin board for announcements and a forum for publicizing theoretical advances and movement news. The anti-rape effort took hold very quickly thanks to the efficiency and diversity of the radical feminist media.

In 1969, the Boston group Cell 16's journal, *No More Fun and Games,* published articles on the importance of self-defense in enabling women to resist male violence. It advocated physical strength rather than "feminine" weakness, self-sufficiency in place of dependency and so-called protection, and aggressiveness instead of passivity. In the publications of Cell 16 appears the oft-repeated statement, "It must become as dangerous to attack a woman as to attack another man" (Densmore and Dunbar 1969; Galligan and Welch 1969). This slogan epitomizes the program of the Boston organization: martial arts, militancy, and aggression as self-defense. While in 1969 the strands of radical feminism varied from region to region, with different groups devising their own agendas, *No More Fun and Games* early on called attention to violence in its advocacy of self-defense and thereby began the first diffusion of anti-rape ideas. Such themes would be repeated and developed as the issue drew more attention from feminist activists.

The first mentions of rape in other journals of the younger branch reflected areas of tension in the thinking about the issue that feminists had begun to develop. One of these points of conflict was race. When feminists first began to politicize rape, New Left and black power ideology saw it simply as a false accusation by white women against black men in the South (Susan Brownmiller, telephone interview, 2 September 1996). In forging a political program that viewed sexual assault as a problem that women share, white feminists were challenging the accepted ideology and exposing themselves to charges of racism for being unsympathetic to the plight of oppressed black men. But some radical feminists did assert that white women were more at risk of rape by men of color than by others. This is evident in an article written by "Erin" for the Bay Area feminist periodical *It Ain't Me, Babe.* She offers a series of pointers for hitchhiking women who want to avoid rape: "[M]en vent their racial hostility against other men by taking it out on 'their' women so don't get in a car with a man of a

race other than your own" (Erin 1970, 17). Another issue of the periodical carries the same suggestion (Disarm Rapists 1970, 13).

Erin's opinions about men who rape women of other races may be
connected to the shocking revelations made by Eldridge Cleaver in
Soul on Ice (1968). In this very popular book, the black revolutionary
explains how he became a rapist: "Somehow I arrived at the conclusion
that, as a matter of principle, it was of paramount importance for me
to have an antagonistic, ruthless attitude toward white women"
(Cleaver 1968, 25). He found rape to be one way of expressing his rage
over his experience of oppression as a black man in the United States.

> I became a rapist. To refine my technique and modus operandi,
> I started out by practicing on black girls in the ghetto . . . and
> when I considered myself smooth enough, I crossed the tracks
> and sought out white prey. I did this consciously, deliberately,
> willfully, methodically—though looking back I see that I was in
> a frantic, wild, and completely abandoned frame of mind.
>
> Rape was an insurrectionary act. It delighted me that I was
> defying and trampling upon the white man's law, upon his sys-
> tem of values, and that I was defiling his women—and this
> point, I believe, was the most satisfying to me because I was very
> resentful over the historical fact of how the white man has used
> the black woman. I felt I was getting revenge. (Cleaver 1968, 26)

Although the author goes on to explain that, in prison, he thought the
better of his rapist past, which destroyed his self-respect, his description
of raping black and white women had damaging consequences. White
men in leftist movements accepted and advanced Cleaver's thesis:
Brownmiller notes that "the sight of white radicals and intellectuals
falling all over each other in their rush to accept the Cleaver rationale
for rape was a sorry sight" (1975, 278). Many women's liberationists
took Cleaver at his word, viewing his revelation as a call to arms to
black men to rape. In the years since, pro-feminist African Americans
have noted that, in spite of the concern with the interracial rape of
white women, all rape of black women is virtually ignored (Salaam

1980, 41). The specter Cleaver had summoned up had a profound impact on the discourse on rape and race in the anti-rape movement.

As mentioned earlier, ideas about rape spread rapidly among feminists through the plethora of movement publications. One article focusing on the safety of hitchhiking (Sisters Pick Up Sisters 1971) and another offering a victim's perspective on rape (Rape 1971) appeared under the heading "Combat Training" in the Los Angeles periodical *Everywoman.* Interestingly, the two were reprinted from an underground, New Left paper, the *Berkeley Tribe.* The rape testimonial, such as the one that appeared in *Everywoman,* became a popular genre within this growing literature. *Everywoman* also reported on the NYRF Conference on Rape held in April 1971 (Conference on Rape 1971), and printed an excerpt from Susan Griffin's landmark essay "Rape: The All-American Crime" of the same year.

On the East Coast, the Baltimore-based periodical *Women: A Journal of Liberation* published a trio of rape articles in a 1972 issue. The first, "Rape: The Experience," provides a victim's account of sexual assault and its aftermath (Anonymous 1972). The second, "Rape: The Facts," reviews rape statistics and the mistreatment of victims by law enforcement (Margolin 1972). Finally, "Rape: A Solution" suggests that a woman's best defense is to purchase and carry a gun (Sheldon 1972). Also in 1972, the *Second Wave* published two selections of feminist attempts to theorize rape (Cohn 1972; Lindsey, Newman, and Taylor 1972). Another theoretical tract that probably enjoyed a wide readership is Barbara Mehrhof and Pamela Kearon's "Rape: An Act of Terror" (1971); there was also Susan Griffin's classic "Rape: The All-American Crime" (1971). As such articles and other information circulated among feminists, the issue gained momentum and the anti-rape movement galvanized.

In large measure, the ideas of feminism spread throughout the United States by way of best-sellers, such as Shulamith Firestone's *Dialectic of Sex* (1970), Kate Millett's *Sexual Politics* (1970), and Robin Morgan's anthology *Sisterhood Is Powerful* (1970). Likewise, information on rape as a women's issue spread throughout the movement and into mainstream American society by way of other popular titles. The women's health volume *Our Bodies, Ourselves* (Boston Women's Health Book Collective 1973) contained a short chapter on rape. The books devoted to rape that brought the issue to a general audience include *Rape: How to Avoid It and What to Do About It if You Can't* (Csida and Csida 1974), *Rape: The First Sourcebook for Women* (Connell and Wilson 1974), *Rape* (Horos 1974), and *Against Rape* (Medea and Thompson 1974). Even as such books carried the issue of rape to a wide audience, they also circulated within the movement and helped to marshal further support there for anti-rape efforts.

Among radical women, and eventually in some older-branch groups as well, the democratic structure of meetings and networks allowed substantial freedom for discussing and acting upon issues. Because participants encouraged each other to articulate the issues of greatest importance to them as individuals, discussions of rape and rape activism could easily involve the whole group. The popularity of the testimonial, in which women wrote about or told of their own rapes, attests to the centrality of experience in radical feminist organizing. This focus on women's experience, and the primacy given to it, predisposed the women's liberationists to analyze and politicize rape as an issue quintessentially grounded in the lives of women.

Another factor in the exchanging of ideas among radicals was the concentration of activism in cities and towns with large college and university populations. The feminist networks connected to the universities, combined with schools' own communications networks, helped to foster the anti-rape movement. For example, the New York Women's Anti-Rape Group led a workshop at a women's health conference held at Queens College in New York City, according to minutes submitted to WARG by Diana Block and Lois Chaffee in November 1971 (NYWAR records). Elsewhere, the collective that founded the D.C. Rape Crisis Center in 1972 sponsored conferences at George Washington and American Universities to reach out to women who might be interested in the rape project (Barker 1972; Kiernan 1972; O'Sullivan papers). In Iowa City, Iowa, Women Against Rape (WAR) formed as part of the women's center at the University of Iowa (*New York Times* 1972). Similarly, in 1973 the University of Wisconsin,

Madison, funded in part the operation of the Women's Transit Authority (WTA), a nonprofit, volunteer-operated collective offering free rides to women at night (Greenwald 1977). In the fall of that year feminist students at Rutgers University's Livingston Campus started a rape crisis center to serve students at three Rutgers branches, adding a hotline the following February (Barrett 1974). Finally, students in the Women's Caucus of the University of Illinois, Circle Campus, began a campaign to sell rape whistles for fifty-five cents apiece, helping students to feel protected and raising awareness of rape (Schreiber 1974). Diana Scully, who went on to become a prominent researcher and to write *Understanding Sexual Violence* (1990), was involved in the whistle campaign as a graduate student.

Anti-rape activism and women's liberation organizing succeeded in university settings for similar reasons. Communications networks in these places were quite strong, making activities and events easy to publicize. In addition, many students, who constituted a receptive audience, could make the time to become involved in the movement. The growing presence of women's centers and women's studies programs further strengthened the anti-rape movement by helping to spread the word about the issue. These characteristics also had their weaknesses, though. College students are a transient population, usually remaining in place for only four or five years, and they are frequently unavailable to work on political causes during breaks and exam periods, both factors that could be the ruin of an organization that relies heavily on student volunteers. University populations also tend to be white, middle to upper class, and otherwise homogeneous, meaning that groups could have some difficulty being taken seriously beyond the walls of the academy. On the whole, however, campus communities not only proved an important source of activists for feminist groups, but existing interuniversity student organizations also offered communications networks to spread the word about the anti-rape movement.

Liberal Feminist Communications Networks

In the older branch of the women's movement, the rape issue was raised first among various NOW chapters. Before 1973, according to

NOWRTF's coordinator Mary Ann Largen, the chapters provided the communications base that enabled liberal feminists to voice their concerns about rape and begin to investigate the issue; some even worked with other feminist groups to found rape crisis centers (Largen 1985, 10). This grassroots organizing forced the issue of rape onto the agenda of the national conference in 1973, when Resolution 148 was adopted, forming NOWRTF. Although a general anti-rape measure had passed at the 1971 national conference, the organization did not commit any resources or energy to the issue at that time. Thus, the chapter organization and conference structure of NOW created the communications network that ushered in liberal feminist activism on rape.

The premier magazine of liberal feminism, nationally circulated *Ms.,* began publishing in July 1972. It first mentioned rape in November of that year in a comic strip, *Mary Self-worth,* which also tackled birth control, abortion, and women's self-esteem. Significantly, the treatment of rape in the strip virtually blames one character for being attacked. The December 1972 issue contains the story "I Never Set Out to Rape Anybody," written by a would-be rapist (*Ms.* 1972b). The magazine's first substantive coverage of the anti-rape movement or of feminist analyses of rape came in September 1973 with "How to Make Trouble: Rape Crisis Centers," a how-to guide for readers considering forming a center. Another rape story in the same issue (*Ms.* 1973) details the unfair treatment of victims who go to court. Because the magazine began to appear only after the women's movement had started to deal with the rape issue, *Ms.* was not on the cutting edge of the anti-rape effort, but it did bring the ideas of the anti-rape movement into a wider public arena.

Second-wave feminism, then, drew upon a communications network that comprised a radical left community (younger branch), various state commissions on the status of women, and several women's organizations that had long been lobbying for the ERA (older branch) (Freeman 1975, 63–67). A thriving movement was built on this foundation, even though it frequently met with resistance. The campaign against rape, by contrast, had a far more supportive and receptive (or "co-optable") communications network on which to draw. By the time

anti-rape actions began in 1971, seasoned activists were already familiar with political action, the political system, negotiating with the
media, organizing meetings and events, and a host of other factors
important to the fledgling movement.

Shared Consciousness

Rape arrived on the feminist agenda by way of the consciousness-raising session. The editors of *Rape: The First Sourcebook for Women* (1974),
an anthology based in part on the 1971 NYRF speak-out and rape
conference, explain the connection between rape and C-R this way:
"[R]ape became an issue when women began to compare their experiences as children, teen-agers, students, workers, and wives and to realize that sexual assault, in one form or another, was common" (Connell
and Wilson 1974, 3). This closely follows the role of consciousness in
the politics of rape as articulated in the NYRF manifesto: "When more
than two people have suffered the same oppression the problem is no
longer personal but political—and rape is a political matter" (quoted
in Connell and Wilson 1974, n.p.). Women who had previously kept
silent about their experiences, or their fears, found in the C-R group a
context for rethinking rape. Instead of internalizing guilt and anxiety,
they encouraged each other to talk about rape as a matter of male
dominance.

The salience of a shared consciousness of common oppression to the
rise of a social movement has been theorized variously by social scientists. Ethel Klein (1984, 93), a political scientist, posits that "the transformation of women's roles and women's understanding of their roles
throughout the [twentieth] century culminated in a feminist consciousness." Other political scientists (e.g., Cook 1989) have gone so far as to
attempt to measure feminist consciousness. This awareness of gender
asymmetry and male dominance was already in place when rape began
to be raised as a women's issue. Rape consciousness grew directly out of
the radical feminist tool for organizing and theorizing, consciousness-
raising, which was designed to elicit democratically from women
which issues were important to them and why. A look at the reasoning
behind C-R, which also served as a means of communicating the anti-

rape message, elucidates the role of C-R in promoting women's shared consciousness of rape.

The objective of C-R was to encourage, as Amy Kesselman explains, "the political reinterpretation of one's personal life" (quoted in Echols 1989, 83). The idea of consciousness-raising did not begin with radical feminists: writers have cited its roots in the Chinese revolutionary tradition of "speaking pains to recall pains" and the black movement's "telling it like it is" (Hole and Levine 1971, 138). In 1968, Kathie Sarachild of the New York Radical Women (NYRW), C-R's principal architect, began to visualize the potential and the need for women to use their own experiences as the foundation for their feminist actions, theory, and politics, to be articulated in the consciousness-raising group. Members of the movement agreed that C-R's purpose was "to find out the truth about women" (Price 1972, 11). Topics for the groups to cover included work, family, sexuality, religion, and anything else that members suggested. It was hoped that C-R would help to bridge the gaps between women, gaps fostered by physical and psychological isolation that traditionally discouraged group consciousness among them (Hole and Levine 1971, 137). Ethel Klein (1984, 97) summarizes the role of C-R as follows: "[P]eople look to political solutions for private problems when they realize that their personal difficulties are shared by other similar people, the group."

Consciousness-raising groups experienced continual tension about their goals. Detractors worried, often with good reason, that the strategy would degenerate into group therapy, aimed at no more than making participants feel better about their own lives, and would never lead to concrete action (Hole and Levine 1971, 140–41). Carol Williams Payne (1973, 283) explains the issues her own group faced: "There was always a conflict between those who favored the personal, psychological approach and those who felt that a women's group should be building a bridge between the personal insight gained by being in a small group and political action with a larger body of women." Such tension was never resolved to the complete satisfaction of either side. Rape is a good example of a consciousness-raising issue that did lead to concrete

action, such as the self-defense collectives and rape crisis centers that
began to be created in 1971 and 1972.

Even though C-R was closely associated with the younger branch of
the women's movement, the rights-focused NOW leadership came to
understand the value of the approach for its own members and eventually offered C-R sessions in its chapters (Freeman 1975, 86). In the late
1960s and early 1970s, C-R formed the core of feminist praxis and
politics, and thousands of women came into the movement by joining
C-R groups throughout the United States. Consciousness-raising is
credited with helping women personally to develop self-confidence and
organizational skills, and collectively to arrive at theoretical insights
that would point the way to political strategy.

Consciousness-raising on rape stressed not only shared consciousness
but also women's shared experience. When Susan Brownmiller's C-R
group first considered the issue in the fall of 1970, three women told
of their rape experiences (telephone interview, 2 September 1996). In
Washington, most of the members of the collective that formed the
D.C. Rape Crisis Center had survived rape and were motivated to
become politically active by discussing their experiences in C-R sessions
(Elizabethann O'Sullivan, personal interview, 8 June 1995). Rape testimonials—victims' stories about their experience and its aftermath—
appeared in various movement publications (e.g., Rape 1971;
Anonymous 1972). Diana Russell's 1975 book, *The Politics of Rape,*
moreover, offers a victim's testimonial in each of its twenty-two chapters. These stories describe the guilt and shame so many women felt,
the disbelief they encountered if they reported having been assaulted,
and the humiliation they endured during questioning by police and
medical personnel. Because consciousness-raising placed experience at
the center of analysis, the testimonial became the most important tool
for understanding the role of rape in women's lives. In addition, like
the founders of the D.C. RCC, many women were led into the anti-
rape movement precisely because they had survived rape: political action was one way to transform a traumatic experience into something
more empowering.

The experiences described through C-R involved stranger, acquaintance, and date rape, coerced sex with psychotherapists, gang rape, rape by family members, intra- and interracial rape, marital rape, attempted rape, and more (Connell and Wilson 1974; Susan Brownmiller, telephone interview, 2 September 1996). But these were not all the stories that women told. They began to tell of the "little rapes"—verbal harassment, street harassment, unwanted sexual contact, and unwanted sexual advances—that are much more common (Connell and Wilson 1974; Medea and Thompson 1974). San Francisco Women Against Rape (1977, 4) asked: "Has a man ever whistled at you while you were walking down the street? Has a man ever made comments about your body while you stood at the busstop, minding your own business? Has a man ever exposed himself to you while you were reading a book on the beach?" The revelations about the little rapes enabled movement women to make connections between such everyday violations—which the vast majority of them had experienced—and larger, more traumatic violations that some had endured. These connections revealed to women the possibility of joining with each other over the rape issue whether they personally had been victims or not. The connections also led to an understanding that abuse includes both verbal harassment and rape, a continuum that left men's behavior and sense of entitlement unchallenged. Also unchallenged was the idea that public space is a male domain; women who occupy it do so at their peril. Understanding such connections proved to feminists that women are subjected to numerous and interrelated forms of sexual abuse; this insight, in turn, helped to garner feminist support for the anti-rape movement.[14]

Before consciousness-raising on rape, the author Susan Brownmiller, like many other women, had perceived it as "a sex crime, a product of a diseased, deranged mind" or as a false charge made by a white woman against a black man. She once believed women in the movement "had nothing in common with rape victims" (Brownmiller 1975, xii). Rape persisted as a topic of C-R and became the subject of widespread movement activity from 1970 to 1973. Consciousness-raising helped women learn about rape from each other; experience formed the backbone of political action. Women's consciousness of sex-

ual assault as pervasive in and destructive to their lives, as articulated
in C-R, provided the first impetus to politicize the issue since the resistance to sexual coercion by women's rights advocates and the black
clubwomen's movement in the nineteenth century. Beginning in 1970,
C-R placed rape squarely on the feminist agenda.

Critical Mobilizing Events

Jo Freeman (1975, 49) hypothesizes that some sort of crisis or pivotal
event is necessary to mobilize the growing discontent among the potential members of a movement. Several political scientists offer as an
example of this sort of event the publication in 1963 of Betty Friedan's
Feminine Mystique, the book that was the first to articulate the sense of
alienation middle-class American women often experienced in their
role as housewives in the 1950s and early 1960s. This best-seller stimulated the feminist consciousness of millions of women who had been
searching for ways to describe their discontent. Together with other
developments such as the passage of the Civil Rights Act of 1964, Friedan's book helped establish the women's rights branch of the second
wave of feminism.

The two critical mobilizing events for the anti-rape movement were
the New York Radical Feminists' first speak-out on rape in January
1971 and their first rape conference in April of that year. What is
noteworthy about the two events was their shared effect of both reflecting and raising rape consciousness, which directed feminist attention to the problem and helped launch the anti-rape movement. In
Freeman's terms, these were efforts used by some of the early campaigners against rape to spark greater interest in the issue among all
members of the women's movement.[15]

According to Susan Brownmiller, after her C-R group began to
discuss rape and her own consciousness had been elevated, she suggested that the New York Radical Feminists host a conference to investigate the issue. The NYRF, however, preferred to hold a speak-out
first, indicating that such an act, in the spirit of the 1969 speak-out on
abortion, was more its style. But the organization did decide to plan
both events (Susan Brownmiller, telephone interview, 2 September

1996). A committee was chosen to arrange the speak-out; among the organizers was Alix Kates Shulman, the writer and activist. The first speak-out on rape took place in St. Clement's Episcopal Church in Manhattan on Sunday, 24 January 1971. Approximately three hundred people crowded the small church. The NYRF decided to admit reporters to the event; all women could attend free of charge (childcare was provided), and men were admitted, only if accompanied by a woman, for two dollars. Twelve women involved in planning the event had prepared to tell of their rape experiences, and twenty-eight others testified spontaneously. NYRF's purpose was clear: women would speak out "to counter the myths that (1) women cannot be raped against their will, (2) women really want to be raped, and (3) women make false accusations. . . . Speaking-out about rape is an attempt to destroy the power of the 'top dogs' to place the blame on women for crimes committed solely by men" (Connell and Wilson 1974, 27). The speakers described various types of violence: rape by acquaintances, strangers, and gangs, sexual harassment, and more. Although the mainstream New York and national press virtually ignored the event, the weekly *Village Voice* did cover it (Susan Brownmiller, telephone interview, 2 September 1996), as did *New York* magazine (Sheehy 1971).[16]

Susan Brownmiller was very active in planning the follow-up rape conference, which took place 17 April 1971. The event was advertised in the New York underground paper *Rat* in an attempt to attract as many interested women's liberationists as possible (Kellogg 1971). The conference was intended to be more investigative and analytical than the testimonial-based speak-out, although it, too, included a speak-out. The conference program outlines a wide variety of workshop topics, including "Legal/Criminal Aspects" of rape, "Incest and Child Molestation," "Survival Now: Community Responsibility and Immediate Demands," "Self-Defense," and "Rape, Sensuality, and Sexuality: Claiming the Sex Act" (Brownmiller papers). Organizers sought to investigate all aspects of rape in the hopes that more knowledge would lead to better organizing strategies and actions against it. Unlike the speak-out, the conference was closed to men; again, childcare was provided. This time the event received coverage in the *New York Times* in a story focusing on the self-defense workshop, by a reporter who continued to write about rape for the newspaper (Lichtenstein 1971). Workshop papers from the conference are collected in Noreen Connell and Cassandra Wilson's 1974 anthology, *Rape: The First Sourcebook for Women*.

The 1971 speak-out and conference both reflected the newly raised awareness of rape as a women's issue and made that issue publicly visible; thus, they served as critical mobilizing events of the anti-rape movement. The organizers of the speak-out explicitly sought to replicate the visible, public impact of the 1969 speak-out on abortion organized by the radical New York group Redstockings (Connell and Wilson 1974, 28; Susan Brownmiller, telephone interview, 2 September 1996). The purpose of both was to bring a taboo subject into the open, declare the question no longer private and specific only to the individual, and encourage rethinking of an issue based on the knowledge of shared experience.

Of course, other developments related to rape took place before 1971, but they cannot accurately be considered critical mobilizing events. For example, during the 1950s, the American Law Institute (ALI) undertook a thorough revision of the Model Penal Code (MPC), including the laws concerning rape (American Law Institute 1980). When the relatively conservative ALI adopted a politically moderate code in 1962, it was not hailed as a first step toward women's liberation from the fear of rape, nor was it denounced as an impediment to justice for rape victims.[17] In fact, it prompted little social-movement response at all and mobilized no significant anti-rape activism. Likewise, reflecting the rising tide of tough-on-crime sentiment among lawmakers, legislatures had begun to change their rape laws within the general context of reform of criminal codes in the 1960s and early 1970s, but without the involvement of the women's movement. New Jersey and Pennsylvania, for instance, altered their rape laws along the lines of the MPC in 1972, before feminist efforts had begun to affect the legal scene. Neither state's law can be considered "radically pro-victim," according to the legal scholar Leigh Bienen (1976, 52). These and similar events can be viewed as significant in the context of the evolution of rape law, but they did not mobilize a social movement against sexual assault.

The New York Radical Feminists' speak-out and conference of 1971 proved to be the catalyst that the burgeoning anti-rape movement required. Although not associated with crisis, as some critical mobilizing events are, these two organized programs uniquely combined consciousness-raising with public exposure to draw the attention of both potential activists and citizens in general to the problem of rape. It was following this mobilization that the women's movement began to commit substantial resources of time, energy, and money to the anti-rape cause. The speak-out and the conference, moreover, caught the interest both of a broad public and of the mass media. Such press attention marked an important step toward putting the problem of rape on the systemic agenda, as I will describe in Chapter 3. The elevated consciousness of the issue as one involving all women, together with the spark of the NYRF's speak-out and conference, gave rise to the feminist anti-rape movement.

The Ideology of the Anti-Rape Movement

The formation of a shared set of political views is a definitive feature of social movements. The political scientist Claire Fulenwider (1980, 22) defines ideology as "a political belief system that makes both cognitive (intellectual) and psychological sense out of political reality." An ideology describes present reality in a new way, evaluates that reality and demonstrates just what is wrong or right with it, and formulates a plan for change consistent with that evaluation (Fulenwider 1980, 23). At the time that rape arrived on the feminist agenda, the women's movement had long been developing its own political ideology. Although the younger and older branches explained women's situation differently and posited different solutions, the radicals and the liberals agreed upon women's subordination to men, their unfair treatment by society's institutions, and the unequal distribution of tangible and intangible resources on the basis of gender. When anti-rape ideology began to be formed, its proponents already shared these beliefs. Thus, the thinking of the women's movement fostered the formation of anti-rape ideology.

Popular perceptions of rape, its victims, and its perpetrators before the anti-rape movement combined elements of sexism, victim blaming, ignorance, and racism. Dispelling the myths about rape provided the conceptual framework for the development of a new belief system to which movement actors subscribed. Figure 1.1 delineates the major "rape myths" that feminists sought to disprove. These myths, as feminists have viewed them, span a broad range of conceptualizations of rape, rape victims, and rapists that campaigners against rape have sought to redefine.[18]

Reconceptualizing Rape

The most important tenet of anti-rape ideology was the assertion that rape is about violence, not sex. Although the idea can be traced to Ruth Herschberger (1948), it is widely attributed to Susan Brownmiller (1975, 439) and rapidly gained wide acceptance at the beginning of the movement. All the other myths derive from the belief that rape is grounded in passion and sexual pleasure: rape is linked to women's attractiveness; women who have had consensual sex cannot be raped; black men desire sex with white women; women say no when they mean yes; women secretly fantasize about and even crave rape. The assertion that rape is violence provided feminists with a whole new framework in which to analyze rape, to remove blame from victims, and to develop a convincing argument to gain acceptance for their claims.[19] In conjunction with the "violence, not sex" argument, feminists also defined rape as any form of unwanted sexual contact, thereby expanding the concept to include forced anal or oral intercourse or contact, penetration with fingers or other objects, and other acts.

Radical women led in developing the emerging rape ideology. In 1971, as the feminist communication network was circulating new ideas about sexual assault, two influential articles appeared: "Rape: An Act of Terror," by Barbara Mehrhof and Pamela Kearon, from NYRF's *Notes from the Third Year;* and the oft-quoted "Rape: The All-American Crime," by Susan Griffin, from *Ramparts* (described by Abe

Figure 1.1 Popular Rape Myths Challenged by Anti-Rape Ideology

On Rape

Rape is a crime of sex
There is no such thing as rape
Most rapes are interracial
Rape exists only in the ghetto

On Rape Victims

It is difficult to rape a woman; if she really does not want
     it, she can resist
Women desire or invite rape
Women say no when they really mean yes
Women's appearance and dress provoke rape
Women of color are very strong, so they handle rape better
Women of color are more sexually promiscuous than other
     women
Women make false allegations of rape out of revenge or
     spite
Only a chaste woman can be raped

On Rapists

Most rapists are black and poor
Black men are predisposed to raping, especially white
     women
All rapists are strangers to their victims
Rapists are sadistic or sex-starved psychopaths
Regular men don't rape or don't need to rape

Peck, a journalist, as "the Bay Area Catholic reform magazine turned radical muckraker" [1991, 29]).[20] These were the first attempts by feminists to theorize—to define, explain, and prescribe solutions to—rape. Mehrhof and Kearon (1971) posit rape as representing the essence of male dominance over women and assert that the fear of it keeps them in a constant state of subordination, unable to resist their oppression.

Griffin views rape as "the perfect combination of sex and violence" by which men express their socially constructed dominance over women (1971, 29). As two of the earliest theoretical tracts to emerge from the anti-rape movement, these articles had a profound effect on the emerging feminist reconceptualization of rape.

The views expressed by Mehrhof and Kearon and by Griffin were echoed in part by Susan Brownmiller in *Against Our Will*. She brought the idea of rape as a form of terrorism in women's lives to a popular audience. When Brownmiller made her famous statement that rape is "nothing more or less than a conscious process of intimidation by which *all men* keep *all women* in a state of fear" (1975, 5; emphasis in original), she reflected the ideological developments that had been taking place since 1970. Women remain "in their place" out of fear of rape. They seek out men's protection from rape by other men, thereby placing themselves in danger of rape by their protectors. All men do not have to rape to produce the desired effect of women's intimidation and passivity. Institutions such as the legal system collaborate with the rapist to ensure that the crime is rarely punished and to deter victims from speaking out. Such thinking, grounded in feminist analysis, helped to locate anti-rape politics squarely within the radical feminist ideology of male dominance and female submission, abetted by a legal system that enforced such dominance.[21] Eliminating rape, then, required transforming gendered social arrangements.

Reconceptualizing Rape Victims

Numerous myths of rape focus a seemingly inordinate amount of attention on its victims. Implicit in these views is the idea that women bring rape on themselves. The 1971 pamphlet *Stop Rape,* created by Detroit Women Against Rape, explains that "all of us [women] everywhere have the fear [of rape,] and it is not an illogical fear because the defining characteristic of the victim is not her reputation, her behavior, her looks, her age or where she lives. It is her sex" ([Detroit] Women Against Rape 1971, 2). Consciousness-raising proved that any woman could be attacked, no matter what her dress, her age, her race, or her past sexual experience. Moreover, C-R revealed that women nearly always blamed themselves for being raped, and consequently remained silent out of shame and guilt. San Francisco Women Against Rape (1977, 11) state, "This society has done a good job of making us into rape victims and then keeping us from rising up in angry protest by making us accept the blame and guilt. . . . A woman must realize that she did not ask to be raped." Women reported that the attitudes of police, hospital personnel, and others to whom they reported rapes perpetuated the feeling of self-reproach by implying or stating explicitly that they had invited their own victimization.

At the same time, women who are older or who don't dress in an obviously provocative manner may see rape as unlikely, an attitude reinforced by myths that associate women's appearance with being assaulted. Anti-rape ideology sought to dispel this misunderstanding as well, starting from the reality of rape in women's experience. For example, the D.C. Rape Crisis Center, declares:

> If a woman is older, sees herself as unattractive or dresses conservatively, she may feel immune to rape. In reality, a woman of any age or appearance is vulnerable to rape. At the Center, we have talked to rape victims in their 80's and 90's. Rapes of children as young as six months have been documented. . . .
>
> Focusing on the condition of the victim leads to a distorted view of rape. It implies that the conditions of the *victim* contributed to the crime. (1977, 1; emphasis in original)

In this way, anti-rape activists attempted to replace a dominant myth—that women's appearance invites rape—with fact: women of all ages, whether they meet cultural standards of physical beauty, are threatened by rape. Culturally imposed notions of passivity and frailty promote the kind of submissiveness that puts them all at risk of being attacked.

In regions where the anti-rape movement comprised a diverse membership willing to focus on black women's experience of rape, other myths were confronted or dispelled. A whole series of them was outlined by Michele Plate of the D.C. Rape Crisis Center (*Feminist Alliance Against Rape Newsletter* 1976, 13):

> People in institutions [such as law enforcement and hospitals]
> perpetuate not only rape myths but also Black myths. They feel
> that *all* Black women are "loose," so what are we complaining
> about. They feel that *all* Black women want sex 24 hours a day,
> so what's the big deal that someone took it with force. They feel
> that *all* Black women are cheap, so they treat Black women as
> tramps and with as little respect as possible. They feel that
> Black-on-Black crime is irrelevant, so why should they take this
> case seriously. (emphasis in original)

Historians have traced degrading beliefs about black women's sexuality as far back as pre-slavery days, when Westerners viewed African
women's semi-nudity and equated it with sexual laxity. Such constructions of black female sexuality were exacerbated during slavery and
indeed survived it (Giddings 1984; White 1985). Black women, then,
faced a different set of myths from those white women confronted,
and some activists in the movement were willing to explore in detail
the ramifications of these conceptualizations.

So, an important feature of anti-rape ideology was to replace victim-
blaming myths with the tenets that women are not responsible for
being attacked and that, since any woman can be raped, there are no
characteristics or behaviors that single out the victim. How a woman
dresses and how she behaves are not related to her vulnerability to
rape, feminists declared. Anti-rape activists also asserted that women
do not lie about rape at a rate any higher than that of other crime
victims. In short, the emerging anti-rape ideology sought to shift the
emphasis from the victim to the perpetrator.

Reconceptualizing Rapists

Some of the most tenacious myths that campaigners against rape confronted in the early 1970s involved society's conception of typical rapists. In one view, they are sexual psychopaths whose desire to rape
emanates from a psychiatric disorder that drives them to commit sadistic acts. The crime, under this conceptualization, was that of a per-
verted and deranged individual. Rape was thought of as very unusual

and rare, and rapists as a small minority of mentally ill men.[22] But as women listened to each others' rape experiences, they noticed that the perpetrators came from every background and appeared to be average American men. In fact, in the experience of the D.C. Rape Crisis Center (1977, 16), the majority of rapists tended to have "normal" psychological and sexual profiles (see also Amir 1971).

Activists also confronted the belief that the rapist was a sex-starved man "suddenly overcome by sexual needs" and driven to satisfy them by force ([Detroit] Women Against Rape 1971, 2). Anti-rape ideology countered this myth, like that of the psychopath, by using existing research and the experiences of victims themselves. Menachem Amir (1971) found that as many as 70 percent of rapists in his sample had planned their crimes, so the spontaneity implied in the sex-starvation myth did not match reality. Instead, according to anti-rape ideology, perpetrators were motivated by a desire for power and control, and they chose violent sex as their vehicle "to brutalize and humiliate women" (D.C. Rape Crisis Center 1977, 1).

Finally, the movement confronted the myth that rape tends to be the act of mainly poor and black men. Amir's 1971 study (which focused solely on men imprisoned for rape) fed into this myth, for it found that the vast majority of rapists were poor and members of working-class minority groups. Some feminists, although cognizant of the history of lynching black men after dubious charges made by white women, preferred to avoid the question of rape and race. Others (e.g., Erin 1970) accepted Eldridge Cleaver's (1968) thesis that black men were likely to rape white women in an effort to lash out against the white man. However, it gradually became clear to feminists in the anti-rape movement that the popular focus on interracial rape diverted attention from the vast majority of rapes, which are intraracial (Connell and Wilson 1974, 241–48).

Members of D.C. RCC note that the myth that black and poor men constitute the greatest proportion of rapists persists since "there are more Black and/or lower class men in jail for rape because women are less afraid to prosecute them because they feel they will be believed. . . . This myth is supported by our legal system in which men without resources to defend themselves are more likely to be convicted" (1977, 16). Anti-rape activists who pursued law-and-order remedies—such as greater police presence for women's protection, tougher enforcement of rape laws, and more appropriate penalties for convicted offenders— were firmly criticized by others who noted that this approach would probably only result in greater numbers of imprisoned black men (Edwards [1976?], 19).

Thus, feminists rejected the dominant myths and stereotypes of the rapist, advancing instead the notion that any man can commit the crime, regardless of his status in the community. While strangers on the street posed a threat to women, acquaintances, dates, and husbands could be equally or more threatening. Along with new research, the basis for this rethinking of popular myths was the information contained in the rape testimonial, whether offered at a speak-out, in women's liberation journals, or in the small-group consciousness-raising session. Revelations about the act of rape, its victims, and its perpetrators combined to form a feminist ideology of rape that campaigners against the crime sought to advance in the wider society. Despite their efforts, however, many of the myths of rape still pervade the American consciousness.

While the nineteenth and early twentieth centuries saw some politicization of the issue of rape, it was not until 1970 that an activist, vocal anti-rape movement began to emerge out of the second wave of feminism. The second wave's organizational base and communications networks provided the social-movement context out of which a more specific effort against rape emerged (albeit one still connected to the larger women's movement). Through the strategy of consciousness-raising beginning in 1970 and the staging of critical mobilizing events in 1971, rape became an issue for feminists, and they began to articulate a new rape consciousness—a politicized understanding of the experience of rape and its role in the larger system of male dominance. Because the women's movement provided this context, the campaign against rape resembled the larger movement in many ways at its inception, particularly in its demographics and its liberal and radical ideologies. A clear structure of thinking emerged to reinterpret rape as an act of power and violence, not of passion and sexuality; to reinterpret victims as blameless; and to reinterpret any man as a potential rapist, in line with the growing consciousness of rape as a problem rooted in male domination of society. This mobilization gave rise to a rich variety of strategies to express the new ideology and to address the problem of rape from a feminist perspective.

2

ANTI-RAPE ORGANIZING
AND STRATEGIES

SINCE THE DAWN of the anti-rape movement, the vast majority of organizing has focused on two related yet seemingly separate activities: establishing and operating rape crisis centers and reforming rape statutes. Here, I survey the many kinds of anti-rape organizing, including self-defense, guerrilla tactics, take back the night marches, rape crisis centers, and law reform efforts. An important goal of this chapter is to examine the ways in which the many forms of organizing—including rape crisis centers and law reform—can be located as related strategies within the wide constellation of events, actions, and activism that comprise the anti-rape movement.

Once rape arrived on the feminist agenda in 1970, the new organizing took many forms. Both liberal and radical women's organizations and C-R groups across the country were taking up the issue, using insights derived from experience to devise strategy. Workshops and conferences were held, often to investigate the possibility of forming an anti-rape project best suited for a particular community. Several strands of organizing, with various goals and objectives, took shape to address the problem in different ways. In this chapter, I look at the roots of each strategy in radical or liberal feminism, and at the ways in which many anti-rape strategies transcended such a distinction. While all the approaches have a common ideology, they do diverge in their methods for addressing rape and in their prescriptions for change.

Self-Defense

Efforts that focused on fighting off attackers were among the first activities by women's groups to call attention to rape. In 1969, as advocates of martial arts training and militancy for women, members of Cell 16 in Cambridge, Massachusetts, were early proponents of teaching self-defense skills to combat various forms of violence against women and to instill in them a sense of self-sufficiency. As rape consciousness spread through the communications network of the women's movement between 1970 and 1973, activists placed greater emphasis on self-defense as one method of preventing rape. Organizing and publications involving this approach were important in the anti-rape movement: through the practice of self-defense, women might reverse or resist their socialized passivity and dependency on men, which contribute to the problem of rape. Taking charge of defending themselves made women feel as if they were making a difference, if only one woman at a time.

Self-defense provided one way for feminists to replace passivity with assertiveness and potentially stem the tide of rape. Organizing focused on martial arts–based training, assertiveness training, and combinations of the two. A 1970 self-defense tract, one that may or may not be connected to Cell 16's activities, appeared in the Boston area underground paper the *Old Mole*. The authorship of the piece, entitled "Kick-Ass for Women" (1970), is claimed only by "a member of the stick it in the wall motherfucker collective." The article argues that women's freedom is severely limited "because the violence of oppression has become so distressingly identical with the possession of a penis." Learning self-defense would not only free women to occupy the public sphere, it would also help to "break down our fear and sense of fragility in our own heads." The author suggests that women use whatever skills they can gain from the traditional martial arts to empower themselves and other women to resist attacks by men.

In the 1960s and 1970s, men dominated the martial arts. Sexism was as prevalent in karate schools as anywhere else, feminists observed (Grimstad and Rennie 1973, 157), and instructors frequently viewed women's fear as little more than a source of profit. To provide a feminist alternative, in 1971 the martial artist Py Bateman founded the Feminist Karate Union (FKU) in Seattle. It began as one project of the University of Washington Women's Commission. The FKU made self-defense classes inexpensive, held consciousness-raising sessions where students could discuss their feelings and experiences, and employed only women instructors.[1] Similarly, the Women's Martial Arts Union was founded on the East Coast to unite feminist martial artists and self-defense instructors in Philadelphia, New York, Baltimore, and Washington, D.C. (Grimstad and Rennie 1973, 157). These unions investigated and shared self-defense techniques and assertiveness skills that would best serve women facing threatening situations in real life. Finally, such periodicals as *Black Belt Woman* of Medford, Massachusetts, and *Fighting Woman News* of New York City emerged in the mid-1970s to connect women in martial arts training and those with an interest in learning to defend themselves.

Many anti-rape projects addressed self-defense as a part of their diverse programs. Organizations such as the D.C. Rape Crisis Center (D.C. RCC), the Los Angeles Commission on Assaults Against Women (founded in 1973), and the East Los Angeles Rape Hotline (also founded in 1973) offered self-defense classes for women from their beginnings or soon after. An investigation of self-defense issues was also mentioned as one of the NOW Rape Task Force's first goals. This strategy was one part of the anti-rape projects' overall program of promoting rape awareness, educating the public about sexual assault, and counteracting women's sense of helplessness about it.

Anti-rape campaigners and other feminists often made self-defense information available through their publications, frequently mentioning particular techniques and offering rape-avoidance advice. For example, *Stop Rape,* by the Detroit Women Against Rape (WAR), an early project, contains a full twenty-two pages of advice (out of fifty pages total); topics include the basics of how to walk more safely at night, deliver a punch, deflect a blow, and turn ordinary objects into weapons ([Detroit] Women Against Rape 1971, 13–34). Pittsburgh Action Against Rape (1975), San Francisco Women Against Rape (1977), and the D.C. RCC (D.C. Rape Crisis Center 1977) make similar suggestions in their manuals. The 1972 version of the D.C. RCC manual, moreover, depicts the outline of a woman, dressed in traditional *gi* (karate garb), on its cover, implying the importance of self-defense to the center's mission. Feminist resource books, among them *The New Woman's Survival Catalog* (Grimstad and Rennie 1973) and *Our Bodies, Ourselves* (Boston Women's Health Book Collective 1973), contain sections on self-defense. Finally, feminist anti-rape books (e.g., Csida and Csida 1974; Medea and Thompson 1974; Brownmiller 1975) paid close attention to self-defense in preventing sexual assault and brought the anti-rape message to a wider audience. Thus, at times, feminists took up self-defense as a goal in itself, as in the FKU project; at other times, they pursued self-defense in conjunction with other strategies against rape.

Self-defense, finally, transcends the differences between radical and liberal anti-rape organizers. Like the anti-rape movement itself, the strategy is rooted in the radical branch of the feminist movement. It allowed women to dare to behave in unfeminine ways, to advocate defensive violence, and to flout conventional assumptions about womanhood. But as an anti-rape strategy, self-defense can be criticized for its liberal assumptions, for it promotes change one woman at a time and seeks to empower individuals to overcome their own passivity and submissiveness rather than rooting out that oppression (but see McCaughey 1997). Self-defense strategies, guided by an anti-rape ideology that linked these violent attacks to the gendered social system, were one way for feminist organizers to effect change.

Guerrilla Action

Unorthodox efforts to combat rape, which have occasionally been romanticized in the feminist literature as the most interesting anti-rape tool (e.g., Castro 1990, 193–95), surely took place among radical feminists at the height of women's liberation. Data on such actions, however, are difficult to locate. Because they were extra-legal or illegal, and usually covert and anonymous, few records involving these strategies remain. One notable, entirely legal exception is the Kitty Genovese Women's Project (KGWP). Here, five feminists spent nearly a year in the Dallas County courthouse poring over Texas criminal records to find the names of all men indicted for rape between 1960 and 1976.[2] On 8 March 1977, the group published a newspaper containing a list of over fifteen hundred names, an act that received attention from the *National Observer* and the *Washington Post*. These white, working-class women from Dallas, some of them survivors of rape, published their list anonymously out of fear of retaliation by men who had been named.[3] The group distributed the paper throughout Dallas and posted it in areas frequented by women.

The KGWP compiled the list "because close to half of all women raped are raped by men they know. . . . [W]e hope to make it more difficult for rapists to operate within a system of anonymity which allows them to continue their violence against women" (Kitty Genovese Women's Project 1977, 1). The group acknowledged that the list represented only a small fraction of all rapists, since most attacks go unreported. The project was criticized within the anti-rape movement for its failure to question the criminal justice system's race and class bias (Ulmschneider 1977; Friedman 1978a). The KGWP paper suggested that women in other parts of the country looking for an anti-rape project might want to follow their example. Deb Friedman (1978a) explains that her group, the D.C. Area Feminist Alliance, considered compiling such a list but chose not to because of the negative implications of a mostly white feminist group taking action against a group of mostly black men. Covert actions targeting individual rapists, then, proved gratifying to some activists but problematic to others.

Like self-defense, guerrilla efforts such as the KGWP's list making might be viewed as liberal strategies practiced by radical women. Because they sought only to expose indicted rapists, rather than analyze and eliminate the sources of sexual assault, the members of the KGWP took an individualistic approach in line with a liberal political strategy. But the members of the Dallas collective viewed their project as a radical action against rape (Nikki Craft papers). They wanted to break the silence that protects rapists and alert the female population to the presence among them of indicted rapists. Although guerrilla tactics hardly bridged the gap between radical and liberal feminism, they did contain elements of both political ideologies.[4]

Take Back the Night

One of the most enduring and identifiable anti-rape collective actions is the take back the night (TBN) march, wherein women (and sometimes supportive men) march in a symbolic reclaiming of the streets and the nighttime hours. Unlike the other strategies discussed here, TBN was usually staged as a single or annual event, not as an anti-rape project in itself. The origins of the phrase "take back the night" are unclear. The *Feminist Alliance Against Rape Newsletter* first used it in the November/December 1977 issue, in the title of a violence-against-women memorial written by Anne Pride of Pittsburgh (Pride 1977). She delivered it at the Pittsburgh Alliance Against Rape's 1977 Women Take Back the Night march. This may have been the first action to go by this title.

But the concept, if not the name, of TBN goes back at least to 1971. That year, *Stop Rape,* a pamphlet published by the radical Detroit WAR, asserted:

> Women have lost a basic civil liberty—the right to be on the street—going to a neighbor's, to the store, or just for a walk. . . .
> A woman alone on the street in the evening is there because she has to be—walking from a building to a car or from one house to another. She is usually clutching her belongings and rushing for fear of potential dangers, especially rape. She can walk calmly only if she is accompanied and protected by a male. (1971, 43–44)

The group suggests that women implement the strategy of "Reinstating the Evening Walk" by gathering four to eight strong to walk or patrol the streets at night. In addition to enjoying the evening air and exercise, participants can escort other women from place to place and keep an eye out for suspicious behavior by men. Because it involves the active reclaiming of the streets at night by women, this strategy has clear connections to TBN.

Another collective action that very closely resembled TBN was the

26 August 1975 woman suffrage anniversary celebration sponsored by
NOW. The lead story of the July/August 1975 issue of *Do It NOW,*
the group's national newsletter, called on chapters to organize protests
aiming to "stop violence against women NOW" by confronting rape
and other violence. In the article (National Organization for Women
1975a, 10), the planners state:

> As the major feminist organization in the nation, we will focus
> public attention on the institutions which perpetrate the victim-
> ization of women and we will demand change in all policies and
> practices derived from the notion of women as "substandard
> person"
>
> TIME: THE NIGHT OF AUGUST 26
>
> PLACE: THE STREETS
>
> ISSUE: VIOLENCE AGAINST WOMEN
>
> NOW's national protest will tell the nation in words and ac-
> tions that we, the women, claim the night and the streets as ours.
> We will "own" the streets on the night of August 26. . . . We
> will take the night for this is the time of danger for all women
> everywhere. We will move together through the streets to stand
> before each of those institutions which have delivered us as vic-
> tims.

Deborah Hart, the national coordinator of the 26 August events in
1975, sent suggestion packets to all the chapters. The next newsletter
presented the highlights of local actions: the Memphis, Raleigh, Cuya-
hoga Falls (Ohio), and D.C. NOW chapters all reported holding events
similar to take back the night (National Organization for Women
1975b, 10–11). Thus, both radical and liberal groups developed and
promoted the concept of TBN between 1971 and 1975.[5] Self-defense,
guerrilla actions, and TBN were but three of the many strategies devised and pursued by the anti-rape movement. In various ways, these
put the anti-rape ideology that had been developing since 1970 into
practice.

The Rape Crisis Center

Because of their prominence among feminists and within communities, rape crisis centers have been the backbone of the anti-rape movement. Accordingly, they merit closer investigation than do such smaller-scale efforts as TBN. Two important themes raised in the scholarly literature on rape crisis centers are the question of definition and the issue of co-optation, involving the degree to which centers have been transformed from feminist spaces into mainstream institutions.

In their study of rape crisis centers across the country, Janet Gornick, Martha Burt, and Karen Pittman (1985, 252) suggest three markers that characterize a true rape crisis center: "(1) some direct services offered to rape survivors; (2) some specific outreach to, and formalized procedure for serving, rape survivors; and (3) some internal education and training on rape." This definition is useful in any analysis of the wide variety of services available for victims in crisis. As an interview respondent points out, "[O]ne or two trained social workers on the staff of a hospital or mental health center is not a rape crisis center, no matter what they call themselves" (Gornick, Burt, and Pittman 1985, 253). Such a distinction is significant for this study of the anti-rape movement: while many centers derive their status and impetus from the movement, they do not necessarily reflect the philosophy behind the majority of rape crisis centers; nor do they necessarily work toward the goals of the anti-rape movement, even as they demonstrate a pro-victim orientation.

The issue of what constitutes a rape crisis center raises the related theme of co-optation. Roberta Ash Garner (1977, 14), a political scientist, defines it as "a structural process of placing movement personnel into elite-sponsored positions," by which radicals and their ideas are absorbed into mainstream institutions without effecting fundamental changes in the social structure. Further, Mayer Zald and Roberta Ash (1966, 327) explain that as a social-movement organization "attains an economic and social base in the society, as the original charismatic leadership is replaced, a bureaucratic structure emerges and a general accommodation to the society occurs." This process, they go on to say, is typically associated with a general move toward conservatism, an emphasis on organizational maintenance and survival, and the development of oligarchic leadership (1966, 327–28).

Rape crisis centers (and similar organizations such as battered-women's shelters), then, can occupy a contradictory position. On the one hand, they have located themselves within the movement to transform society and its institutions by advocating change in the gender relations that allow rape to occur. On the other hand, to be able to secure funding, attract volunteers, and enjoy a collegial relationship with law enforcement and hospital personnel—that is, to be able to function—rape crisis centers must collaborate with the very institutions they intend to transform (Morgan 1981). In Los Angeles, for example, the organizations' original focus was transformed from a "political agenda of changing [the] consciousness" that permits rape to a "social service agenda of helping victims manage the trauma they experience" (Matthews 1994, 149). A closer look at the birth and growth of rape crisis centers, their prominence in the anti-rape movement, and the tensions they have experienced will shed light on this phenomenon.

The first rape crisis center was founded in 1972 in Washington, D.C. While other anti-rape projects preceded it, the range of services and the philosophy of the D.C. Rape Crisis Center (D.C. RCC) closely resemble those of similar groups now operating, and they fit the definition of a rape crisis center devised by Gornick, Burt, and Pittman (1985).[6] This first center was the result of efforts to address the problem of rape as radical feminists understood it, according to Elizabethann O'Sullivan, a founding member of the D.C. RCC identified with the radical branch of the women's movement (personal interview, 8 June 1995). In addition, the pamphlet *How to Start a Rape Crisis Center,* published by the Washington collective in 1972, states that the center's original participants "identify themselves as 'feminists' or 'radical feminists' " (D.C. Rape Crisis Center 1972, 35).

The decision to form an organization to respond to the needs of rape victims in the District of Columbia grew out of a January 1972 meeting of radical women to discuss forming a women's center; a related topic to be considered was a rape project (Elizabethann O'Sullivan, personal interview, 8 June 1995). Bear in mind that the D.C. organizers did not invent the idea of the rape crisis center. For example, as early as the New York Radical Feminists' (NYRF) 1971 conference on rape, members of the workshop "Survival Now: Community Responsibility and Immediate Demands" proposed setting up an information and support hotline, establishing police and hospital escorts for women in crisis, and undertaking community education (Connell and Wilson 1974, 181), all services that came to be offered in rape crisis centers. Thus, the concept had been circulating for some time, but the D.C. women were the first to put it into practice.

Having determined the most effective use of their anti-rape energies, the organizers chose a central location (one member's house) that would serve as the rape crisis center, operating separately from the women's center (Elizabethann O'Sullivan, personal interview, 8 June 1995). They then began to research the medical and law enforcement aspects of the rape victim's experience to assess the availability of resources in the area and to determine the center's role in the community. The women met regularly to share their findings and make plans. Between April and June 1972 the project's organizers virtually became lay experts on a wide range of rape-related issues. They compiled information on hospital protocol, sexually transmitted diseases, pregnancy and the morning-after pill, police questioning, rape counseling, the media, and a host of other matters. Then, in a gesture more traditional than one would expect from a radical collective, the group adopted bylaws (see Appendix 2) on 24 May. After a training period with a practicing therapist, the D.C. Rape Crisis Center began operations one week later, on 1 June 1972 (O'Sullivan papers).

The organization's purpose, as stated in the bylaws, was "to provide necessary assistance to rape victims and victims of sexual attacks, and to provide the community with information on rape" (O'Sullivan papers). The center offered emergency phone service, discussion groups for rape victims, transportation to the police or a hospital, emergency housing for women who had been assaulted, and public information and education on rape. Like many radical experiments of the 1970s that employed the principles of participatory democracy, the center was designed to operate as a collective; all members shared responsibilities and made decisions jointly. (A loose, nonhierarchical committee structure was in place by February 1973.) The initial collectivist spirit underlay not only the practical operation of the center, but also the choice to organize politically: the D.C. RCC embodied the feminist politics of "I do for you, you do for others" (D.C. Rape Crisis Center 1972, preface, n.p.). The women's long-term goal was to "abolish rape in our own lifetimes," as they declared in the policy statement included in meeting minutes of 15 September 1972 (O'Sullivan papers). In 1972, when the revolutionary politics of the 1960s still held sway among radical activists, such a goal seemed attainable.

The Washington organization enjoyed balanced and fair media coverage in its first months of operation (*Washington Post* 1972a, 1972b). There were a large number of idle news reporters in town to cover the 1972 presidential campaign; this stroke of good fortune gave the collective access to persons who worked in a variety of news media. These print and electronic journalists helped in gaining mostly positive coverage of their anti-rape efforts and in spreading the word of the new community resource (Elizabethann O'Sullivan, personal interview, 8 June 1995). The center's activities were even reported as far away as Chicago (Goodyear 1973) and the West Coast (*Los Angeles Times* 1972). According to meeting minutes, the word also spread through the thriving D.C. activist channels and through sponsorship of rape conferences at American and George Washington Universities and of women's group meetings (Barker 1972). However, O'Sullivan recognizes that too much publicity in the center's early months could have impeded the fledgling organization's success: she notes that the women were probably unprepared to handle a heavier load of calls and requests for referrals and information than they were already receiving (personal interview, 8 June 1995). Clearly, so novel a concept as a rape crisis center needed time to put down roots before it could attain a wide base of community use and support.

O'Sullivan further notes that the radical politics of the D.C. RCC predisposed it to considerable distrust of "establishment" institutions (personal interview, 8 June 1995). The collective's circumscribed relationship with such authorities as police departments, hospitals, and district attorneys' offices was informed by this distrust. For example, by 1972 anti-rape activists had amassed enough anecdotal and other evidence to conclude that unenlightened attitudes toward rape and its victims pervaded police stations, hospitals, and prosecutors' offices. The D.C. RCC's policy was to take a neutral stance on whether women should report rape; the collective simply provided victims with information on what was likely to result. They neither encouraged nor discouraged reporting, which, because of their retrograde attitudes, could expose a victim to even more pain and suffering. This policy was in line with the center's philosophy of helping the rape victim to take control of her life by deciding for herself what steps she would take. This approach guides rape crisis centers across the country even today.

The Washington collective's distrust of governmental institutions was also manifest in the choice to avoid close interaction with the establishment by using only private funding for as long as possible. This was slightly ironic for radicals, whose socialist and collectivist tendencies might have led them to demand full state support for their organization. The women's collaboration with public institutions, initially tenuous at best, gradually became more collegial during the center's first year, although the position on reporting rape to established authorities remains unchanged to this day.

Perhaps one of the most important documentary projects the members of the collective undertook was writing, printing, and distributing the pamphlet *How to Start a Rape Crisis Center*. The women began working on the piece only two months after the center opened, demonstrating at once a sense of history, a collectivist spirit of sharing experience and insights, and an urgency to address the problem of rape beyond the local level.[7] The members hoped and believed that their experiences and insights might prove useful to fellow activists elsewhere. The pamphlet was widely disseminated throughout the United States and was revised and expanded in 1977.

How to Start a Rape Crisis Center (D.C. Rape Crisis Center 1972) gives much insight into the philosophy behind the organization. Significantly, its members saw part of their job as providing advocacy and encouraging self-help. They worked as liaisons between victims and police, hospital, and, if necessary, prosecutors. In this role, the women provided information about these institutions to those who had been attacked and made their own expertise on rape available to agency personnel. Notably, the rape crisis center espoused a philosophy of self-determination, restoring to the victim a sense of control over her own life (D.C. Rape Crisis Center 1972, 23).[8] This theme, too, still characterizes rape crisis centers today.

As the D.C. RCC evolved, its focus and politics grew to reflect the demographics and the needs of the Washington community. By 1975, the collective structure had been replaced with a more traditional structure, with a board of directors, state funding, and paid staff. In an important move, the center chose to make the hiring of women of color for paid staff positions a priority, although the board remained primarily white. In 1976, Nkenge Toure, who had been active in the organization since 1975, was hired as the first African American rape crisis center director in the country (Nkenge Toure, telephone interview, 9 January 1997). Loretta Ross, another African American woman, who had been recruited in 1977 by Toure, became director in 1979. As the center evolved and worked to respond to the needs of the city's predominantly black population, it came to take a more expansive view of violence against women, incorporating more economic and race analysis in its approach to the issue. This led to a significant extension of its efforts into issues involving sexual harassment and poverty. As Ross observes, a black woman was more likely to be evicted by her landlord than to be raped, so the center had a better chance of connecting with poor and working-class women if it remained mindful of the reality of their daily lives (personal interview, 16 October 1995).

Loretta Ross describes working in the D.C. RCC in the late 1970s and early 1980s as at once full of possibility yet fraught with frustration for African American feminists. It had become, in her words, the center of black feminist organizing for the country. For example, during her tenure, the D.C. RCC planned and hosted the first National Conference on Third World Women and Violence, held 21 to 24 August

1980. The board of directors was reluctant to permit an activity that was closed to an entire group—white women—but the conference, attended by 125 women, including 30 to 35 Latinas, was a success in Ross's estimation.

During Ross's tenure the D.C. RCC also made the controversial decision to begin a study group with men incarcerated at Lorton jail who had approached the center about starting a group called Prisoners Against Rape. Although the membership was wary of working with men, and particularly of committing resources to them, they eventually agreed to the arrangement and cooperated successfully on rape issues with the prisoners. Although it broke with the radical feminist tradition of refusing to work with men, Ross sees this effort as a major advance in men's involvement in issues of sexism and of stopping sexual assault. While this pioneering effort was going on, the black women at the center were experiencing some tension about their roles: Ross explains that they were frequently accused of not being feminist enough for the mostly white feminist community and not being black enough for the black community (personal interview, 16 October 1995).

Although the D.C. Rape Crisis Center was the first such group to open its doors in the early 1970s, less than two years after its founding similar organizations had been established throughout the United States. Tucson; Chicago; Ann Arbor, Michigan;[9] Berkeley, California; Chapel Hill, North Carolina; Seattle; Palo Alto, California; Santa Cruz, California; Boston; Madison, Wisconsin; Brevard County, Florida; New York City; and Pittsburgh were among the locales with centers operating by the end of 1973. By the next year, rape crisis centers had been formed in forty-three states (Halpern 1978). The same ideology that inspired the D.C. RCC collective—an approach that is pro-woman and pro-victim, and that stresses self-help—informed the operations of the new groups around the country, and it remains the driving force behind the Washington organization today (Denise Snyder, personal interview, 9 August 1995).

The D.C. Rape Crisis Center led the national anti-rape movement in the years following its opening and continues to do so. As the first organization of its kind and as creator and distributor of the widely read *How to Start a Rape Crisis Center,* the group was recognized very early as both a model and a resource for information. And the D.C. RCC welcomed the opportunity to serve the larger anti-rape community. Its bimonthly newsletter began to be nationally distributed in 1972, and regularly featured notes on D.C. RCC developments, suggestions for organizing rape conferences, legislative updates, announcements of events and publications, national news, and, always, a listing of publications available by mail from the center. Demonstrating the organization's interest in continuing to serve the national network of anti-rape projects, the May/June 1974 newsletter asked readers: "If you are working with a rape crisis center or other project related to rape, please send us news, articles about the changes you've gone through, what you're doing now, publications you have available, etc. It's important for Rape Crisis Centers to be communicating and sharing ideas" (O'Sullivan papers).

In early 1974, the D.C. RCC developed a national directory of rape crisis centers. This fostered the growth of a communications network for rape crisis centers and, more broadly, the anti-rape movement. As a social movement its effectiveness and success depended upon the formation of a communications network linking like-minded actors who held the common goal of stopping rape.

Feminist Alliance Against Rape

Anti-rape activists working in isolation quickly came to understand the value of forming coalitions to advance their struggle. By joining with others of like mind, they were able to share resources, strategies, and ideas and to present themselves as a united band of citizens working on a single issue. It soon became clear to the D.C. RCC staff that something more than a single rape crisis center was needed to nurture connections among the growing numbers of centers and anti-rape activists throughout the country. In mid-1974, the Feminist Alliance Against Rape (FAAR) was founded. Its purpose was to serve as an "autonomous organization of community-based and feminist-controlled anti-rape projects"; the group would represent feminist interests in the growing field of anti-rape work, which by then involved government agencies, professionals, and other individuals and institutions (Feminist Alliance Against Rape Staff 1974). FAAR intended to serve as a clearinghouse for information, news, and opinion for this expanding network of rape crisis centers, hoping to aid in establishing a true grassroots alliance.

Membership was open to individuals and groups. From 1974 to 1987 the *FAAR Newsletter,* the centerpiece of the alliance's activities, sustained communication among them. As other issues concerning violence against women appeared on the feminist agenda, FAAR evolved, merging with other organizations. These included the Association Against Sexual Coercion (AASC), devoted to fighting sexual harassment, and the National Communication Network (NCN), a domestic violence group. After FAAR merged with NCN in 1978, the newsletter was renamed *Aegis: A Magazine on Ending Violence Against Women* to reflect its parent organization's broadened scope. The *FAAR Newsletter* offers a unique glimpse into the rape crisis center movement, particularly in the years 1974 to 1978, when rape was the exclusive focus. Because of FAAR's mission to represent grassroots, feminist-identified projects, the pieces it published provide a wealth of information on groups that maintained a feminist philosophy closely resembling that of the first rape crisis centers. After 1978, the content of *Aegis* reflected the confluence of anti-violence issues that began to dominate the feminist agenda in the late 1970s (Schechter 1982).

In its first issue, July/August 1974, the *FAAR Newsletter* raised questions about professionalization and co-optation, topics that would surface repeatedly in the rape crisis center literature. In an article on S. 2422, a bill sponsored by Senator Charles Mathias (R-Md.) to establish the National Center for the Prevention and Control of Rape (NCPCR), the FAAR staff welcomed the possible opportunities for funding that such a center might offer, but presciently expressed concern that Mathias's bill "would be implemented in a way which is likely to discriminate against non-degreed paraprofessionals involved in the issue of rape. Those of us who have been responsible for the increased 'concern' for rape victims may be squeezed out of that picture" (Feminist Alliance Against Rape Staff 1974, 11). Early on, FAAR found that rape crisis centers—born of feminist impulses and an ideology that saw sexual assault as a symptom of male dominance and not as a single problem in need of treatment—were in danger of being co-opted by social service professionals who had joined the cause without ever subscribing to its feminist ideology and politics. A member of the FAAR staff, Deb Friedman (1975, 1), elaborates the point in another article:

> As more and more professionals are becoming involved in anti-rape work, . . . there is an increasing tendency to *defer* to professional leadership in anti-rape projects. While professional skills and knowledge are valuable resources in a project, there is no valid reason for professionals to *control* rather than work as peers within the rape issue. (emphasis in original)

For FAAR, as for many other activist groups, the specter of professionalization, and the co-optation of the rape crisis center that it represented, proved alarming and ran counter to the principles on which these organizations had been founded. Moving away from their feminist roots was unconscionable to rape crisis centers that had arisen from the women's movement (Friedman 1975). Institutionalization was the opposite of the original goal of institutional transformation.

FAAR's alarm was warranted. As the issue of rape attracted increasing attention from policy makers, monies from two major funding sources—the Law Enforcement Assistance Administration (LEAA) and, later, the NCPCR—were channeled in expected directions. Funds went primarily toward research, projects, and programs headed by degreed professionals; projects that were willing to accept stipulations to grants that might compromise the welfare of the rape crisis client (e.g., programs that required a victim receiving services to report her rape to law enforcement); and projects directed in conjunction with law enforcement. These financial choices were often made at the expense of community-based anti-rape projects with feminist leanings. Until the late 1970s, the sole public funding source not connected with law enforcement—allocated by the Labor Department under the Comprehensive Employment and Training Act (CETA)—was intended to

provide monies for community groups to hire and train former recipients of public assistance only, not for comprehensive services or other
staffing needs. Thus, a distrust of institutions—grounded in the tenets
of the radical movements that shaped the radical branch of the wom-
en's movement—informed the relationship of rape crisis centers to
their major sources of funding. For many centers, to yield to the bu-
reaucrats' demands was unthinkable.

By FAAR's standards, professionals planning anti-rape projects
from the top down, divorced from grassroots organizers in the communities they were to serve, would never be able to address the needs
of most women in those communities. Likewise, rape studies conducted without the involvement of local activists would prove useless
to the victims they purported to help, because grassroots campaigners
against rape were first to research the issue, first to form alliances with
women who had been attacked, and first to raise public awareness of
rape.

Compromises inherent in funding grants posed, for FAAR members, another impossible breach of faith with rape crisis center clients.
This was particularly so in the matter of the neutral stance taken by
most centers about reporting rape to law enforcement agencies. The
experience of the Stop Rape Crisis Center (SRCC) in Baton Rouge,
Louisiana, highlights this issue. In 1976, an item in the *FAAR Newsletter* reported that the SRCC, a recipient of federal LEAA funds through
the local district attorney's office, had been instructed by District Attorney Ossie Davis to discontinue services to nonreporting victims and to
victims who reported but whose cases had been concluded (Feminist
Alliance Against Rape Staff 1976). When the director of the center was
fired for objecting, and the entire staff and volunteer corps resigned in
solidarity, the paid workers were replaced with criminal justice professionals and new volunteers began to be recruited. These events took
place because government funding contingent upon reporting rape to
the police was incompatible with the original organizers' goals of placing the victims' needs ahead of law enforcement's "purely prosecutorial
objective" (Feminist Alliance Against Rape Staff 1976). A few years
later, in 1980, the SRCC was named an "exemplary project" by the

National Institute of Justice (NIJ), LEAA's successor as the major Justice Department funder (U.S. Department of Justice 1980, 6).

The *FAAR Newsletter* also featured debates over whether close connections with law enforcement would discredit the rape crisis centers' long-standing suspicion of the criminal justice system as an institution that exacerbates race and class inequities in the United States. This was a particularly controversial issue for the alliance and many of its members, as reflected in the thirteen years of publication of the *FAAR Newsletter* and *Aegis*. The debate concerned not only liberal versus radical feminist strategies and goals (as many understand the primary split within feminism to be), but also the role of the anti-rape campaign in the context of the larger progressive movement and the question of reform versus reformism in feminist politics.

The member-activists of FAAR were divided over strategies they understood to be radical and liberal. While rape crisis center activists were generally associated with radicalism, many other women advocated using criminal justice agencies, even though this represented working within the system to achieve movement goals, and even though radicals typically dismissed working within the system as so much liberalism. Members of the San Francisco Women Against Rape (SFWAR), for example, stated that they "support a woman's right to strike back. If a woman wants to use the courts as a means of redress (and it is practically her *only* means), we are not going to lay yet another guilt trip on her by labelling her behavior anti-revolutionary. Besides, by prosecuting a rapist in her own and other women's defense, she is advancing her own revolution, which is *our* revolution too" (San Francisco Women Against Rape 1974; emphasis in original). Some rape crisis centers, then, viewed the criminal justice system as a viable—even potentially revolutionary—resource for rape victims.

But other activists opposed this approach because of the criminal justice system's historic mistreatment, scapegoating, and oppression of such disenfranchised groups as the poor, African Americans, and Latinos. Viewing the choice to report to criminal justice agencies as a "personal decision of the victim, not as a political solution or a responsibility to other women," they maintained a neutral policy on whether to refer victims to the authorities (MacMillan and Klein 1974). Rape crisis center advocates who viewed themselves as part of a larger progressive movement seeking to overthrow all sexist, classist, and racist hierarchies believed involvement with criminal justice agencies was futile. According to Robin McDuff, Deanne Pernell, and Karen Saunders of Santa Cruz Women Against Rape (SCWAR), in an editorial in the *FAAR Newsletter,*

> those convicted of rape are most likely to be Third World and/ or poor white men, as is true of convictions of nearly all other crimes. In order for a D.A. to "win" a rape case he (or rarely she) must use sexist, racist, and classist stereotypes and assumptions, thereby supporting the worst aspects of the system. If the goal of this process is fighting and ending rape, it is bad and self-defeating to use racist and classist means to get to that end. The process is crucial to the true success of the end. (1977, 3)

To these and other activists, working with the criminal justice system betrayed the progressive movements against the related oppressions of racism, classism, and sexism, and betrayed everyone subject to these oppressions.

Finally, some FAAR members framed the argument as a matter of pursuing reform strategies versus reformism. Borrowing an analysis of these two possible movement goals (see Bunch 1987), the FAAR staff (1975) distinguished between a reform designed to ameliorate a situation, and a reformist ideology, which "assumes women can be liberated within the existing social, political or economic system, through a series of reforms." Reformism, the FAAR staff stressed, can never eliminate rape or any other major problem facing women. Individual reforms, however, "can be important steps in a process of change" that maintains its commitment to the larger goal of social transformation. In this view, anti-rape activists could work on specific reforms without fear of total political compromise and also still work for the eradication of rape. The strategies and goals espoused by FAAR's leadership and by many members incorporated this perspective.

National Coalition Against Sexual Assault

NCASA was founded in 1978, when fifty-seven rape crisis center representatives from twenty states attended a meeting of the National Organization of Victim Assistance (NOVA) and decided that their centers needed an independent network. The organizers included Anne Pride of Pittsburgh Action Against Rape (PAAR), Sandy Lambert of the Pennsylvania Coalition Against Rape (PCAR), and Pam Klein and Mary Wood of the Rape and Sexual Assault Care Center of Edwardsville, Illinois. According to the coalition's first newsletter, dated September 1978, the goals of the National Coalition Against Sexual Assault were

1. To end sexual violence and rape in our society
2. To unite all centers
3. To establish a national communications network
4. To serve as a lobbying unit
5. To develop a forum for discussion of issues concerning sexual assault and to present positions on those issues
6. To investigate funding sources for the continuation of programs and rape crisis centers. (O'Sullivan papers)

Membership was open to individuals and groups involved in providing direct or indirect services to rape victims. Four committees were established: communications, funding, legislation, and "special issues." Before its first conference in August 1979, the coalition had signed up seventy-two member programs.

It is clear from its goals and structure that NCASA reflected a more bureaucratized, social service approach to rape crisis work than FAAR, which was oriented toward the grass roots and political organizing. Minutes of the planning session for the group's first meeting list as two of the conference's goals "To provide the mutual strength and support needed by the professionals who provide . . . services to victims" and "To take the professional status due to each rape crisis center, victim advocate, and community educator" (minutes, 10 March 1979, O'Sullivan papers). Thus, NCASA seeks to elevate rape crisis center staff to professional status, in marked contrast to FAAR's skepticism about the role of professionalism in the grassroots movement. The documentation of the coalition's founding makes no mention of its relationship to the criminal justice system or of its position on the role of rape in systems of oppression such as racism and classism, issues important to FAAR.

Statewide Coalitions

In addition to the national organizing efforts of FAAR and NCASA, rape crisis center coalitions were formed in various states. The oldest of these, still in existence, is the Pennsylvania Coalition Against Rape (PCAR), founded 4 August 1975. At its initial meeting, a steering committee that included Mary and Joe Gillespie of the rape crisis center in West Chester, Cheryl Engel of the State College center, and Denise Shull and Letty Thall of the Philadelphia center was appointed to guide the coalition's establishment. The organization's mission was to "work to eliminate all forms of sexual violence and to advocate for the rights and needs of victims of sexual assault" (PCAR records). Similar coalitions formed in California, Illinois, Georgia, and elsewhere to unite local rape crisis centers in their efforts to secure funding and provide services to victims.

In spite of organizational tensions, fears about and the realities of co-optation, clashes over strategy, and problems with funding, rape crisis centers have proven to be a vital resource of the anti-rape movement. They have provided a number of organizational resources that are, if not essential to the survival of the movement, significant in its continued success. For example, the centers afford the movement a centralized location, so that movement actors have a physical space in which to gather, collect other resources, and receive inquiries about the center itself and about rape in general. Coalitions among them, moreover, provide for the lines of communication that are vital to a social movement's success. Most rape crisis centers have paid staff members who can do the work of the anti-rape movement without the fear of burnout that can accompany strictly volunteer involvement, even though this arrangement can carry a political cost (Staggenborg 1988). Many centers have speakers' bureaus and other outreach programs that seek to educate the community, capture media and political attention, and keep rape on the public agenda. Based on these resources, the centers are still the sites and agents of crucial anti-rape activism.

Rape Law Reform

In recent decades, the law has been an effective means for social-movement groups to seek their desired changes and influence public policy (Handler 1978). The pursuit of women's issues through the courts (O'Connor 1980) and through legislative reform (Boneparth 1982) has met with significant success. Matters such as abortion, sexual harassment, employment discrimination, pregnancy discrimination, and equitable divorce have come to the legal arena owing primarily to the efforts of women's rights activists. Indeed, one explicit purpose for the founding of the National Organization for Women (NOW) in 1966 was to replicate the legal and legislative achievements of the National Association for the Advancement of Colored People (Davis 1991, 53). In the late 1960s, NOW and other women's rights groups embarked on a plan to introduce gender equity into constitutional and statutory law.

The reform of rape laws did not begin with the advent of the anti-rape movement or the women's movement more generally. When the elite and conservative American Law Institute (ALI) first drafted its Model Penal Code (MPC) for rape in 1955—it was made final in 1962 and published in 1980—several states began to revise their statutes in accordance with the ALI's suggestions (Estrich 1987, 58–59). The code effected a departure from the common-law approach to rape previously used in most jurisdictions. Under that definition, "a man commits rape when he engages in intercourse (in the old statutes, carnal knowledge) with a woman not his wife; by force or threat of force; against her will and without her consent" (Estrich 1987, 8). This definition, as the legal scholar Susan Estrich sees it, remains the guiding force behind even the reformed laws of most states. Thus, the common law of rape merits closer investigation.

According to Estrich (1987, 40), rape convictions under common law relied upon affirmative evidence of nonconsent on the part of the accuser, usually in the form of evidence that she had resisted attack. This is a standard nearly unmatched in criminal law. Even in states that abandoned the resistance requirement in favor of the standard of force (by the assailant), prosecutors could use evidence of resistance (by the victim; bruises, for example) only to establish that force had been used (Estrich 1987, 60). Furthermore, as a counterpart to the resistance requirement, common law in many jurisdictions required corroborating evidence of a victim's testimony to establish that a crime had been committed. The most obvious exception to the law of rape is stated explicitly in the common-law definition: a man cannot be accused of raping his wife. Evidence concerning a victim's sexual history was routinely admissible under common law. Commentators have noted that all of the rules governing the common law of rape converge to codify both distrust of women's charges and widely held assumptions about the significance of a woman's sexual experience to a rape charge (Estrich 1987; Sanday 1996).

The Model Penal Code for rape, an explicit departure from the standards of the common law, is nonetheless guided by the gender assumptions behind it, albeit more fairly applied. Written in the mid-1950s and accepted at the 1962 annual meeting of the American Law Institute, the MPC defines rape as forced vaginal or anal penetration. It classifies the crime as a felony in the first degree if the victim is a stranger to the perpetrator or if serious bodily injury is inflicted, and a felony in the second degree if no such injury is inflicted or if the perpetrator was the "voluntary social companion" of the victim. Moreover, the MPC maintains a marital exemption, a corroboration requirement, a prompt-complaint provision, and a cautionary-instruction (from judge to jury) requirement, all holdovers from the common law.

The intention of the MPC was to provide a template on which the states could base their criminal statutes. According to the ALI, the rape laws of Delaware, Hawaii, Maine, Massachusetts, Missouri, North Dakota, Ohio, Texas, Vermont, and West Virginia have been influenced by the code (American Law Institute 1980, 299–300). Hawaii,

Maine, New York, and Pennsylvania adopted the MPC as part of an overall reform of their criminal codes (Field and Bienen 1980, 190). No state borrowed the MPC for rape whole cloth, only choosing portions, such as the criterion for serious bodily injury.

What distinguishes the Model Penal Code, and statutes modeled closely after it, from feminist rape reform is perspective. The legal scholar Leigh Bienen (1976, 52) characterizes the MPC as not "radically pro-victim." Certainly the period of its drafting—the 1950s—and the conservatism of the ALI influenced the language and implications of the MPC. Moreover, women's and rape victims' perspectives were all but ignored when it was being written: the name of one woman is listed on the MPC's Criminal Law Advisory Board—Florence M. Kelly of the Legal Aid Society of New York (Bienen 1976, 53).[10] Had women been involved in the drafting, the code might well have read differently.

Thus, a pro-victim perspective was absent both from the common law of rape and from MPC-based rape reform. Many attempts at revising such statutes absent involvement of the women's movement reflected a tendency among legislators to project a law-and-order, tough-on-crime image to their constituents. Rape laws that disproportionately favored criminal defendants were an easy target for them. But with the advent of the women's movement, which aroused public attention to gender asymmetry in the law and elsewhere, and with the growing campaign against rape, which set out to dispel the "rape myths" that prevailed in the popular discourse and even legal codes, the legal community was presented with a new perspective.

By 1970, many feminists had begun to understand rape as a problem having both personal and political dimensions; the crime had become an issue for the women's movement. Feminist activists and writers recognized that only a cursory glance at state rape laws, accounts of the humiliation endured by victims in court, and shockingly low conviction rates revealed that, with regard to criminal justice, rape was "only slightly forbidden fruit" (Mehrhof and Kearon 1971, 80). Legislative reform was a logical place to begin to address these problems:

improved rape laws would send the message that sexual assault would not be tolerated.

In the view of radical anti-rape activists, antiquated laws and unresponsive institutions were of a piece with pervasive rape myths and an anti-woman, anti-victim mentality. The earliest radical actions against rape served as the venues for the first feminist explorations of rape laws and the need for reform. As the women's liberation branch of the movement grew and gained momentum in the late 1960s, its adherents were better known for bucking the existing legal and political system than for working to reform it. But the program of the April 1971 rape conference organized by the New York Radical Feminists, the first such meeting on record, shows that the NYRF planned a "Rape and the Law" workshop as part of the conference, and Edith Barnett, an attorney, presented the short paper "Legal Aspects of Rape in New York State" (Connell and Wilson 1974, 134–36). In 1971, New York's rape law was biased toward defendants; its standards of proof were among the strictest in the country, making convictions virtually impossible. Particularly onerous was the law's corroboration provision, enacted in 1967 as an MPC-based reform. It required corroborative evidence of three material elements of the crime—force, penetration, and identity of perpetrator—before a prosecutor could bring a case to trial. The Empire State's severe rape law soon became notorious among feminists.[11] At the conclusion of the NYRF workshop, a paper entitled "Suggestions on the Elimination of Rape" was drawn up "as a guide for future action" (Connell and Wilson 1974, 267–69). Although the long-range strategy for eliminating rape, according to the "Suggestions," is to eradicate sex roles, the short-range tactics include reforming rape laws. While it may appear ironic that the NYRF and the conference's radical participants recommended a reform approach, it is quite possible that, as a sophisticated feminist understanding of the complexity of rape developed, strategists saw that only a multifaceted movement—one that included legal change—could address the problem effectively.

Many radical feminists supported law reform. Barbara Mehrhof and Pamela Kearon's 1971 article "Rape: An Act of Terror" pointed out that, despite supposedly stringent laws against the crime, very few accused men were arrested and fewer still were convicted. In "Women Speak Out," Helen Katopoulos (1971) criticizes the legal system for effectively condoning rape and failing to protect women. She refers to spousal rape as "legal rape" and indicts the law for failing to treat it as a felony. On the West Coast, the feminist group Women for a Free Future in Berkeley addressed the city council to demand changes that would help to protect women from rape in the streets and in their homes, according to the *San Francisco Chronicle* (1970). Susan Griffin (1971) uses the example of a celebrated California rape trial, *People v. Plotkin,* in which the complainant's sexual history cast doubt upon her claims, to demonstrate the sexual double standard codified in the rape laws and trial process. Finally, the radical group The Feminists, organized in New York City, protested at the trial of a sixteen-year-old accused of rape (Price 1971).[12] Thus, surprisingly, rape law reform efforts drew significant energy from radical feminists.

Two other important feminist struggles were taking place in the state legislatures at about the time rape law reform came under consideration: ratification of the equal rights amendment and legislative debates over abortion (prior to *Roe v. Wade* in 1973). In 1972 the New York legislature nearly succeeded in repealing the liberalized abortion law that had passed two years earlier. The near loss of abortion rights brought an active feminist lobbying force to Albany, including Barbara Shack, a member of the Manhattan Women's Political Caucus (Greenhouse 1974). Likewise, the process of ratifying the ERA in the states motivated women's rights advocates to learn to use the political system to their advantage. This new women's lobby developed the political savvy and skills necessary to pursue a number of other feminist causes in the state legislatures, among them the issue of rape.

An important group within this cadre of legislative activists was the growing number of women in the legal profession in the 1970s. Judith Hole and Ellen Levine (1971, 350) describe their low numbers and low status in the United States only a few years earlier: in the late 1960s women constituted "only three percent of the nation's lawyers; of 2708 lawyers employed by 40 top law firms in six major cities, only 186 were women. . . . [O]ut of nearly 9700 judgeships in the United States, only 200 are held by women."

This picture changed as women began to enter law schools in massive numbers with the rise of the feminist movement. According to Cynthia Fuchs Epstein (1993, 4), by 1976 they made up 9.2 percent of the country's practicing lawyers. And not only were women newly entering a profession in which they had been heavily underrepresented, but many brought with them a commitment to women's rights that had been all but absent from the legal field. According to one woman lawyer, in 1971 every coeducational law school had a women's group, and many of these students had chosen to go into law as a way to work for women's rights (Hole and Levine 1971, 351–52). Pressure from this new and vocal population inspired law schools to begin to offer courses on women and the law, and moved professional organizations such as the American Bar Association (ABA) and the Association of American Law Schools to form women's committees in 1970. In Michigan, New York, and elsewhere, efforts to reform rape law created a classroom of sorts for a number of feminist law students.

Together, these lawyers, law students, activists, and lobbyists, some new to the field, others seasoned by earlier legislative battles, brought a pro-victim perspective to reforming rape laws. This point of view led them to direct their efforts toward a number of related goals, according to Patricia Searles and Ronald Berger (1987, 25), including:

> (1) increasing the reporting of rape and enhancing prosecution and conviction in rape cases; (2) improving the treatment of rape victims in the criminal justice system; (3) achieving comparability between the legal treatment of rape and other violent crimes; (4) prohibiting a wider range of coercive sexual conduct; and (5) expanding the range of persons protected by law. These goals were to be achieved through changes in the following areas: redefinition of the offense, evidentiary rules, statutory age offenses, and penalties.

Such intentions stand in contrast to the revisions conceived by the writers of the Model Penal Code. A new kind of rape reform was under way in the 1970s.

The corroboration provision of the New York State law, mentioned earlier, presents a good example of the differences between a law-and-order and a feminist approach to rape law reform. New York's statute required that the state corroborate the identity of the accused, the fact of penetration, and the victim's nonconsent before proceeding with prosecution. During the first round of reforms in March 1971, the state assembly passed a bill to relax these requirements. The bill eliminated the requirement that a prosecutor corroborate the identity of the assailant with independent evidence, which in effect required an eyewitness or a confession to the crime. The sponsors stated that the bill's passage would make convictions for rape more feasible; it had the support of various district attorneys, and the opposition of the Legal Aid Society (Ledbetter 1971). The bill failed in the senate in 1971.

In spite of this failure, the corroboration issue remained on the legislative agenda. In the fall of 1971, members of women's rights groups (now involved for only a few months in investigating rape laws) testified in the senate in favor of a bill to relax the corroboration provision while still pushing for repeal. Several students at New York University Law School, along with attorneys interested in the project, had studied the state's rape law in the Clinic on Women in the Law during the summer of 1971. Participants, identified in the press as speaking "for the women's liberation movement," testified before the senate committee in support of repealing the corrobation requirement, even though repeal was not at issue in the bill (*New York Times* 1971b).

In New York City, the Women's Anti-Rape Group (WARG), forerunner of the New York Women Against Rape (NYWAR), an organization associated with the radical branch of the women's movement, also advocated repealing rather than modifying the corroboration requirement. The legislature voted to remove the eyewitness provision in 1972, but the requirement that a victim corroborate penetration and lack of consent remained. According to an editorial broadcast by New York City's WPIX-TV on 23 March 1972, that year's reform bill had the support of the New York State District Attorneys Association, but was generally opposed by feminist groups (NYWAR records). On 28 March 1972, a WARG member presented an editorial favoring total corroboration repeal, and opposing reform, on the same station (NYWAR records).[13] Overall, then, legislators made only small changes in the corroboration requirement with little involvement from the women's movement. Only repeal, not modification, of corroboration would satisfy activists.

Women's participation changed the terms of the debate over New York's corroboration law. The feminist Anti-Rape Squad organized an "Assault on the State Legislature to Repeal the Corroboration Requirement," an open meeting to explore what political tactics would best convey the repeal message to the lawmakers, on 6 January 1972 (NYWAR records). The next year, activists in several feminist and anti-rape groups formed the Women's Anti-Rape Coalition to begin a media and legislative campaign to address problems in the rape laws.[14] Organizations including NYWAR (formerly WARG), New York NOW, the Manhattan Women's Political Caucus (MWPC), and NYRF sent representatives. According to the coalition's statement of purpose, dated 26 June 1973 (NYWAR records), its goals were "1. Raising the public consciousness of rape; and 2. Working toward the repeal of the corraboration [sic] requirement for rape cases." Working under a loose committee structure, this coalition was perhaps most notable for the diversity of its members groups: NYWAR operated one of the city's first rape crisis centers; NYRF had planned the first speak-out and conference on rape; and NOW and the Manhattan Women's Political Caucus took on a whole range of legislative issues in the state, including rape, abortion, passing the ERA, and gay rights (Greenhouse 1974, 28). Later, the National Black Feminist Organization (NBFO) got involved. The collaboration of the rape crisis center group with the law reform project is discussed at greater length below.

The coalition set forth on a campaign to raise public consciousness of rape by holding workshops and conferences, with the press invited to all events. Declaring August as Rape Prevention Month provided a specialized topic on which the media could focus (Lewis 1974). Having called attention to the issue, and having garnered much public support, including John Lindsay's creation of the Mayor's Task Force on Rape, the coalition next began lobbying the state legislature for the full repeal of the corroboration requirement in a campaign led by Sally McGee of the MWPC. When joint committee hearings on repeal began on 15 November 1973, the coalition amassed thirty speakers to testify in favor of the bill, as reported in the *New York Times* (Montgomery 1973b). The Legal Aid Society persisted in defending the existing law; the New York chapter of the ACLU shifted its position from opposing repeal to neutrality. The bill eliminating the provision for corroboration passed both houses unanimously without debate. It was signed by the state's Republican governor, Malcolm Wilson, "who had never uttered a word about the issue of rape in public," according to Nancy Lewis (1974, 6). Later, when Wilson exaggerated his involvement in the repeal effort in a campaign advertisement, New York NOW rebutted him, asserting that he had "little to do" with the legislative victory, according to the *New York Times* (Clines 1974).

While New York activists and legislators were debating corroboration reform, other legal struggles were beginning elsewhere. Michigan's 1974 Criminal Sexual Conduct Law (discussed below) is one of the most comprehensive and well documented rape reforms that has taken place to date. Whereas the Michigan Women's Task Force on Rape accomplished a complete overhaul of the rape statute with a single bill, activists in most other states had to take on their states' laws one provision at a time. The reforms most frequently sought were redefining rape, graduating (or "staircasing") offenses, easing extreme evidentiary burdens (including corroboration and resistance requirements), limiting the admissibility of evidence of the victim's sexual history (rape shield), repealing mandatory instruction from judges to juries, and removing the spousal exemption.

As legislative reform efforts got under way in the states, and as it became clear that its membership was increasingly concerned with rape laws, NOW took up the cause of reform. At its 1973 national conference, Resolution 148 was passed, by acclamation, to create the organization's National Rape Task Force (NOWRTF); this suggests the importance the issue had attained in just over two years. Moreover, Resolution 148 had been submitted by the Women and Justice Workshop, indicating that the national group would treat rape as a matter of law and justice. Given this development, delegates to the conference were irked by the reporters who showed up primarily to cover the meeting's three titillating themes—rape, lesbianism, and prostitution—and ignored the less exciting issues raised (Shanahan 1973).

The goals of the NOWRTF, as outlined in Resolution 148, were

1. To define the crime of rape
2. To research existing laws covering rape and related crimes against women and children
3. To propose a model guide to be recommended to state legislatures for adoption into their criminal code
4. To research and recommend follow-up procedures, i.e., psychological effects and assistance, to help the victim
5. To explore effective forms of resistance
6. To explore possibilities of a coalition with existing rape groups for exchange of resources and support. (NOW records)

To some extent, the NOWRTF accomplished all these objectives. The provisions that it define rape and research the laws (provisions 1 and 2) led to the completion of provisions 3 and 4, the design of a model rape law and the recommendation of follow-up procedures. The task force explored effective forms of resistance (provision 5) by creating and developing a self-defense committee. The formation of coalitions with other organizations concerned with rape (provision 6) is evident in the large amount of membership crossover, and in the extensive communication, networking, and resource sharing between the NOWRTF, state and local organizers, and groups outside NOW.

Because of NOW's democratic chapter structure, its rape task force had less direct grassroots organizing influence in the states, serving mostly as a clearinghouse for information and efforts in support of reform. All chapters were encouraged to create their own RTFs and to work on issues specific to their regions, including, but not limited to, legislative reform. Mary Ann Largen, the first NOWRTF coordinator, viewed the local task forces as the real centers of action; this was logical, since nearly all rape laws are state laws (Largen 1985, 10). However, she and the national task force also worked on federal projects related to rape.

One of the ways feminist activists confronted the problems inherent in the existing statutes was to devise "model," alternative rape laws that reflected the new feminist understanding of the crime from the victim's point of view. These were generally designed in conjunction with feminist lawyers and law students who were familiar with legal language and the history of rape laws, and who could put into words the pro-victim spirit behind the changes they proposed. These activists learned to strike a balance between their radical, anti-rape impulses and the political demands of a law reform strategy. Several models emerged.

New York University's Clinic on Women in the Law, mentioned above, was a student-led initiative to examine various aspects of women's legal status. It began in 1971 as a summer course taught by Kristin Glen and Anna Garfinkle, both attorneys in private practice. Told that no money was available from the law school, students obtained funding for the course from the New York Foundation, a philanthropic association. The clinic was accepted as a law school course that fall (*New York Times* 1971b). One of its projects focused on writing a model rape law that would change the problematic provisions of the New York statute. Among other activities, student experts from the clinic testified at the state senate committee hearing in favor of the modification of corroboration under review.

Like other reform statutes, the NYU model law expands the definition of the crime to include forced anal and oral, as well as vaginal, intercourse. The authors propose moving the rape law to the section of the state criminal code that covers "assault." This neutralization through using a more benign term is evident in a number of reform proposals. It represents three statutory goals: first, to avoid the emotional connotations of the word *rape;* second, to arrive at a broader concept of the crime that accounts for the various forms of unwanted sexual violence; and finally, to account for the possibility of female perpetrators and male victims (a goal that a gender-laden term such as *rape* does not meet, according to proponents of the change). Perhaps most important, and most in line with reforms sought in other states, the model law provides a staircase of offenses, eliminates the marital exemption for rape, prohibits the introduction of evidence of the victim's sexual history, and removes the requirement that a victim resist. And, significantly for New York, the model statute makes no mention of corroborating evidence (Connell and Wilson 1974, 164–69).

The comprehensive reform law passed in Michigan has served as a model for other states. According to Jan BenDor, an activist there, the involvement of lawyers and law students proved particularly fortuitous to the design and passage of landmark reforms in that state (1976, 150). BenDor (1976), Leigh Bienen (1980), and Susan Estrich (1987) all indicate that the Michigan Criminal Sexual Conduct statute has been widely hailed as even a "feminist" rape reform. The Michigan Women's Task Force on Rape (MWTFR) was a group of activists and counselors originally organized through the multiservice Women's Crisis Center of Ann Arbor. When they decided to embark on a law reform strategy, the members of the task force found a willing and able advocate in Virginia Nordby, a part-time law instructor experienced in drafting legislation. She enlisted the help of law students, who researched the statute and became advocates of the reform law themselves (BenDor 1976). This example demonstrates the mutuality of anti-rape activism: successful strategies required a certain amount of expertise on the part of the actors seeking the changes; at the same time, working with the activists provided training for up-and-coming experts, the law students. The MWTFR ultimately convinced the state legislature to pass their model law.

As its name implies, Michigan's Criminal Sexual Conduct statute expands the definition of rape to account for a wider range of sexually violent acts and to treat them in a gender-neutral manner. The law provides for four degrees of sexual assault, with a staircasing of penalties; eliminates the resistance requirement; and prohibits the introduction of evidence concerning the victim's past sexual history involving anyone but the defendant. A clause removing the spousal exemption for rape was included in the MWTFR version, but it was dropped during deliberations; reformers accepted the compromise to ensure passage of the rest of the bill (Marsh, Geist, and Caplan 1982, 15). Because the reform law was relatively complete, revising Michigan's rape statute with one clean sweep, it became a dream law for reformers in other states, where decisive elements of the statutes had to be dismantled one by one in a longer, exhausting process. Statutes influenced by the new Michigan law include those of Colorado, Minnesota (whose statute is nearly identical to Michigan's), Nebraska, New Jersey, South Dakota, and West Virginia (American Law Institute 1980, 299–300).

NOW's rape task force wrote a third significant model statute. In fact, the first job the NOWRTF took up was to draft such a law as a guide for state activists. In 1974, it was adopted as Resolution 20 at NOW's national conference. The model law proposes a comprehensive set of reforms that would, among other goals, revise evidentiary requirements that place the victim on trial (rape shield); seek a general reduction of penalties to encourage convictions (particularly the elimination of the death penalty, which was not declared unconstitutional for rape until the 1977 Supreme Court decision *Coker v. Georgia*); incorporate a graduated structure of offenses; expand the definition of rape to include forced oral and anal intercourse; and eliminate the spousal exemption for rape (NOW records). These objectives have formed the centerpiece of most efforts to change state laws since 1974, many of which have met with some success.

The collective efforts of the reformers brought nearly immediate results in the states: by November 1974, Michigan had a completely new rape law; Ohio, Texas, New York, Indiana, Connecticut, Florida, Iowa, and California had changed their statutes to some extent; and reform bills were pending in eleven other states. By 1980, all of the states and the District of Columbia had passed or considered changes of some sort. Reforms in the spousal exemption for rape continued through the 1990s: Georgia removed its spousal exemption in 1996.

A number of observers (Loh 1981; Marsh, Geist, and Caplan 1982; Spohn and Horney 1992) have documented the impact of various efforts to modify rape laws. The symbolic impact of the Michigan reform is clear: so comprehensive a code sends a message about the seriousness of the offense of rape and reinforces the law's intolerance of the mistreatment of rape victims, according to the researchers Jeanne Marsh, Alison Geist, and Nathan Caplan (1982). To assess the instrumental impact of the new law, these authors undertook both a time-series analysis of rape statistics and a number of interviews with law enforcement and criminal justice officials, rape crisis advocates, and anti-rape activists. They found that both arrest and conviction rates improved under the reform statute. The interviews showed that most defense and prosecuting attorneys believed that the new law, particularly its rape shield provision, improved a district attorney's chances of achieving a rape conviction.

In their study of six jurisdictions before and after rape reform, Cassia Spohn and Julie Horney (1992) found that although the reform statutes had little or no effect on convictions, they did have some impact on rape indictments, varying with the relative strength or weakness of the measure enacted. Finally, Wallace D. Loh (1981) discovered that, in at least one jurisdiction, reform laws yielded no change in indictment or conviction rates, but did improve the accuracy of criminal charges. Analyses of the impact of rape reform statutes agree that their greatest value lies in the potential for educating the actors within the legal system and the citizenry at large about the seriousness of the crime and for dispelling at least some of the prevailing myths about rape.

The rape law reform project formally begun by feminists in the early 1970s is not over. Although all fifty states have adopted changes of some sort, those in which only nominal reforms have passed are now seeing a resurgence of interest in making more-comprehensive revisions incorporating many of the elements of the model laws outlined here. In Georgia, for example, where the rape statute had been updated in 1976 only to provide a relatively weak rape shield provision, the anti-rape coalition Georgia Network to End Sexual Assault (GNESA) has worked in coalition with state legislators in the 1990s to pass a bill to eliminate the spousal exemption. Currently, students at Emory University Law School have joined with prosecutors and legislators to create and enact a complete overhaul of the state's rape law, which was

adopted in 1865. Considering the incremental nature of changes in
public policy (Boneparth 1982), these and other efforts are not evidence
of the failure of the early law reform movement. They are its legacy.

Joint Efforts: Rape Crisis Centers and Rape Law Reformers

By 1976 four hundred rape crisis centers had been established in the
United States (Largen 1981), and by 1980 rape statutes had undergone
some type of pro-victim reform, or such reforms had been considered,
in all fifty states and the District of Columbia (Bienen 1980). Activists
in both camps had virtually transformed the victim's post-rape experience. They had provided counseling, support, and advocacy through
the rape crisis center and the rape hotline and had changed the law to
reduce the misery of court proceedings for the victim who reports to
law enforcement. Moreover, both law reform and rape crisis center
efforts served an educational function by focusing on the need for
changes in public attitudes toward sexual assault. Because they challenged a political system that effectively excused all but the most brutal
of rapists and blamed all but the most innocent of victims, their goals
lay well within the parameters of the feminist ideology of rape that
emerged in the early 1970s.

The rape crisis center and rape law reform projects did not function
in isolation from each other, but instead operated within the wider
constellation of efforts to address the issue of rape. Because crisis center
activists and law reformers shared a pro-victim orientation and an active desire to mitigate her post-rape experience, their ideological expressions also often shared consistent themes. And because both groups
have been interested in taking steps toward reducing or eradicating
rape, their activities, diverse as they are, have frequently overlapped
and converged. As anti-rape projects grew in number and political
sophistication, alliances between rape crisis centers and law reformers
were strengthened, even as their strategic choices remained diverse.

As anti-rape projects matured politically throughout the 1970s, the
sharp distinctions between liberal and radical feminist strategies diminished. As rape crisis centers became less informal and more professional to be able to secure funding, a service-provision model began to

replace the radical feminist model that had originated in 1972 (Gornick, Burt, and Pittman 1985). This gradual shift toward a less radical political program involved cooperation with governmental institutions and frequent collaboration with the criminal justice system's approach to crime. However, actions such as the corroboration repeal effort in New York, described above, retained a radical feminist flavor; activists refused to settle for the incremental changes preferred by legislators and held out for the total elimination of the requirement. The anti-rape movement promoted such cross-fertilization of groups and strategies because of its guiding pro-victim orientation.

In a number of cities, anti-rape campaigners of various stripes joined forces to engage in public events and actions to call attention to sexual assault as an issue and to pressure policy makers to respond to the needs of victims and anti-rape workers. To raise rape consciousness among varied feminist groups, anti-rape projects often used their public education talents to address women's organizations (in Jo Freeman's sense of the word) that might prove co-optable to the anti-rape cause (Freeman 1975). In October 1972, for example, "Karen" and "Emily" of the D.C. RCC attended a meeting of Northern Virginia NOW to talk about rape, the rape crisis center, and self-defense, an event that was covered in the *Washington Post* (Kiernan 1972). The two women intended to introduce NOW members to the issue of rape in the hopes of attracting greater interest in the anti-rape cause.

In other areas, various women's groups formed coalitions around the issue to increase their numbers, call greater public attention to rape, and lobby for an institutional response to the problem. As discussed above, in New York members of the Women's Anti-Rape Group (WARG), precursor of the New York Women Against Rape (NYWAR) crisis center collective, attended a gathering of New York NOW to discuss a variety of anti-rape strategies in 1973. According to the NYWAR meeting minutes for 24 May 1973, the session's leader, Mary Vasiliades, head of the NY–NOW Ad Hoc Committee on Rape, warned participants that "as for stopping rape, the task will be a lonely one" and that leadership would not come from elected officials (quoted in NYWAR records). Vasiliades also told the group that NY–NOW's focus was on prevention, education, and legislative change. Evidently, these goals meshed with NYWAR's agenda as a rape crisis center.

The collective, in fact, became quite active in the local effort to reform rape laws. One NYWAR member, Emma, worked with NOW and other women's groups interested in forming a rape coalition, as recorded in meeting minutes of 8 June 1973 (NYWAR records). On 26 June 1973, the Women's Anti-Rape Coalition (WARC), the resulting organization, held its first meeting, declaring as its purpose raising public awareness of rape and repealing the corroboration requirement (NYWAR records). At least five groups made up this coalition at its inception: NYWAR, NY–NOW, New York Radical Feminists, and the Manhattan Women's Political Caucus (a chapter of the National Women's Political Caucus). Two more feminist associations, the National Black Feminist Organization (NBFO) and the Coalition of 100 Black Women, joined within a year. The Women's Anti-Rape Coalition declared August Rape Prevention Month, engaged in a media campaign to call attention to rape, and successfully lobbied the legislature to repeal the corroboration requirement of New York's rape law. At WARC's 1975 conference, the various women's groups in attendance were united in their call for federal funding for feminist rape crisis centers, increased numbers of women officers in New York City's rape investigation units, and electing more women to the state legislature who would work for improved rape laws (*New York Times* 1975). It is clear that WARC viewed reforming the law and supporting crisis centers as complementary and compatible.

In a similar effort in Chicago, such diverse groups as the League of Black Women, Chicago NOW, Chicago Legal Action for Women, the Women's Rights Committee of the ACLU, and Rape Crisis, Inc., joined to form the Chicago Coalition Against Rape. Its goals included investigating needed legal changes and how rape cases were handled by area hospitals, reported the *Chicago Tribune* (Schreiber 1974). The Chicago and New York examples illustrate that, while the rape crisis center and rape law reform projects were carrying out different tasks, and while both came to anti-rape work from divergent feminist standpoints, they did not see their projects as mutually exclusive, and they took advantage of the impact of coalition work to raise public consciousness.

Rape crisis center workers recognized early on the need for effective rape laws to enhance their ability to work as advocates for victims; this constituted a large part of the motivation for the centers' law reform efforts. Center staff and volunteers had a vested interest in the passage of fair, pro-victim laws that directly benefited their clients. The centers also recognized the importance of legal expertise to the process of treating rape victims. The D.C. Rape Crisis Center collective asserted in the pamphlet *How to Start a Rape Crisis Center* that

> without a doubt, the most valuable resources available to the Rape Crisis Center are lawyers. . . . [I]t is necessary to establish contacts with criminal lawyers and attorneys working in the prosecutor's office as quickly as possible. For it is these lawyers that are used to dealing with rape cases, who are aware of special problems, and who have the most concrete, specific information. Generally, the Center refers all questions involving an actual victim's case to a practicing attorney. (1972, 14)

Such views highlight the reciprocal relationship between the legal profession and rape crisis centers, even those as closely affiliated with radical feminism as was the D.C. RCC.

Beyond benefiting from improved rape statutes, the crisis centers, because of their proximity to victims, were also well situated to locate weaknesses in the laws. In Washington in 1973, a representative of the D.C. RCC served on the D.C. Task Force on Rape, organized by Councilman Tedson Meyers to investigate the legal and institutional response to rape victims there. Other members of the young collective testified during the task force's hearings before the Public Safety Committee, as reported in the *Washington Post* (Scharfenberg 1973b). The task force's final report, according to the D.C. RCC newsletter of July/August 1973, carried an edge of radicalism because of the five-to-one ratio of women to men on the body, but the newsletter describes the report as "reformist," not radical (O'Sullivan papers). The document covers police, hospital, and court procedures for dealing with rape victims, and the law of rape in the District of Columbia. Although the outcome of the work of the task force was not ideal by the center's standards (for example, the task force declined to recommend eliminating the spousal exemption for rape), it is clear that the center saw the legal reforms as necessary for the proper treatment of rape victims. In Washington and elsewhere, rape crisis center workers took an active role in reforming rape laws.

In the case of the Michigan law reform, the expertise accumulated by advocates at the Women's Crisis Center (WCC) in Ann Arbor led to the decision to set up the Michigan Women's Task Force on Rape (MWTFR); it was this group that initiated the landmark law reform effort there. By working in a "delicate" alliance with city officials based on appeals to a law-and-order sensibility, WCC activists gained legitimacy for the anti-rape cause and called public attention to the issue (Marsh, Geist, and Caplan 1982, 13). Because of ongoing frustrations with an inadequate statute that made rape convictions unlikely, the WCC group formed the MWTFR, setting off the reform process. In Michigan, then, disgruntled rape crisis center advocates were responsible for starting the law reform. But, say commentators, "not all of those present at the initial meeting were convinced that law reform would be the appropriate avenue for change. Several radical feminists dissociated themselves from this effort, questioning the efficacy of a social change strategy to be implemented by a male-dominated institution" (Marsh, Geist, and Caplan 1982, 14). This indicates only that the rape crisis center's involvement in the reform effort, ideologically unpalatable to some of its members, was never an uncontested strategy.

In another example of rape crisis center activism in law reform, the Pennsylvania Coalition Against Rape (PCAR), made up of crisis centers, worked in 1976 to pass sweeping new legislation. According to "History of PCAR, 1975 to 1995," the proposed law eliminated the corroboration and victim-resistance requirements, a ninety-day statute of limitations on reporting rape, and cautionary instruction from judges to juries; it also contained a rape shield provision that made a victim's sexual history inadmissable except as it involved her and the accused (PCAR records). This was the first organized action on the part of the coalition, which indicates the importance that rape crisis centers placed on pro-victim legislation.

Finally, much legal information, based on the experiences of their workers, is to be found in rape crisis center publications. *Not a Fleeting Rage,* the handbook of one hotline operation, the San Francisco Women Against Rape (1977), offered detailed information about the legal process the victim would encounter if she reported being attacked. In another handbook, *How to Organize a Women's Crisis-Service Center,* the Women's Crisis Center of Ann Arbor (1974) details the legal procedure on reporting a rape. In Washington, Nkenge Toure of the D.C. RCC wrote "District Attorney's Guide to Dealing with Sexual Assault Victims," an article offering prosecutors pro-victim advice in taking on rape cases, for *FAAR Newsletter* (Toure 1978). Whether or not individual crisis center workers agreed with a strategy of law reform, they understood that many of their clients would pursue their cases through police and prosecutors, and they were at the very least sympathetic to efforts to enact pro-victim legislation. Crisis centers have long sought to offer rape victims as many options as possible, among them reporting to the police, having an exam at an emergency room, and pressing charges. Reformed rape laws have helped them to present victims with an even greater number of choices.

Evidence of the reciprocity between the law reform and crisis center strategies can be found in the records of both sets of groups. For example, NOW's records document the frequent interaction between them. Mary Ann Largen of NOWRTF printed in the task force's July 1974 newsletter an excerpt from the D.C. Rape Crisis Center's testimony before the city council's Public Safety Committee Task Force on Rape, entitled "Rights of Rape Victims" (NOW records). Further, in a letter of welcome to the members of the NOWRTF (not dated), Largen suggests that they might be interested in starting rape crisis centers in their own regions as a task force project (NOW records). And in 1974 she detailed the "Rape Revenue Sharing Guidelines" for all members of NOW, explaining how to obtain federal funds for local projects such as rape crisis centers, governmental task forces on rape, and victim compensation programs (NOW records). Some chapters took Largen's advice; for example, NOW—Trenton, New Jersey, opened a rape crisis center in 1974. Largen was clearly enthusiastic about crisis center efforts.

The working relationship between the NOWRTF and the D.C. Rape Crisis Center is further documented in the latter's papers and newsletters. The February/March 1974 newsletter, for example, included a short article by Largen entitled "Telephone Counseling of Rape Victims" (O'Sullivan papers). Moreover, the D.C. RCC meeting minutes contain occasional references to her and Northern Virginia NOW's rape task force, indicating an alliance between these ideologically divergent groups as early as 1973.

Elsewhere, proponents of law reform and rape crisis centers frequently united for public events and investigative efforts. Diverse groups in New York City staged a Women's Walk Against Rape through Central Park to protest the de facto exclusion of women from use of the park at night owing to the high incidence of rape. This event, the city's fourth annual Rape Prevention Month action, prompted letters of support from Representatives Elizabeth Holtzman (D-N.Y.) and Bella Abzug (D-N.Y.) (*New York Times* 1976b). In Houston, at the first National Women's Conference in 1977, delegates passed a resolution endorsing the wholesale rewriting of rape statutes to represent a pro-victim stance. They also called for the establishment of rape crisis centers, complete with services for bilingual, "bicultural" communities, and for state and federal funding of them (*Ms.* 1980, 176). And in 1975, at the Sixth Alabama Symposium on Justice and Behavioral Sciences, whose topic was "Rape: Research, Action, Prevention," conferees represented many strands of anti-rape activism and research, including law reform efforts, rape crisis centers, and medical and university communities. The meeting's organizer, Mary Ann Largen, made sure to send copies of the conference's resolutions on 28 January 1975 to Senators Edward M. Kennedy (D-Mass.) and Charles Mathias (R-Md.), frequent sponsors of rape legislation in Congress (NOW records).

Finally, rape crisis center activists and law reformers had a common sympathy for rape victims and for women. Although their ideologies often diverged markedly (for example, the view of many early crisis center activists that the criminal justice system was incapable of promoting social change), both were intent on dispelling rape myths, offering alternative conceptualizations of sex, violence, and power, and making the post-rape experience as easy as possible for the victim. The law reformers sought to demonstrate how statutes codified rape myths and victim blaming, and to make the changes that would render these statutes more neutral, at least on their face.[15] The rape crisis center activists followed the principle of "I do for you, you do for others" (D.C. Rape Crisis Center 1972, unnumbered page, preface), and worked with police, hospitals, and prosecutors to ensure fair treatment of victims. Both sides have used community education to raise public awareness of the rape issue. And both have met many of their initial goals.

The relationship among the anti-rape strategies and strategists of the 1970s can be variously interpreted. First, liberal and radical activists viewed the panoply of possible approaches as interconnected and necessary. Statutes alone are sterile without community-based organizations in place to hold lawmakers and law enforcement officers accountable for their actions. Conversely, crisis centers would be reluctant to refer a victim to the police or district attorney to report a rape if the statutes that guide the actions of law enforcers remain decidedly victim unfriendly. Second, as the anti-rape movement mobilized, and as the complexity of the problem became more evident, the nature of sexual assault prompted a response so serious that it brought together ideologically diverse feminists determined to prevent or eradicate it. Both factors appear to be in play among anti-rape activists. Thus, the divisions among different groups or different strategies may be less important to the effectiveness of the overall anti-rape movement than the features they share.

From the inception of the campaign against rape, the issue was articulated on the feminist agenda as a complex problem calling for attention and action at all levels of society, including changes in individual consciousness and in institutional response. So complicated an issue required a multifaceted approach. Together, adherents of both radical and liberal political programs played significant roles in promoting fundamental social change and in attempting to attract the attention of policy makers and the public at large.

3
HISTORICAL DEVELOPMENT: RAPE ON THE PUBLIC AGENDA

THE HISTORY OF the impact of women's movement organizations on public policy is a complex fabric of successes, failures, and compromises. Some perceive this impact as historic: according to Susan M. Hartmann, "The women's movement and its allies in the 1970s worked a modest revolution in public policy" (Hartmann 1989, 127); Margaret Conway, David Ahern, and Gertrude Steuernagel (1999) refer to the policy changes wrought by women as "a revolution in progress." Indeed, it cannot be disputed that the activities of the women's movement and its organizations have had a marked impact on U.S. policy making, even when outcomes have fallen short of stated goals.

A great many policy efforts and issues count among the wide constellation of public policies affecting women. Examples include abortion rights, equitable divorce settlements, educational parity, family and medical leave, and greater access to credit, all policy gains resulting directly from second-wave feminist activity.[1] According to Ellen Boneparth and Emily Stoper (1988, 1), "The challenge for the women's movement in the 1970s was to convert those issues into actual changes in public policies in the form of new laws, judicial decisions and executive implementation. By giving birth to a series of interest groups, and by expanding its base, the movement met that challenge quite successfully." Organizations in the women's movement disagreed on which issues to politicize, how to devise strategy, and what goals to pursue. Clashes over issues related to race and poverty, in particular, led to deep divisions among activists (Carden 1977, 40). However rare consensus may sometimes have been, considerable change on behalf of women has resulted from such policy efforts.

Rape is one feminist issue that commentators cite as an important success in measuring the effect of the women's movement on public policy: Boneparth and Stoper (1988, 23) state that "women acting on behalf of women achieved some major successes: . . . a new public awareness and some innovative new policies in the area of violence against women (rape and battering)" among them. Hartmann (1989, 121–22) asserts that "the women's movement and its allies lifted the veil of secrecy from these taboo subjects [rape and wife battering], pushed them onto the national agenda, and promoted policy initiatives designed to assist the victims and to lessen the incidence of violence against women." There is widespread agreement that feminists succeeded in establishing a new awareness of, and approach to, the rape issue on the policy level in the United States. But despite public policy scholars' apparent consensus on the importance of anti-rape public policy, little attention has been paid to the details of this breakthrough.

As I will demonstrate here, a major achievement of the anti-rape movement has been to move the issue from the strictly feminist agenda to the national policy agenda. I trace this process by using the methods of policy studies to define and describe this effort and the changes it has effected. The beginning of this story has already been told in my discussion of the development of the campaign against rape as a social movement. I now turn to the role of the rape issue in public policy making in the 1970s, and the impact of the movement on policy. The policy developments of the 1980s, 1990s, and beyond are the subject of Chapter 4.

Defining Public Policy

The political scientist James Anderson (1994, 5–6) defines policy as "a purposive course of action followed by an actor or set of actors in dealing with a problem or matter of concern. . . . Public policies are those developed by governmental bodies and officials."[2] He points out that this definition emphasizes the deliberate actions that are intended to achieve certain goals over random occurrences ("public policies . . . do not, by and large, just happen"), focuses on the long-term process of addressing a problem instead of a single action or decision, and implies that policies frequently are made in response to interest groups' demands.

Anderson's definition is particularly helpful for understanding the public policy changes effected by the anti-rape movement. First, from the earliest considerations of how to address the social problem of rape, attempts at establishing new policies have always been goal oriented. Such ends have ranged from the immediate (such as making the victim's hospital experience as comfortable as possible, or attaining funding for rape-related research) to the long-term (the prevention and control of rape). Moreover, the campaigners against rape demanded a complex policy response to the issue—no single governmental action or body could sufficiently address a problem so deeply ingrained in our culture, one that has defied any simplistic approach promising an easy solution. Finally, because the anti-rape movement has been credited for bringing the issue into the public discourse and to the attention of policy makers, this definition highlights the demands made by its members and acknowledges the role of its activists in bringing about institutional change. These persons created the impetus and momentum that policy makers tapped for their initiatives.

The Policy Process and Agenda Setting

Political scientists have used various ways to describe how policy makers identify public issues for action (Anderson 1994; O'Connor 1996).[3] Beginning in 1970, the rape issue followed a trajectory much like that of other policy questions. This chapter focuses on the phases of the process that are particularly useful for understanding how policy makers came to take up the issue of rape: problem recognition and definition, agenda setting, policy formulation, budgeting, and policy evaluation. I intend to make clear the mutually reinforcing—and frequently mutually exclusive—relationship between the feminist agenda and the public one.

All agendas are not equal, of course. Roger Cobb and Charles Elder (1972, 85–87) consider in detail the characteristics of the public agenda, proposing that there exist a systemic agenda and an institutional, or formal, agenda—related and not entirely separate. The broader, systemic agenda includes all items a particular community considers to be matters of concern. Three subjective "prerequisites" must be fulfilled before an issue arrives on the systemic agenda:

> (1) widespread attention or at least awareness; (2) shared concern of a sizeable portion of the public that some type of action is required; and (3) a shared perception that the matter is an appropriate concern of some governmental unit and falls within the bounds of its authority. . . . An issue requires the recognition of only a major portion of the polity, not the entire citizenry. (Cobb and Elder 1972, 86)

By contrast, the institutional (or formal) agenda consists of all items that have been singled out explicitly for "active and serious" consideration by local, state, or federal governments (Cobb and Elder 1972, 86). Questions on the systemic agenda can be broad or abstract, but the items on the institutional agenda are more specific and concrete. In the 1970s, rape appeared on the systemic agenda when feminists began to politicize and call attention to it; rape became an item on the institutional agenda when anti-rape activists channeled the particular issues involved to policy-making bodies.

Problem Recognition and Definition

Because feminist groups were articulating rape as a matter that had never before been viewed as a political problem, the first stage in the policy-making process is critical to understanding the politics behind rape activism. The importance of this phase is highlighted by the sensitive nature of the issue. Before rape consciousness developed among feminist activists, the topic, like many others raised by the women's movement, was generally taboo in public discourse. But because rape has been a question for criminal law even before the twentieth century, it occasionally became a matter of public interest, unmediated by feminist activism until the 1970s.

Lynching is an example of such public discourse. During the period when many black men and some women were being lynched in the United States, rape was often used to justify what were in fact brutal gang murders. Whites, outraged by the supposed tendency of black men to rape white women, made a public spectacle of the lynching to warn black men to resist these presumed urges. As evidenced by the investigative journalism of Ida B. Wells, public attitudes toward lynching and rape had little to do with reality. Although the mainstream press contributed to the growing attention to the link between rape and lynching, it often did so in ways that promoted, rather than reduced, mob violence (Benedict 1992). Since legal charges were rarely filed against the accused, and since the claims of rape and the lynchings served purposes other than the cause of justice, the public discourse left little room for discussions of the real rapes of women (black or white) or of the impact of the crime on its victims. The imagined effect of black-on-white rape, from a white male point of view, dominated the discourse. Although activists were able to get lynching on the institutional agenda (Baughman 1966; Grant 1975; Ferrell 1986), its corollary issue—rape—did not enjoy that status.

Likewise, given the psychiatric profession's dominance of the discourse surrounding rapists and criminality throughout much of the twentieth century, rape was also sometimes presented as the deviant act of the sexual psychopath, the "ravenous brute," or the sexually aberrant male. The stereotype of a man with overwhelming sexual urges or an unresolved childhood psychodrama stems from this discourse and remains with us today.[4] Before the consciousness-raising work of the anti-rape movement, then, a pro-victim approach to sexual assault was absent from public discourse, let alone the formal public agenda. The campaign against lynching did not address the experience of rape, and the psychiatric approach individualized and psychologized the rapist, treating him as aberrant and unique, but failing to address the problem from a victim's point of view.

The introduction of the rape issue to the policy process coincided with its arrival on the feminist agenda in 1970, when radical feminists and consciousness-raising groups took up the task of politicizing the personal. Because an analysis of male dominance was already taking place in the movement and its writings, definitions of rape fit into a growing body of theory and served to advance radical feminist approaches to patriarchal politics. Activists recognized the depth of the problem of rape based on victims' reports of the trauma it caused, the insensitivity of the members of public institutions charged with responding to victims, and the fear of rape that nearly all women seemed to share. They educated themselves on the breadth of the issue with legal and medical research and further consciousness-raising.

Feminists' recognition of rape was reflected in their definition of the problem. As they understood it in the early 1970s, rape was a problem of both personal and political dimensions. Their anti-rape ideology viewed rape as a crime of violence, not of sexuality and passion, and as an expression of male dominance designed to keep women subordinate to men. The new feminist understanding proved to be the first step toward moving the problem onto the public agenda.

1970s' Approach to Crime: Get Tough

Wider trends helped to define further the national context for the recognition of the rape issue. In addition to the growth and increasing influence of the women's movement, the 1960s and 1970s saw a new focus placed on crime and criminals in the United States. Governmental support for some goals of the anti-rape campaign has been important to the successes it has enjoyed. This support came in the form of federal, state, and local funding and the willingness of legislators to re-examine rape statutes. Because of the law-and-order, tough-on-crime political climate of the 1970s, including Richard M. Nixon's own famous anti-crime platform in the 1972 presidential election, public officials were now lending a sympathetic ear to the claims of anti-rape activists. The law-and-order attitudes among the general population and the legislators who represent it fostered increasing alarm over rape just as the women's movement began to call new attention to the issue. Although crime has been a policy matter since the framing of the Constitution, an intensive concern with it began in the 1960s and gained momentum throughout most of the 1970s.[5]

According to a Justice Department (DOJ) report, crime became an issue on the public agenda during the presidential campaign of 1964, emerged as a major public concern in the opinion polls of 1966, and had become significant in the federal budgetary process by the late 1960s. Around that time, President Lyndon Johnson proclaimed his grandiose goal of "not only reduc[ing] but banish[ing] crime" altogether (U.S. Department of Justice 1975, 1). In 1968, Congress passed, and Johnson signed, the Omnibus Crime Control and Safe Streets Act (P.L. 90-351), creating the Law Enforcement Assistance Administration (LEAA) within the Department of Justice. Amended several times in the 1970s, the act delineated the parameters of federal involvement in crime and law enforcement efforts across the nation. LEAA was the central funding source for various local and state anti-crime, policing, corrections, and research projects for fourteen years. Its establishment is the most tangible mark of the arrival of crime on the institutional agenda at the federal level.

By the time Richard M. Nixon took office in 1969, a full-blown "national attack" was deemed necessary. According to a report issued under Richard G. Kleindienst, an attorney general during the Nixon administration (and himself later jailed as a result of the Watergate scandal), "Under the leadership of the President, the Federal Government mounted the most comprehensive and vigorous attack on crime in the history of the Nation. . . . The president ordered an all-out assault . . ." (U.S. Department of Justice 1972, vi). Such militaristic rhetoric reflected and reinforced the sense of alarm typical of the law-and-order atmosphere of the day.

In 1972, President Nixon characterized the 1960s as a decade of immense criminal activity, and the 1970s as the time for action. Encouraged by early reports of a reduction in crime rates for 1971, the president remarked that

> this represents truly significant progress in this Administration's determination to turn back the wave of crime which swept our nation in the 1960's. It is the best news yet on the crime front. . . .
>   . . . Another key ingredient in the crime fight has been the development of a new, less permissive public attitude. The American public is now fully awake to the social menace of crime, and fully determined that criminals must be defeated if America is to make social progress. . . .

. . . Together, . . . let us show that the day of the criminal is
past in America, and the day of the citizen is here. (quoted in
U.S. Department of Justice 1972, 1)

By the early 1970s, then, public policy–making activity was more focused on reducing and preventing crime than ever before. Policy makers viewed crime and law enforcement as local issues that required a
federal response, as is evident in the LEAA budgets for the decade. As
a new agency, it received relatively low funding at its inception in 1969,
$63 million. But LEAA's budget enjoyed increases over the next six
years, jumping to $895 million in 1975. When the agency was phased
out in 1980, the figure was still a relatively high $642 million.

In addition to developing and funding LEAA, the Department of
Justice further demonstrated the new policy focus on crime by sponsor-
ing the National Crime Victimization Survey (NCVS), starting in
1972. The survey is the collaborative effort of several government
agencies, including the Bureau of the Census and the Bureau of Justice
Statistics (U.S. Department of Justice 1994a, 1). At first administered
under LEAA, and originally called the National Crime Survey, the
NCVS fell to the BJS when the Justice Department was restructured
under the Justice System Improvement Act of 1979 (U.S. Department
of Justice 1981). The NCVS polls 100,000 people to gather data on
victimization by personal violence and property crimes (U.S. Department of Justice 1994b). The survey is intended, among other things, to
provide an alternative or a supplement to data collected in the FBI's
Uniform Crime Reports, which has tabulated crimes disclosed to the
police since 1930. The NCVS reflects both the U.S. government's acknowledgment that a high percentage of crimes go unreported and its
desire to compile comprehensive data on victimization.[6]

The 1970s' focus on crime followed closely on the heels of major
advances in civil rights and overall equality for African Americans.
The late 1960s was a period of militant social movements, including
the Weather Underground, the Black Panthers, and other groups and
figures who advocated "any means necessary"—including armed resistance—to achieve radical goals such as racial equality and the over-

throw of capitalism and imperialism. This militancy confirmed the worst suspicions of racist and conservative whites in the United States that black people and the members of the counterculture posed the greatest threat to the safety and livelihood of the law-abiding majority. Thus, the law-and-order agenda of the 1970s was informed by a pronounced white fear of minority criminality.

This new attention being paid to crime and crime rates set the stage for policy makers' responsiveness to the issue of rape as raised by activists and lobbyists from the women's movement. Candidates for public office—most notably and visibly President Richard M. Nixon in his bid for a second term in 1972—declared crime a national crisis, pledged to reduce it and "make the streets safe" (McGinniss 1969), and promised to appoint only judges with a tough-on-crime record to the federal bench to reverse the trends begun during the liberal Warren Court. An explosion of anti-crime legislation followed. Lawmakers carefully avoided casting any votes that might lead to allegations of being "soft" on crime. Because actors in the anti-rape movement were hard at work advancing policies that were gentle on victims and tough on assailants, their legislative proposals often appealed both to feminist activists and to policy makers.

The politics of law and order and the politics of rape intersected at all levels of government. The bill to repeal New York's corroboration requirement sparked a controversy that called into question the extent to which policy makers could use their involvement in the rape issue to advance their own political careers, not to mention their own political agendas. In 1974, Governor Malcolm Wilson signed the corroboration repeal bill for which the Women's Anti-Rape Coalition had lobbied so intensively, and which the state legislature passed unanimously. Despite his silence during the repeal bill debate, Wilson attempted to capitalize on the public attention being paid to the rape issue; he enlisted a rape survivor to speak in a televised campaign advertisement for his 1974 election bid.[7] This commercial, in which a victim recounts her experience, implied that the governor had been a primary and vocal proponent of the bill and a supporter of anti-rape and anti-crime legislation. New York NOW quickly refuted these questionable claims, stating that Wilson had "little to do" with reforming the state's rape law. In his defense, the governor's representatives responded that Wilson "did not sign [the bill] reluctantly" (Clines 1974). If nothing else, the use of the advertisement demonstrates rape's presence as a campaign issue (albeit in terms unacceptable to movement activists) and one candidate's appeal to anti-crime sentiments and the women's vote.

Supporting anti-rape initiatives was logical and relatively easy for legislators of the tough-on-crime school. Activists, however, frequently had to choose between making political compromises to achieve some degree of reform and pursuing a purer political agenda that avoided all complicity with the system. The *Feminist Alliance Against Rape Newsletter* (later *Aegis*) was one forum in which this tension was quite pronounced. The members of FAAR frequently criticized others in the anti-rape movement for their willingness to work on policy and to try to reform a male-dominated political and legal system rife with extreme class and race bias. For example, the Washington, D.C., activist Loretta Ross (1982, 40) explained:

> In . . . America, Third World women must struggle against brutal acts of racial and sexual violence, while facing the systematic denial of society's benefits. . . . [W]e are the targets of rape and sexual abuse by all men, not only men of our races. . . . We are the poorest of the poor, and are considered defenseless, which is why we get attacked so often. We have little or no redress through a criminal *in*justice system that at all times continues the oppression of our peoples. (emphasis in original)

Ross and other FAAR members viewed the problem of sexual assault as women of color experience it to stem from the combined oppressions of racism, sexism, poverty, and imperialism. This contrasted with early feminists' framing of rape as a manifestation of male dominance, unmediated by other forms of oppression. Moreover, Ross pointed out (1982, 45), "The racist nature of the criminal justice system still has a drastic impact on Third World communities as non-white men are disproportionately jailed for sexual assault." In her view and that of other activists, because the agents of this oppression are the very people responsible for making laws and meting out criminal justice, and because law reform strategies that refuse to confront systemic racism will simply perpetuate this oppression, a policy approach that ignores systemic racism will fail to address the problem of rape for women of color.

Other commentators were careful to acknowledge the dilemma inherent in cooperating with law-and-order legislators. For example, the journalist Daniel Ben-Horin, writing in the *Nation,* questioned the merits of policy victories won at the cost of making activists complicit with conservative legislators who saw reformed rape laws, not as an assertion of the female right to bodily integrity, but as a chance to "protect our women" (Ben-Horin 1975, 113). In his feminist-sympathetic view, "The problem with riding on someone else's coattails is that your control of direction is limited," which could lead, for instance, to legislation that seeks only more protection of women within the traditional constructions of male aggression and female passivity (Ben-Horin 1975, 114). Viewed in this light, the tough-on-crime and feminist approaches to rape appear to be only marginally compatible.

The paradox of the law-and-order approach as both bane and boon to anti-rape organizing was not lost on movement activists, who understood the limits of reform policies and legislation. Even liberal feminist proponents of reform looked on this approach as inherently limited. Mary Ann Largen, the first coordinator of the National Organization for Women Rape Task Force, explained that "while the women's movement continues to focus upon the societal sexism inherent in rape, society itself is taking up the rape issue under the 'law and order' banner. This banner provokes emotion but fails to deal with the source of the problem; it is a Band-Aid solution to a problem which requires major surgery" (Largen 1976, 72). Her words capture the marked discontinuity between feminist articulation of rape as the symbolic and real domination of women by men, and the status of rape in the policy arena as just another crime. Movement activists themselves remained wary of the political compromises necessary to bring the issue to the institutional policy agenda.

The Media and the Anti-Rape Agenda

Many social scientists have commented on the importance of media coverage to social movements, agenda setting, and public policy (Molotch 1979; Linsky 1986; Iyengar and Kinder 1987; Kingdon 1989; Iyengar 1991). Once feminists discovered rape as an issue in the early 1970s and set out to research and define it, an onslaught of coverage in the mass media quickly followed, helping to put the issue on the systemic agenda. Then, as the ideology of the anti-rape movement started to develop, print and electronic news organizations began to pay even more attention to the problem and the new politicization of it. Through this media coverage—both print and broadcast—rape came to be defined as a major social problem.

To be sure, rape and other "sex crimes" (a euphemism widely used in journalism and law enforcement) have been a staple of twentieth-century reporting. According to Helen Benedict, author of a study on rape coverage in newspapers and magazines from 1900 until the mid-1950s, sex crimes were reported almost exclusively in relation to lynching and interracial rapes in which black men were accused. White-on-white rape was covered rarely, black-on-black rape was ignored, and white-on-black rape was not covered at all until the 1950s (Benedict 1992, 27). Because of the growth of the civil rights movement and widespread attention to racial inequality, Benedict finds, by the 1950s journalistic accounts of the rape of white women by black men tended to focus on false allegations and virtually blamed white women for black men's disenfranchisement. The tactic that dominated press coverage of the day was to "defend the accused by denigrating the victims." As usual, the rape of black women continued to be virtually ignored. In the 1960s, the press exhibited growing sensitivity to racism, but understood very little of sexism: rape stories of that decade, according to Benedict, either ignored the victims altogether or described them with infantilizing or mocking language, referring to young adult victims as "girls" or "coeds," and to middle-aged single women as "spinsters" (1992, 37–39). In the print media during the first seven decades of the twentieth century, not one word of this amounted to any serious consideration of rape as a social problem affecting women.

Once rape had become a feminist issue, reporting of it began to change. Table 3.1 suggests that press attention to sexual assault increased dramatically in the early 1970s and remained relatively high throughout the decade.[8] Coverage peaked in 1974, the year that statutory reform efforts were under way in several states, the year Congress was considering the Rape Prevention and Control Act, the year after NOW voted to establish its first Rape Task Force, and two years after the first rape crisis centers were established.

News coverage of rape in this period was by no means uniform. Many stories indexed under that heading are simple accounts of reports to police, arrests, convictions, and appeals. Such stories might be catalogued in the index as "Queens (NYC) woman raped by unidentified assailant on roof of her apartment house." These reports do, however, demonstrate the growing importance of the crime as a public issue, because they mark a greater willingness on the part of the press to cover it in ways that neither blame its victims nor advance racial stereotypes. They also demonstrate new trends in reporting rape: while it remained one of the crimes least likely to be taken to the police, com-

Table 3.1 New York Times *Coverage of Rape, 1968–1980*

Year	Number of Stories on Rape
1968	18
1969	29
1970	26
1971	44
1972	65
1973	108
1974	117
1975	88
1976	73
1977	97
1978	105
1979	94
1980	67

mentators and analysts agreed that the growing attention to rape in the early 1970s probably made women more likely to file charges than they had been in previous years (Brownmiller 1975, 191). The number of these simple reporting stories, then, is closely related to the new attention to rape and helped shape public attitudes.

Other newspaper accounts of rape, new to the 1970s, can be classified as episodic and thematic stories (Iyengar 1991, 14). These are a direct result of, and evidence of, rape's arrival on the public agenda. Episodic stories use a specific incident of rape or a victim case study to illustrate the problem. Not only was it now possible to talk about rape in victim-sympathetic ways, but new attention was being paid to the systematic and structural obstacles facing women who had been attacked—sneering police officers, judgmental medical staff, reluctant prosecuting attorneys, sex-biased judges, procedural difficulties in courtrooms, impossible legal standards of proof, and general lack of support from the community, among others. An example of an episodic story appeared in the *Los Angeles Times* as "Rape: Does Justice Turn Its Head?" (Stumbo 1972). The article began with the rape account of "Janet," who could not find justice in the California legal system. It went on to investigate the problems inherent in prosecuting rape charges in that state. Such articles proliferated in local and national newspapers throughout the 1970s.

Thematic news stories examine some aspects of rape, such as trials or police procedures, in a more "general or abstract" context, using "collective or general evidence" (Iyengar 1991, 14). For example, a 1972 article in the *New York Times,* "Law of Rape: Because Ladies Lie," investigated the problem of the general refusal to believe rape victims and how the legal system reinforced this disbelief (Oelsner 1972). Although less common than episodic, thematic stories became more visible as rape grew in importance in the public mind; they represent the important new trend of presenting sexual assault from the victim's point of view.

Another interesting development in the print media's treatment of rape, whether episodic, thematic, or otherwise, is the amount of attention paid to the anti-rape movement. In February 1971, Gail Sheehy, writing about the New York Radical Feminists' (NYRF) rape speak-out of 24 January for *New York* magazine, declared that "the next major focus of the women's movement [is] rape and protection against it" (Sheehy 1971, 26). Articles in such diverse publications as the *Progressive* (Wasserman 1973), *Intellect* (Hartwig and Sandler 1975),[9] *Time* (Welch 1973; Millett 1974), *Reader's Digest* (Rowan and Mazie 1974), the *New York Times Magazine* (Lear 1972; Lichtenstein 1974), and the *Nation* (Ben-Horin 1975) described the problems facing rape victims and the unfairness of the legal codes and went on to discuss efforts by the women's movement to call attention to the problem and to achieve policy changes. Much of the media coverage even gives credit to feminists for removing the taboo from the public discussion of rape. This type of coverage informed the citizenry that changes were taking place and helped create a climate in which victims might be more likely to report rapes to the authorities.

Further heightening this new public profile, the print media began to cover events and developments in the anti-rape movement. For instance, a rape conference at George Washington University was reported in the *Washington Post* (Barker 1972). The newspaper also described the opening of the D.C. Rape Crisis Center and published a positive editorial on it (*Washington Post* 1972a, 1972b). The *New York Times* reported on the NYRF conference of April 1971 (Lichtenstein 1971), a critical mobilizing event for the anti-rape movement, although it ignored the January 1971 speak-out. The *Times* also meticulously covered developments in the effort to repeal the state's corroboration requirement, spearheaded by feminists, throughout the 1973–74 legislative session. An editorial supporting the repeal appeared while the legislature was considering the measure (*New York Times* 1974a). The *Times* even reported on the NOW conference of 1973, when a resolution forming the national rape task force was passed (Shanahan 1973). For its part, the *Los Angeles Times* stated that "Rape Concern Reaches the Federal Level," noting developments such as the introduction of the Rape Prevention and Control Act by Senator Charles Mathias (R-Md.) (Cimons 1974). Through their coverage, newspapers kept rape on the systemic agenda, and they also conveyed to their readers the idea that policy changes in how sexual assault was dealt with were possible, forthcoming, and necessary.

Print was not the only news medium to be a source of rape information and awareness.[10] Beginning in 1972, movies, documentaries, and specials produced for television increasingly focused on rape. In that year, Washington's WRC-TV aired "The Lonely Crime," a two-part news program on rape, in which D.C. Rape Crisis Center staff members and rape survivors spoke openly in interviews (Carmody 1972a, 1972b). Also in 1972, CBS stations around the country broadcast the special "Rape" (Murphy 1972). The television movie *A Case of Rape,* starring Elizabeth Montgomery, aired in February 1974. It was perhaps the first victim-sympathetic fictionalized depiction of rape on television. This program received the highest Nielsen rating of any TV movie that had yet been broadcast (Brown 1974). Other awareness-raising programming included ABC's documentary "The Rape Victims," shown in May 1977 (O'Connor 1977). And last, in a marked conflation of mass entertainment and policy making, a special one-hour episode of the situation comedy *All in the Family,* portraying the attempted rape of a central character, Edith Bunker, aired in October 1977. The week before its national broadcast, a private showing was held for 175 Capitol Hill regulars, including rape crisis volunteers from the Washington area. The screening was hosted by Representatives Herbert Harris (D-Va.) and Peter Rodino (D-N.J.), co-sponsors of Representative Elizabeth Holtzman's (D-N.Y.) federal legislation to protect rape victims' privacy, discussed below (Shales 1977). Anti-rape movement response was lukewarm: FAAR appreciated the consciousness-raising value of the episode and the credible performance by Jean Stapleton as Edith, but they criticized producer Norman Lear for over-simplifying the issue and the resolution—reporting the assault to law enforcement (McDonald 1977).

The mass media, then, played a significant role in spreading anti-rape ideology, providing information about the movement, and covering the issue. This involvement reflected both the growing attention to issues of crime control and the new rape consciousness inspired by feminists in the anti-rape movement.

Highly Publicized Rape Cases and Trials of the 1970s

Continual media attention has kept rape at least on the systemic agenda since it arrived there in 1970. Contributing to newly raised public awareness, well-publicized trials kept the issue alive for months at a time in ways that expressed a newfound sympathy with victims. Perhaps ironically, in two of the three most celebrated early cases charges of rape were never filed, and women defendants became the focus of public attention. The third case involved a civil suit by a celebrity for a rape that was reported to authorities but did not result in an arrest. The first two cases prompted feminist support, although they enjoyed no public consensus on guilt or innocence. Both controversial, they received so much media attention precisely because they raised complicated issues. These two early cases also involved women of color, and both broached the question of the extent to which a woman has the right to defend herself against rape. All three trials captured national attention and brought the issues of rape, self-defense, and criminal justice to the forefront of public consciousness.

According to Inez Garcia, on 19 March 1974 she was raped at her house in Monterey, California, by Louis Castillo while his friend Miguel Jimenez watched and prevented her from fleeing. About twenty minutes after the rape, she located a gun and tracked down and shot at the two men, killing Jimenez. At her much publicized trial, attended daily by supporters from the Berkeley women's liberation community, Garcia was represented by the radical lawyer Charles Garry, famous for his defense of the Black Panthers Huey Newton and Bobby Seale. Once the mass media picked up the story, according to one source, "Inez Garcia was not just a name but a national symbol: the rape victim who fought back" (Blitman and Green 1975, 50). Feminists in California formed the Inez Garcia Defense Committee and worked to win public support for her, raise money for her defense, and promote the notion of Garcia as a symbol (Free Inez! 1974). The judge in the case complicated matters with a controversial decision to prohibit Garry from introducing evidence of the rape.

On 21 October 1974, Garcia was found guilty of second-degree murder and sentenced to five years to life in prison, prompting public protests by women's groups across the country (Bright-Sagnier 1974). In December 1975, the conviction was overturned on appeal owing to a technicality. At her second trial, in 1977, Garcia was represented by a feminist lawyer, Susan Jordan;[11] on 4 March 1977, she was acquitted of all charges, a victory hailed by feminists around the United States (*Washington Post* 1977). In May 1977, public television stations nationwide aired *The People vs. Inez Garcia,* a docudrama based on the 1974 trial.

In August 1974, Joann Little,[12] an African American, was being held in the Beaufort County, North Carolina, jail. Little said that on the night of 27 August, she killed a white prison guard, Clarence Alligood, with his own ice pick during a struggle as he raped or attempted to rape her. Alligood's body was found in Little's cell, naked from the waist down. Little fled the jail, but was soon captured and sent back to face first-degree murder charges, which were later reduced to murder in the second degree.

Little's defense drew support from a number of politicians and organizations. For example, the Southern Poverty Law Center issued a statement in her support in January 1975 (Guillory 1975). On 7 February 1975, Representative Elizabeth Holtzman (D-N.Y.) joined twenty-eight other members of Congress in sending a letter to Attorney General Edward Levi requesting an investigation into the charges against Little and her assertion that she and other women inmates had been sexually assaulted at the Beaufort County jail (Holtzman papers). On 15 April 1975, Representative Shirley Chisholm (D-N.Y.) issued a press release on the Little case, calling attention to the rape issue, the racial dimension of the situation, and the right of women to defend themselves against rape (NOW records). On 31 March 1975, Afi Phoebe of the National Black Feminist Organization (NBFO) called on NOW to join her group in a public protest at the courtroom in Beaufort County where Little would be tried. The NOWRTF, headed by Mary Ann Largen, became a supporter of Little and included information about the case in the task force's newsletter (NOW records). In June 1975, an article by the radical activist Angela Davis, "JoAnne Little: The Dialectics of Rape," appeared in *Ms.* magazine. On 15 August 1975,

Little was found not guilty; the jury had deliberated for seventy-eight minutes (NOW records). The events surrounding both Garcia and Little highlighted the complexity of the rape issue as one involving not only male dominance, but race- and class-based oppression.

The third case to receive substantial media attention in the mid-1970s was the rape of the popular singer Connie Francis by an intruder in a Westbury, New York, Howard Johnson's Motor Lodge in November 1974. No arrest was ever made. The incident made headlines when Francis sued the hotel chain for $6 million for failure to provide adequate security. A New York jury awarded her $2.5 million, one of the largest monetary compensations ever made in a rape suit. The jury also awarded Francis's husband, Joseph Garzilli, $150,000 for the loss of his wife's services, according to a 2 July 1976 article in the *New York Times*. Fearing that these sums would be set aside on appeal, Francis later settled out of court for approximately $1.5 million, the *New York Times* reported on 23 February 1977.

These three cases attracted ample media coverage and raised significant questions about rape and race. Both Little and Garcia were women of color, and race was a significant component of their trials. But the Francis civil suit involved a well-known white woman and an unidentified, unapprehended perpetrator. To create a media sensation in the mid-1970s, a rape trial did not have to involve a person of color, but Francis's celebrity surely accounts for some of the public interest in her case. Perhaps most significantly, not one of these three cases brought an accused rapist to trial in a courtroom.

Rape on the ABA Agenda

Another step in making rape a public agenda item was the passage of a resolution urging rape law reform by the American Bar Association (ABA) in 1975. The organization has long taken policy stances on issues it deems important to law and justice (Grossman 1965). At its February 1975 meeting, the ABA House of Delegates adopted a resolution urging

> a redefinition of rape and related crimes in terms of "persons" instead of "women," and revision of rules of evidence in order

> to protect the prosecuting witness from unnecessary invasion of
> privacy and psychological and emotional harm by: (1) elimina-
> tion of corroboration requirements which exceed those applica-
> ble to other assaults, (2) revision of the rules of evidence relating
> to cross-examination of the complaining witness, (3) re-evalua-
> tion of rape penalties, (4) development of new procedures for
> police and prosecutors in processing rape cases, [and] (5) estab-
> lishment of rape treatment and study centers to aid both the
> victim and the offender. ("House of Delegates" 1975, 465)

The resolution, and the report that accompanies it, were submitted by
the ABA Law Student Division (LSD) and presented to the delegates
by Connie K. Borkenhagen, an LSD member. The most telling evidence of the intersection of the ABA's resolution and the institutional
agenda was Representative Elizabeth Holtzman's presentation of the
resolution and report to the House in support of her proposed legislation to amend the federal rules of evidence to include a rape shield
provision (U.S. Congress, House 1976b).[13] As the issue gained greater
visibility in a variety of public forums, rape was recognized as an
agenda item with ramifications reaching far beyond the concerns of
the feminist groups that first called attention to it.

Judicial Quips

Another issue involving the law that kept rape on the systemic agenda
at the end of the 1970s was a series of statements about sexual assault
made by judges in jurisdictions across the United States. Jurists, whose
comments are nearly always public, and whose views are presumed to
be impartial, fair, and without political motivation, have occupied a
lofty position in the minds of Americans. The falls from grace experienced by several of them reflect both the growing concern about rape,
its victims, and the fairness of rape trials, and the betrayal of trust these
insensitive remarks represent.[14]

One of the first examples of such callousness came to light in San
Francisco in early 1971, when the California Supreme Court censured
Judge Bernard B. Glickfeld of the superior court for speaking harshly

to a victim who claimed that the sentence he gave her two confessed rapists was too lenient (*New York Times* 1971a). But the case that perhaps received the most national media attention was that of Judge Archie Simonson of Madison, Wisconsin. In a 1977 ruling, he stated that a fifteen-year-old boy who raped a girl in a high school stairwell was reacting normally to relaxed cultural attitudes about sex and the recent fashion of more-revealing clothing for women. Area activists, including the members of the local NOW chapter, were incensed by Simonson's attitude and by the lenient sentence he gave the boy. Consequently, a protest was mounted, including the circulation of petitions demanding the judge's resignation or recall. Moria Krueger, reported to have pro-feminist sympathies, was chosen to replace Simonson in a recall election in September 1977.[15]

In a somewhat different ruling, a court of appeals in California reversed the conviction of a man for raping a female hitchhiker, stating that a woman who enters the car of a stranger must expect sexual advances (Blake 1977).[16] This case, too, prompted feminist protest, highlighted by a Los Angeles demonstration that drew a crowd of three hundred and featured the attorney Gloria Allred, then president of Los Angeles NOW, and Joan Robins of the Rape-Crisis Hotline, as speakers. Feminist groups compared the court's statements to those of the notorious Judge Simonson of Wisconsin, and demanded the recall of the writer of the decision, Justice Lynn D. Compton (*Los Angeles Times* 1977). Later, in another case, the judicial review board of Connecticut privately censured Judge Walter Pickett Jr. of the state superior court for remarking that "you can't blame somebody for trying" while presiding over a trial for attempted rape (*New York Times* 1979). Similar judicial quips in the courts of Indiana, Colorado (by a federal district court judge, John Kane), and again in Wisconsin drew national media attention and sparked feminist outrage.

Such incidents, as offensive and contrary to movement goals as they were, actually served useful purposes. Of course, these judges' attitudes and remarks had, at the least, immediately harmful consequences for the rape victims involved. But such horrendous statements allowed feminists to point out how pervasive the myths of rape still were. Even supposedly enlightened, educated pillars of society were capable of the kind of thinking that the movement had been working for years to change. Women were mobilized to protest, demonstrate, and speak out against the public attitudes the judges represented. More important, movement activists saw these comments as blatant statements about how the jurists involved viewed the women who came into their court-rooms to testify about having been raped. Here was concrete evidence of how the courts can be biased against rape victims. Feminists seized the opportunity these events offered to renew public attention to sexual assault.

Agenda Setting

Although women activists had intensively investigated and defined the problem of rape before the public agenda had reflected a new under-standing of it, the degree to which their attitudes would be reflected in the new policy approach remained to be seen. When campaigners against rape captured the attention of legislators and other decision makers, they brought with them feminist definitions and theories of sexual assault that had been developed in tandem with analyses of male dominance, and they hoped for policy responses on their own terms. Once the issue of rape reached the institutional agenda in 1973, it be-came clear that such would not be the case.

Feminist Agenda vs. Public Agenda

Although activists were effective in moving rape to the systemic and then the institutional agenda, the radical feminist formulation of the problem did not survive the transition intact. The ideas of the anti-rape movement that circulated through feminist networks in the 1970s surely intrigued policy makers, but the resulting policies were a far cry from how feminists understood the problem when it was originally recognized and defined. While participants in the women's and anti-rape movements accomplished much in putting the issue on the policy agenda, the terms in which the rape problem was considered changed once it reached the public agenda.

This phenomenon is not surprising, and results from the nature of both the policy process and the radical branch of the women's movement. The sociologist Jessie Bernard (1971, 39) explains: "All protestors [*sic*] disturb policy makers; [radical] Movement Women more than others. They challenged the sexism-tainted scientific facts on which policy makers have traditionally had to rely. They refused to see our society through establishment eyes. . . . Movement Women were, in brief, troublemakers for the status quo. And they meant to be." Much as law-and-order thinking did not reflect many anti-rape activists' disdain for the oppressive elements of the criminal justice system, so the formal agenda did not reflect many aspects of the feminist ideology of rape (although it did include some of these elements in diluted form). But both the law-and-order agenda and the public agenda of rape helped anti-rape campaigners to advance significant policy goals. The most important of these was passing pro-victim legislation aimed at making the experience of women who had been raped less traumatic, whether in emergency rooms or courtrooms. The major differences between feminists' and policy makers' approaches are outlined in Figure 3.2.

The aims of the anti-rape movement evolved and contracted to accommodate the framing of the issue on the public agenda. While the initial radical goal was to eradicate rape and reclaim the bodies of all women from the threat of rape, such an objective had to be modified for the policy arena. New goals emerged to fit the rape issue more carefully into the range of possibilities in public policy: changing the treatment of victims by medical and law enforcement personnel, securing funding for research into the crime's incidence and prevalence, increasing the abysmal conviction rates for rape, and heightening public awareness of the problem. All of these have proved far more attainable, tangible aims for the policy arena than eradication.

Women in Public Office

The growing number of female officeholders is often cited by political scientists as a crucial factor in the attainment of public goods for women. The liberal branch of the contemporary women's movement has made achieving movement goals through the electoral process the centerpiece of much organizing activity. For example, in 1967 the

Figure 3.2 Rape: Changing Definitions from Feminist Agenda to Public Agenda

Feminist Agenda	Public Agenda
Rape	**Rape**
• is an expression of patriarchy	• is a heinous crime
• is a problem of gender hierarchy	• is primarily an urban problem
• is pervasive in women's lives	• is infrequent
• is a metaphor for the oppression of all women	• is a matter of law, medicine, and psychology
• is men's tool for the control of women's bodies	• is the province of a few criminally minded individuals
• is grounded in women's socialized passivity and men's socialized aggression	• cannot be explained
• will cease to exist with the demise of patriarchy	• can be controlled with tough laws, funding, and research
• can be committed by any man	• is committed only by strangers
• curbs women's freedom	• threatens the safety of "our" women
• is a growing problem	• is a growing problem

NOW Task Force on Political Rights and Responsibilities endorsed integrating women into political parties, ensuring their equitable representation on committees and other policy-making bodies, and placing the NOW Bill of Rights for Women into the hands of all candidates (Carabillo, Meuli, and Csida 1993, 208–9). Organizations such as the National Women's Political Caucus (NWPC), founded in 1971, and EMILY's List, founded in 1985, were formed with the explicit goal of supporting and funding women candidates and improving women's political representation.

But the role women play once in office presents another issue. For instance, the impact of gender on legislative voting patterns, and the question of whether female legislators are more likely than their male colleagues to vote in favor of pro-woman bills, has been widely investigated (Mezey 1978; Carroll 1984; Welch 1985; Dodson and Carroll 1991; Thomas 1994). Political scientists agree that women legislators tend to vote to improve the status of women or women's rights, and may, in fact, be "reshaping the [legislative] agenda" in the United States (Dodson and Carroll 1991). But it is by no means a given that a woman in public office will advance the anti-rape agenda any differently from her male counterpart.

In the 1970s, female officeholders did take a visible role in pushing for pro-victim rape legislation. In 1976, Representative Elizabeth Holtzman (D-N.Y.) became the first woman in Congress to introduce federal rape legislation when she introduced a bill to amend the Federal Rules of Evidence to restrict the introduction of a victim's sexual past in all federal rape trials. With approximately one-third of the women in the House as co-sponsors, the bill ultimately became the Privacy Protection for Rape Victims Act (Holtzman papers) (see Appendix 4). Another advocate of rape reform, Representative Bella Abzug (D-N.Y.), co-sponsored such legislation as Holtzman's and kept in touch with anti-rape groups in her district and elsewhere (*New York Times* 1976b).[17]

Female legislators were vital in advancing federal anti-rape policy, but because of their small numbers in Congress in the 1970s they were not the first to put rape on the national institutional agenda. For example, in the Ninety-First Congress (1969–70), women occupied only 2.1 percent of the seats; by the Ninety-Fifth Congress (1977–78), this figure had only risen to 3.7 percent (McGlen and O'Connor 1995, 77). Female officeholders at the federal level helped define pivotal rape issues for the legislature, and they responded to the demands of the polity by introducing pro-victim legislation that mirrored the bills then passing in many states. Moreover, the growing presence of women in policy-making bodies traditionally dominated by men has helped to keep male lawmakers accountable to their female constituents and has helped to keep "women's issues" such as rape on the legislative agenda. Once public awareness of sexual assault was raised, women in Congress responded to the anti-rape movement's demands for action.

Rape on Campus

The university was another major social institution whose agenda reflected the growing concern with rape. In Chapter 1, I noted the fundamental role of colleges in providing a useful communications network on which anti-rape activism could draw, particularly between 1972 and 1974. This student-led initiative did not evoke a concerted response from university officials immediately, however. Rape first became an issue for administrators to grapple with once it had become established on the wider systemic agenda. Since then, the university has become a unique locus of anti-rape organizing and policy.

For a number of reasons, campus rape has taken on a meaning all its own. First, because they are often uniquely self-contained communities, universities have had to construct rape policies much in the same way that states and local governments have. As quasi-governmental policy-making bodies, universities share some characteristics with these jurisdictions. Second, colleges and universities in the United States to some extent still maintain an *in loco parentis* relationship with their students, whereby the administration acts essentially as a temporary parent, assuming a protective and disciplinary posture toward students. Third, activists involved in the student movements of the 1960s made a point of holding universities accountable for what they saw as corrupt, exploitive, or repressive policies, and thereby won political legitimacy for campus-based actions. Finally, concerns over liability and public relations issues have led universities to take active measures to reduce crime out of their own self-interest.

College officials began coming to terms with rape as a security matter in the mid-1970s, when highly publicized assaults of female students sparked outrage on campus and drew community attention in a number of cases. In December 1974, at a meeting of security officers of the Midwest's Big Ten universities, concern about rape was declared to be "first on the agenda and the number one priority" among campus security issues, according to a *New York Times* report (Maitland 1975). Reported rapes of students at North Carolina Central University, the City College of New York, the University of Florida, San Diego State University, New York University, Yale University, Barnard College, and elsewhere prompted officials to introduce such measures as increased police patrols, safety lights (the infamous "blue lights"), restrictions on access to dormitories to limit the presence of nonresidents, and escort services for women (Maitland 1975; *New York Times* 1976a). The administrative response to the growing concern about rape, then, was to enhance the security of women on campus.

Student initiatives such as helplines, self-defense lessons, and workshops on rape complemented these institutional efforts. Students also pressured administrators when they perceived inattention to the rape issue. For example, one hundred students at Hunter College in New York City stormed the office of the president to demand improved security in the wake of three reported rapes in the college's main building (McFadden 1975). In Washington, D.C., students at George Washington University and Howard University held a take back the night march and a rape crisis forum (respectively) in response to reported sexual assaults on and near campus (Katz 1981). Such efforts by administrators and students were limited to addressing the problem of rape by strangers or by men outside the college community. Finally, in 1976, when a court ordered Catholic University to pay $20,000 in damages to a law student who had been raped in a campus locker room, institutions of higher education became acutely aware of the need to address rape and provide improved security (Robinson 1976). These actions reflected not only the traditional concern with keeping students safe, but also a common public perception of rape in the 1970s as a crime committed primarily by men who were strangers to their victims.

The agenda-setting phase in the development of anti-rape policy led to no uniform understanding of or approach to rape, either on university campuses or among policy makers. Those in the anti-rape movement—crisis center members and staff, law reform activists in the states, and others—possessed an understanding of rape that differed tremendously from that of most people. Their understanding reflected the general tenets of anti-rape ideology: that victims are not at fault in their own rapes; that rapists are "normal" men, not sex-crazed socio-paths; and that rape is an act of violence and power, not of sex and passion. While the appearance of the issue on the public agenda in the 1970s marks an important development in the anti-rape movement, this agenda reflected a narrower, less radical stance on rape than did the feminist one.

Policy Formulation

Developing policy involves designing acceptable courses of action or options for dealing with an identified issue (Anderson 1994, 102). It takes place in a variety of arenas and at all levels of government: fed-eral, state, and local. At this stage in the anti-rape policy process, wom-en's groups devoted an immense amount of their energy to initiating policies that would best advance movement goals. Rather than focus on stopping rape altogether, a goal too unwieldy for a single policy initiative, anti-rape activists and their governmental and institutional supporters devised approaches that aimed to address rape, promote awareness of and research into it, and make the experience of reporting and prosecuting sexual assault easier and less humiliating for victims. Anti-rape activists, such as NOW's Mary Ann Largen (1985), pursued complex policy strategies in the hopes of achieving incremental change while still working to realize the movement's larger goals.

The nature of the federal system in the United States has deter-mined in large part the range of courses of action available to those policy makers and anti-rape activists determined to devise a policy re-sponse to the rape issue. The framers of the Constitution, in seeking to define the parameters of federal and state powers, left a number of governmental functions primarily to the individual states. One of these was the creation and enforcement of criminal law codes, which are maintained and negotiated in the various legislatures; hence, reforming criminal law is primarily the responsibility of individual states. Whereas other women's movement issues—most visibly the relegaliza-tion of abortion by the Supreme Court in 1973 (O'Connor 1996)—have alternated between a national and a state focus, policy changes concerning rape have been more concentrated in the states. Although statutory reform efforts there have constituted the largest part of anti-rape policy, both local and federal initiatives have also been involved.

Local Developments

Most local anti-rape policy activity involves institutional, as opposed to legislative, reform. Often led or supported by movement activists, such initiatives sought to change the rape-processing protocols followed by hospital and law enforcement personnel and to engage local leaders in examining the issue of rape as they never had before. Cities across the United States became involved in this process beginning early in the 1970s. In one of the first actions to promote a local policy initiative, women's liberationists in Berkeley, California, demanded that the city council hold hearings to give voice to "all of the raped women in Berkeley," who would be best suited to make demands for greater protection by the city (*San Francisco Chronicle* 1970). While this effort was movement led, other municipal governments soon began to initiate policy discussions in response to anti-rape activity and the new public awareness of rape.

Elsewhere on the West Coast, in 1974 the Los Angeles City Council's task force on rape, made up of representatives of city agencies and women's groups, proposed a package of changes in the handling of rape cases there; it included provisions concerning medical care, police procedure, grant seeking, and self-defense training in schools, according to the *Los Angeles Times* (Baker 1974). In August 1975, the Los Angeles Commission on Assaults Against Women, the city's first rape crisis center, held a demonstration at city hall to introduce a whistle alert system, encouraging women to purchase their one-dollar safety whistles. Two women on the city council—Pat Russell and Peggy Evenson—introduced a resolution declaring 9 August "Blow the Whistle on Rape Day," then joined the group on the city hall steps to purchase whistles of their own (*Los Angeles Times* 1975). Finally, in 1976 District Attorney John Van de Kamp of Los Angeles announced a new policy for prosecutors: one deputy D.A. would follow a given rape case from start to finish, eliminating the possibility of cases changing hands repeatedly, and special training would be provided for handling rape cases, according to the *Los Angeles Times* (Farr 1976).

In the Northeast, an early local policy effort that brought together movement activists and representatives of New York City agencies established an all-woman rape investigation unit within the police department. The unit, at first led by Lieutenant Julia Tucker, was created in late 1972 and had a special phone number for rape reports, 577-RAPE (Knight 1973). During her brief tenure, Tucker was prominent in anti-rape politics in the city, even attending the 24 May 1973 joint meeting of the New York Women Against Rape and the Ad Hoc Committee on Rape of New York NOW (NYWAR records). Tucker also represented the New York squad before other cities considering such units. In another development, the district attorney's office in Nassau County, New York, was the first in the country to form its own rape squad; it was headed by Assistant District Attorney Lynn Siudak (*New York Times* 1974b). These events represent local efforts to change the way rape cases were handled by law enforcement.

In August 1973, as part of the city's publicity for rape prevention month, Mayor John Lindsay of New York announced the formation of the Mayor's Task Force on Rape, an interagency group appointed to create better procedures for processing rape cases (*New York Times* 1973). Intended to bring together city agencies and movement groups active in rape law reform, the task force would come to include representatives from New York NOW and the Manhattan Women's Political Caucus. It enabled the mayor to lobby for the repeal of New York's corroboration requirement in the state legislature. In 1977 Lindsay's successor, Mayor Abe Beame, announced the establishment of city-run crisis centers in four boroughs (Staten Island was excluded), funded through a CETA grant from the Department of Labor (Breasted 1977). Significantly, feminist groups grew less and less enthusiastic about the bureaucracy the task force became, and eventually withdrew their support (Friedman 1978b). These organizations, represented by Sally McGee of the Manhattan Women's Political Caucus, were repeatedly disappointed by the task force's failure to provide funding for feminist rape crisis centers, such as that of NYWAR. They were also disappointed in the city's failure to appoint more women officers to the police department's sex-crime squads (Maitland 1974b).

In Washington, the city council created the D.C. Public Safety Committee Task Force on Rape; like its New York counterpart, it was composed of representatives from public and private groups, including Billie Malkin of the D.C. Rape Crisis Center and Mary-Helen Mauntner of the Women's Legal Defense Fund (Scharfenberg 1973a; Sigal 1973). Other D.C. RCC members also testified at the task force's hearings on rape laws. In a related development, in 1974 the D.C. Medical Society urged the city council to create rape treatment centers in five area hospitals and called for special medical training for dealing with victims and for performing exams (Cohn 1974). Elsewhere in the Washington area, Maryland's Prince Georges County Council commissioned a rape task force in 1972, sponsored by Councilwoman Gladys Noon Spellman, to investigate the treatment of victims and make recommendations for changes in police, hospital, and court procedures. When the group presented its report to the county council in 1973, seventy-five members of the Prince Georges League of Women Voters attended the meeting to witness the proceedings (Mitchell 1973).

In the Midwest, the Chicago City Council Police Committee held hearings in 1973 on a proposal to form an all-woman unit for rape investigations. Marjorie Witty of the South Side Rape Action Project and Helen Aarli of the North Side Rape Crisis Line testified that all rape cases should be investigated by women police officers, prosecuted by women district attorneys, and heard by women judges, the *Chicago Tribune* reported (Schreiber 1973). Lieutenant Julia Tucker of the New York Police Department rape investigation unit also testified. The next year, again according to the *Chicago Tribune* (Orehek 1974), the city council's Committee on Health declared twenty-eight Chicago hospitals rape treatment centers, providing privacy and counseling for victims. In St. Paul, Minnesota, the Committee on Sex Offenses announced a plan to design a comprehensive rape victim treatment program for Ramsey County, hoping that it would be supported by LEAA funds (*Minneapolis Tribune* 1974). One of the first actions of the Iowa City Women Against Rape (WAR) was to present a list of demands to their city council, asking for improved street lighting, greater patroling in high-crime areas, extended hours for public transportation, advocacy for rape victims at police departments, and city-sponsored self-defense classes for women (*New York Times* 1972).

These and similar efforts across the nation mark local policy makers' attempts to improve the institutional response to rape. They indicate a new awareness of sexual assault and a new seriousness in discussing it. Local policies hold special importance because, since they mandate precisely how police, hospitals, district attorneys, and others would treat women who have been raped, they have a direct impact on the victims' experience. One of the most notable accomplishments of the anti-rape movement has been a marked reduction in the suffering of victims, at least that suffering caused or aggravated by institutional actors.

Developments in the States

Anti-rape policy gains have largely been won in state legislatures. Efforts to reform the rape statutes began with a handful of initiatives to effect incremental changes in antiquated, victim-unfriendly laws, often in line with the recommendations of the American Law Institute's Model Penal Code (MPC). Such initiatives went much further when independent women's movement actors, who viewed the victim-unfriendly statutes as cases of unacceptable discrimination, lobbied for pro-victim changes to state criminal codes. These changes—reviewed in Chapter 2—included redefining the crime of rape (often expanding its scope to include male victims and implementing a gradation, or "staircasing," of offenses); modifying the rules of evidence (by, for example, eliminating the corroboration requirement, replacing the existing standard of resistance with a standard of force, and limiting the amount of evidence involving the victim's sexual past admitted at trial); eliminating cautionary instruction from judges to juries; and reforming (usually reducing) penalties to encourage conviction (Searles and Berger 1987, 25). State-level reforms are arguably the most important, visible, and controversial of the anti-rape policies that have been enacted.

Federal Developments: Legislative

The national government has become involved in anti-rape policy in a number of ways. While criminal law remains primarily the responsibility of the states, Congress does maintain a federal criminal code. It applies to crimes committed in areas not governed by states, such as federal lands and holdings (including Indian reservations), national parks and forests, federal buildings (such as post offices), and military bases. This is in addition to federal court involvement in the enforcement of constitutional issues that may bear on rape cases and rape law, and Congress may enact legislation on rape.

One of the earliest federal efforts at policy change was the introduction of the Rape Prevention and Control bill in the Senate on 17 September 1973 by Senator Charles Mathias (R-Md.). It would amend the National Mental Health Act to establish the National Center for the Prevention and Control of Rape (NCPCR) within the National Institute of Mental Health (NIMH) in what was then the Department of Health, Education, and Welfare. Representative H. John Heinz III (R-Pa.) sponsored the bill in the House. Significantly, Senator Mathias used information gleaned from the Prince Georges County Rape Task Force and the D.C. Public Safety Committee Task Force on Rape, both mentioned above, to make his case when he first submitted the bill (U.S. Congress, Senate 1973). This illustrates the interplay between the different levels of government in forging anti-rape policy.

Senator Mathias's choice of language in presenting his bill to Congress reveals much about the translation of rape from the feminist to the public agenda. For example, after establishing the crime's astonishing prevalence with statistics borrowed from the (Maryland) Governor's Commission on Law Enforcement and the Administration of Justice, the senator went on to make a paternalistic, protectionist argument to bolster the bill's chances with his colleagues:

> [I]f there is one thing that American males have always prided
> themselves on, it is that more than any other group of men on
> earth we "care for our women." If we slave and we sacrifice and
> we struggle, it is not for ourselves but so that our women can

enjoy advantages far greater than those we, ourselves are able to enjoy. We fight no war, adopt no program, create no law that is not ultimately and unselfishly aimed at making life better for our women. We have, it would appear, every reason to believe what we have said of ourselves: that we are a woman-oriented society; that women are the center and circumference, the Alpha and Omega of our lives. Yet such a belief must be confronted with stark reality. (U.S. Congress, Senate 1973, 29830)

Mathias's "stark reality" was that "our" women face a constant fear of rape, that laws throughout the land are biased against them, and that the emotional trauma following a rape is tremendous. The reality he presented, however, ignored both the well-documented discrimination against women that belies men's best efforts to "mak[e] life better" for them, and the fact that the majority of American women live unpampered, sometimes difficult lives. Nonetheless, the senator's speech advocated pro-victim rape law reform and demonstrated a higher level of rape consciousness than had been shown before in a federal governmental setting. The bill passed Congress twice as a part of the larger Health Services Act and was vetoed twice by President Gerald R. Ford, who preferred a less costly measure that would make block grants to the states (Lyons 1975). In July 1975, Congress overrode the second veto, and the legislation became Public Law 94-63 (see Appendix 3).

Other advances in rape policy at the federal level include passage of the Rape Victims Privacy Act, first introduced in the House by Representative Elizabeth Holtzman (D-N.Y.) and forty-five co-sponsors in March 1976. Senator Lloyd Bentsen (D-Tex.) introduced the bill in the Senate. It would amend the federal rules of evidence to prohibit the introduction of evidence concerning a victim's sexual past in a federal rape trial. Holtzman's language in introducing the legislation was far more pro-victim than that used by Senator Mathias less than three years earlier. She specifically mentioned the degradation and pain a victim often feels during questioning about her prior sexual conduct and the reluctance of women to report rape when they anticipate such treatment. She also cited the recent developments in rape shield legislation in state legislatures such as that of California (U.S. Congress, House 1976a, H3926). To lend the bill further legitimacy, Holtzman submitted to the House the text of the American Bar Association's resolution on rape and its accompanying report, discussed earlier in this chapter. The ABA document summarized the rape reform approach and provided an overview of the major revisions passed or considered in the state legislatures (U.S. Congress, House 1976b). The Holtzman bill was approved by both houses and was signed into law (as P.L. 95-540) by President Jimmy Carter on 30 October 1978 (see Appendix 4).

Federal Developments: Judicial

Decisions handed down by the federal courts can be powerful tools in advancing public policy in the area of women's rights (Rosenberg 1991; O'Connor 1980). However, very few Supreme Court rulings have dealt with the law of rape; those that have done so have reflected evolving public attitudes about the crime, but they have had little effect on rape policy.[18]

Cox Broadcasting Corporation v. Cohn. In this 1975 decision, the Supreme Court held that the press has the constitutional right to publish the names of rape victims in spite of some state laws that prohibit the practice to safeguard the privacy rights of citizens. The case involved Atlanta's WSB-TV, owned by Cox Broadcasting, and a Georgia statute preventing the media from publicizing rape victims' names. Cox argued that information revealed in a court of law was publicly available and therefore fair game for news organizations. This decision settled the important issue of whether the press might disclose victims' names under the First Amendment, but left open the ethical question of whether it should do so.

This issue has a long history and divides feminists even today. Most news organizations have internal policies that guide their decisions in making rape victims' names public. In 1978, the publisher Herman Obermayer provoked a varied response when he announced that his newspaper, the *Northern Virginia Sun,* had adopted a policy of identifying victims by name in reporting rape charges and trials (McAllister 1978). Some feminists oppose naming victims on the grounds that such policies discourage them from reporting rape out of fear of public scrutiny. They argue that rape should be treated differently from other crimes (whose victims' names can be published) because it is different from other crimes; rape is one of the few crimes that puts the victim on the defensive and calls her personal conduct and sexual past into question (Taylor 1978). On 17 January 1978, Northern Virginia NOW wrote a letter to the *Sun* to recommend changing the policy (NOW records). Others have argued that women who have been sexually assaulted should be named because the stigma of rape will only be removed when more victims are willing to come forward publicly (Susan Brownmiller, telephone interview, 2 September 1996). *Cox* demonstrates that, debates aside, the Constitution remains the final arbiter for this question, although by no means does it require the publication of victims' names. This issue was hotly debated at the time of the Big Dan's gang rape of 1983, the rape of the Central Park jogger in 1989, and the rape charges brought against William Kennedy Smith in 1991 (discussed in Chapter 4).

Coker v. Georgia. This 1977 decision ruled the death penalty for rape unconstitutional under the Eighth Amendment's prohibition of cruel and unusual punishment. Women's organizations filing amicus briefs included the ACLU Women's Rights Project (WRP), NOW, the Women's Law Project, the Women's Legal Defense Fund, and Equal Rights Advocates, Inc. The WRP's amicus brief encouraged the Court to examine closely the issues of rape and race, to consider carefully statistics showing that harsh penalties for rape are disproportionately meted out to black men, and to find the death penalty for rape unconstitutional. (This brief was filed under the WRP leadership of Ruth Bader Ginsburg.) The women's organizations' main concern, though, was that juries would be far less likely to convict in rape cases if a death penalty might result. Apart from these two rulings, and because of the nature of the federal system, the Supreme Court had little else to say on the issue of rape in the 1970s.

Budgeting

How anti-rape programs targeted at victims, prevention, and research have been funded is an interesting example of budgetary policy at work. When rape first became a concern on the national institutional agenda in 1973, LEAA was a source of monies for anti-rape projects, insofar as they reflected that agency's law-and-order approach. In 1974, through its Office of National Priority Programs, LEAA made a $238,000 grant to the Center for Women Policy Studies (CWPS) for research "to locate promising rape reduction and victim assistance programs in the areas of law enforcement, health care, and community group activity" (U.S. Department of Justice 1974a, 26, 28).[19] The CWPS published its findings, *Rape and Its Victims: A Report for Citizens, Health Facilities, and Criminal Justice Agencies,* in 1975. Grassroots activists were critical of the center's biases toward professionalism and law enforcement (MacMillan 1975; Warrior 1977). LEAA also funded a rape study conducted in 1974 and 1975 by the Queen's Bench Foundation, an organization of women attorneys in California. Its findings were published in the group's 1976 report *Rape: Prevention and Assistance.* Like that of CWPS, the Queen's Bench study was criticized by movement activists for its methodology (fifty-five rape victims interviewed), criminal justice bias, and racial bias (San Francisco Women Against Rape 1975).

Another research-funding office within LEAA, the National Institute for Law Enforcement and Criminal Justice, highlighted its financial involvement with rape studies in its annual reports for 1974 to 1977 (U.S. Department of Justice 1974b, 4; 1975, 20; 1976, 2; 1977, 10–11); its outlays included grants in 1975 and 1976 to the Battelle Human Affairs Research Center in Seattle, Washington, to investigate problems in the criminal justice system's response to rape. The Battelle study resulted in LEAA's publication of *Forcible Rape: Medical and Legal Information* and *Forcible Rape: A National Survey of the Response by Police,* among other reports. LEAA also made block grants to regions and states, which could be disbursed according to local need and demand. Community anti-rape projects were eligible for funding through the recipient states. Crisis centers in such cities as Baton

Rouge, Louisiana; Des Moines, Iowa; and Seattle, Washington, took advantage of this opportunity. Another source of money for rape crisis centers came through the Comprehensive Employment and Training Act (CETA), passed in 1973 to provide recipients of public assistance with jobs and job training in social service agencies.

In spite of the budgetary gains just cited, note that funding of anti-rape projects has often held a strong bias toward law enforcement, which grassroots rape crisis centers and other organizations opposed. For example, the activist Mary Ann Largen notes (1974) that the structure of LEAA, coupled with the agency's own bias, hampered anti-rape projects in securing grants. LEAA discretionary funds—available to support large projects such as the CWPS study—represented only 15 percent of the agency's total budget, and these were to be distributed by state and local governments. Largen points out that no policy that would hold these governments accountable to private groups was in place in 1974. Moreover, such private groups, rape crisis centers among them, were required to apply for funds only in conjunction with a police department or a hospital; since many rape crisis centers then had tense relationships with such institutions, even the prospect of a joint application was impossible. Accordingly, feminist crisis centers were outraged that anti-rape projects were virtually excluded from government funding unless they were willing to accept compromises.

This problem was alleviated somewhat by the passage of the Crime Control Act of 1976, which amended the law that created LEAA. The new act set up the Office of Community Anti-Crime Programs within LEAA, which would allocate $15 million per year to community-based anti-crime projects. Grants were made to incorporated nonprofit organizations that addressed crime on more than one level, such as self-defense, counseling, and community education. Funding was also limited to agencies that employed a full-time executive director and operated with the guidance of a board of trustees or some other community group. Hence, the need to acquire money on these law-and-order terms was a major factor in formalizing the structure of rape crisis centers.

The Mathias Act of 1975, creating the NCPCR, involved mostly budgetary issues: in passing it, the House and Senate were making a real, albeit modest, financial commitment to the study of rape. Congress initially appropriated $4 million for its work; after the center was recommended for de-funding under the Reagan Administration, this amount was reduced to $2.9 million. Because the primary purpose of the center was to provide financial support to researchers investigating various aspects of the rape issue, a solid budget was essential to its effectiveness and survival. In the first round of grants in 1976, funds were awarded to such anti-rape research luminaries as Diana Russell, Pauline Bart, Martha Burt, and Peggy Reeves Sanday, and funding for creating educational materials went to the Women's Crisis Center of Ann Arbor, Michigan (Friedman 1976). Thus, the budgeting stage was central to establishing the NCPCR. Between 1982 and 1987, during the various executive branch reorganizations under the Reagan Administration, the center was essentially phased out, and it no longer exists.

Policy Evaluation

The issue of rape presents some interesting questions for the evaluation stage of the policy process. What constitutes success? What is the measure of evaluation? It appears logical that, to assess the effectiveness of rape policies as a whole, one could simply measure incidence rates: if they increase or remain static, the policies have failed; if they decline, the policies have succeeded. Such an approach, however, would be highly problematic, for the relationship between official reports of incidence and the actual numbers of rapes is highly speculative. The FBI, a major compiler of crime statistics, itself estimates that perhaps one rape in ten is reported to authorities (U.S. Department of Justice 1973, 15). In fact, increases in official reports of rape should more appropriately be viewed as a mark of the effectiveness of rape policy. Because improving the treatment of victims by criminal justice agencies and personnel was an original goal of the anti-rape movement, an increase in reported rapes may indicate that the policy is succeeding. Table 3.2 tracks the incidence of the crime from the years before the rise of the anti-rape movement through the period covered in this chapter.[20]

Table 3.2 FBI Uniform Crime Reports, *Incidence of Rape, 1967–1980*

Year	Total Number of Rapes Reported	Number of Rapes per 100,000 Females
1967	27,100	27
1968	31,060	30
1969	36,470	35
1970	37,270	36
1971	41,890	40
1972	46,430	43
1973	51,000	47
1974	55,210	51
1975	56,090	51
1976	56,730	52
1977	63,020	57
1978	67,131	60
1979	75,989	67
1980	82,088	71

Whether these growing rates indicate an actual increase in numbers of rapes is impossible to know.

Individual policies have been variously studied and evaluated for their effectiveness. For example, the rape reform statutes in particular states have been examined for their impact on arrest and conviction rates (Loh 1981; Marsh, Geist, and Caplan 1982; LaFree 1989; Spohn and Horney 1992). If any consensus has emerged from these studies in the states, it is that reform statutes have at least the symbolic effect of raising public awareness of rape and encouraging its reporting and prosecution. Moreover, the consideration of reform statutes in all fifty states in the 1970s—and their passage in forty of them—suggests considerable success in improving the system's responsiveness to rape victims.

Throughout the 1970s, anti-rape policy evolved considerably from the day in 1971 that New York Assemblyman Guy R. Brewer (D-Queens)

remarked of the women's liberationists who were supporting a corroboration reform bill under consideration, "From what I've seen of those
horrible-looking bags, I don't think they have to worry about being
victims of rape" (Ronan 1971). In the space of a decade of lobbying
and politicizing the issue, the anti-rape movement managed to place
rape squarely on both the systemic and institutional agendas in the
United States. While policy activity has ebbed and flowed, and while
policy advances have been only incremental, a clear pro-victim approach has replaced the silence (at best) and the defendant bias (at
worst) that once informed what little policy activity there was on the
question. The effectiveness of the various policies adopted, though ad-
mittedly difficult to measure, has been limited by a problem that wom-
en's movement activists had pointed out from the beginning: changes
in policy without simultaneous, sweeping changes in attitudes would
have, overall, only a modest effect on the incidence, prevalence, and
impact of rape. Movement women also noted that the racist bias of the
criminal justice system would limit the impact of reforms. While the
incidence of rape (through 1980) recorded in the *Uniform Crime Reports*
shows a marked increase from the years before sexual assault appeared
on the public agenda (Table 3.1), it is impossible to determine whether
this growth should be attributed to more rapes or to greater reporting
of them because of heightened awareness. But the policy history of the
rape issue demonstrates that policy makers were willing to bring about
substantive changes when it was within their power to do so, particularly given the convenient fit between the politically practical goals of
the anti-rape movement and the dominant tough-on-crime mood of
the larger society.

4

THE ANTI-RAPE AGENDA FROM THE 1980S TO TODAY

ONCE SOCIAL-MOVEMENT ACTORS succeed in bringing an issue to public consciousness, they face the task of keeping it there. Anti-rape activists found that the problem of rape did not diminish with the raising of awareness and the flood of public policy making that resulted from the initial drive for change. Indeed, as feminists and their sympathizers developed a more nuanced understanding of rape in the 1980s, often with the help of studies funded by public grants, more policy possibilities opened up to them. New developments in research and feminist understandings of sexual assault led to new forms of anti-rape organizing. As this work began afresh, society's attention was drawn again to the issue, with its attendant function of raising public consciousness, and the interest of policy makers was sparked once more. Thus did the issue of rape enter and re-enter the public agenda over the next two decades (and beyond), restarting the policy-making process in each incarnation. Picking up where Chapter 3 left off, I now will investigate the various ways that rape has reappeared on the public agenda since the late 1970s.

By the beginning of the 1980s, rape was not the "hot" issue it had been in 1972. The American public's outrage at rape had diminished, as had the shock value of news coverage of the issue. The persistence and success of activists in making it an issue in the 1970s removed the taboo from public discussion, and culminated in a certain boredom once the topic's novelty had worn off. In the late 1970s and early 1980s, other types of violence, such as child abuse, child sexual abuse, sexual harassment, and wife battering, began to enjoy the kind of policy response that rape had seen during the preceding decade.

The 1980s were at once years of growth and consolidation for rape crisis centers and anti-rape coalitions throughout the United States. The National Coalition Against Sexual Assault (NCASA) saw its membership rise to represent nearly half the rape crisis centers in the country. Although some of the centers founded in the 1970s were closing their doors because of lack of funding or support, others sprang up to serve victims and offer community education. Political and legal efforts had yielded an immense amount of rape reform legislation by 1980, and some further reforms and refinements continued into the 1980s and 1990s. With regard to the major efforts of the activists of the 1970s, rape crisis centers and statutory reform, the movement by the 1980s had reached the stage of abeyance. Organizations were operating in a "holding pattern," devoting energy to maintaining hard-won gains rather than undertaking new challenges to the established order (Taylor and Whittier 1997, 545). This trend became even more apparent given the growing conservatism of American politics during the Reagan era. But although abeyance also signifies a period when a movement no longer attracts new recruits or seeks political innovation, the anti-rape campaign continued to do both in the 1980s and 1990s, largely in the form of organizing college students and pressing for federal legislation. Moreover, these years have witnessed new trends in the discourse of rape within feminist circles and in popular culture, with greater attention being paid to pornography and minority sexuality by feminists and a backlash of sorts developing in the mass media. Thus, while the novelty of the issue of rape had worn off by 1980, and confrontational actions were less visible, the movement maintained itself and adapted to a changing political climate and other developments.

Rape Categories

As the 1970s came to an end, anti-rape activists went on challenging the myths that continued to hold sway despite heightened public awareness of the issue. The most important myth to come under scrutiny in the second decade of rape activism was that of the rapist as stranger, the man who attacks his victim in the bushes (parking garage, alley) late at night, brandishing a weapon. While such attacks do happen, studies began to reveal that a majority of rapes are committed by men known to their victims, such as lovers, husbands, friends, and other acquaintances, who do not use weapons or extrinsic violence (Russell 1984; Koss 1988). Radical feminists had long been asserting that any man—even one's husband—is a potential rapist: in a 1973 publication, Dana Densmore of the Boston-area radical group Cell 16 observed that "there is a continuum of rape situations, beginning with one's husband, working through lovers, dates, friends, acquaintances, men known slightly outside the home, and finally complete strangers. On this continuum, most rapes are by the men in the first categories" (Densmore 1973, 73). Likewise, the term *date rape* had been used as early as 25 August 1974 in a flyer advertising a speak-out on rape and sexual abuse organized by the New York Radical Feminists (NYRF) and the National Black Feminist Organization (NBFO). Date rape was named as a type of sexual abuse in a list that included gang rape and incest (Brownmiller papers). But this element of feminist anti-rape ideology did not carry over to the public agenda until the 1980s and remains controversial today.

A significant development in the evolution of the public understanding of the issue was a growing tendency to classify rape. This trend began in the late 1970s and developed further in the next decade; it reached the forefront of the public agenda in the 1990s with two very public date rape trials involving celebrities and the rise of an anti–anti-rape backlash. "Rape" unmodified increasingly came to be replaced by "acquaintance rape," "date rape," and "spousal (or "marital" or "wife") rape." Activists began to take a new message to the media: a rape is a rape is a rape, they asserted, and each type is equally traumatic to its victims, is equally worthy of rape crisis services, and is an equally serious matter of criminal justice.

Despite the feminist insistence on similarity among the varying types of rape, the notion of a continuum that includes husbands, boyfriends, and strangers did not translate well onto the public agenda in the first phase of popular awareness. Rarely did discussions of non-stranger rape take place in public forums. But attention to these cases began to grow in the late 1970s, when Nebraska became the first state to remove the spousal exemption for rape, which under common law granted husbands immunity from prosecution for forced intercourse with their wives. In 1978, the year after Oregon's law changed, Greta Rideout became the first woman in that state to charge her husband with rape. John Rideout was acquitted after a nationally publicized trial.[1]

These emerging categories proved at once useful and problematic for the anti-rape movement. The presence of terms such as *acquaintance rape* in the mass media afforded these concepts a sense of legitimacy and reflected a reality that rape crisis centers had long been witnessing: rape by acquaintances was more common than rape by strangers and just as traumatic. And, certainly, the seriousness being accorded to marital rape was a mark of progress.[2] Women interviewed in one study explained that, without concepts such as acquaintance rape, they were less likely to view an incident as rape, even though they felt violated; as one of them explained, "I felt raped, but I didn't realize I had been raped" (Warshaw 1988, 48). The growing understanding of the emerging categories gave such women a language with which to describe their experiences. The trend toward "typing" rape, then, has served a useful purpose by lending these long-ignored phenomena legitimacy and seriousness in the public consciousness.

But such classifications have also had a negative effect on the movement. *Date rape* and similar terms have frequently trivialized the issue in the public's perception (Mary Beth Carter, telephone interview, 13 January 1997). Mary Koss and Sarah Cook (1993, 108) point out that date rape "comes to signify 'rapette' in many minds," that the act seems not as traumatizing as being attacked by a stranger. Susan Estrich amplifies this view, noting that acquaintance rape is perceived by agents of law enforcement as (1) a private crime with no bearing on the public, (2) less serious than stranger rape, (3) somehow involving the contributory fault of the victim, and (4) less frightening than being assaulted by a stranger (Estrich 1987, 23–25). This perception has led to the dismissal of some kinds of rape as trivial and unworthy of public

outrage. The emergence of these rape categories, then, has not revolu-
tionized how certain types of rape are perceived in the public sphere.

There is no doubt, however, that the new attention to date and
acquaintance rape has reinvigorated the anti-rape movement, renewed
media coverage of sexual assault (see Table 4.1), and led to further
policy initiatives. Important legislation such as the Violence Against
Women Act (VAWA) of 1994 and the Drug-Induced Rape Prevention
and Control Act of 1996 recognize the problems of date and acquaintance rape. The VAWA makes specific provisions for "Safe Homes for
Women" and "Safe Campuses for Women," acknowledging that these

Table 4.1 "Date Rape" and "Acquaintance Rape" in Headlines and Lead
Paragraphs, 1979–1999

Year	Date Rape	Acquaintance Rape	Total
1979	0	1	1
1980	0	0	0
1981	0	0	0
1982	0	0	0
1983	0	0	0
1984	1	0	1
1985	5	1	6
1986	3	5	8
1987	15	3	18
1988	22	4	26
1989	47	8	55
1990	50	8	58
1991	250	49	299
1992	165	15	180
1993	323	15	338
1994	151	5	156
1995	85	11	96
1996	197	16	213
1997	161	6	167
1998	194	7	201
1999	285	8	293

are both places where women are at risk. The second of these laws (also known as the Rohypnol Act) came in response to the use of new odorless, tasteless drugs to incapacitate potential rape victims such as dates and partygoers. The anti-rape movement, then, has challenged Americans to acknowledge the significance of attacks by acquaintances and re-think our deepest beliefs about the crime.

Sensationalized Rape Trials

As discussed in Chapter 3, highly publicized events involving sexual assault have served as major consciousness-raising vehicles for the anti-rape movement. In the 1970s, the Inez Garcia, Joann Little, and Connie Francis cases received more than ample news coverage that called attention to the rape issue in the first years that it was on the public agenda. In the two decades since, similarly well-publicized, even sensationalized, trials have kept the anti-rape agenda alive and in public view.

Court cases can play a number of roles in the development of a social movement and the life of a social issue. In a study of three widely publicized rape trials, Lisa Cuklanz (1996) offers a typology of popularized trials in general. They may be social-movement strategy trials (or test cases), such as *Roe v. Wade* and *Brown v. Board of Education;* political trials, such as those of Ethel and Julius Rosenberg and Angela Davis; celebrity trials, such as the Claus von Bulow and O. J. Simpson cases; or issue-oriented trials, which are not planned as social-movement strategies but take place as the result of a movement. The three cases discussed here—involving Big Dan's Tavern, Mike Tyson, and William Kennedy Smith—can be considered issue-oriented trials, although those of Tyson and Smith also involve celebrity. The publicity generated by these three trials and others has played an important role in advancing the public discourse on rape.[3]

One of the most infamous rape cases to make headlines in the United States was a gang rape at Big Dan's Tavern in New Bedford, Massachusetts. On 6 March 1983 a woman, aged twenty-one, entered Big Dan's to buy cigarettes and have a drink. She was prevented from leaving by two men who dragged her to a pool table, and she was subsequently gang-raped by at least four men while perhaps another twenty or more bar patrons looked on and cheered. News of the incident traveled quickly. Area feminists, previously uninvolved in anti-rape activism, formed the Coalition Against Sexual Violence, led by Rita Moniz, a professor of political science at Southeastern Massachusetts University. Eight days after the rape, approximately forty-five hundred sympathizers held a candlelight march outside the New Bedford city hall to protest the gang rape and all violence against women. A telegram of support from Gloria Steinem was read aloud. The coalition went on to establish New Bedford's first rape crisis center six months later. One year after the assault, in two separate actions, four men were tried for aggravated rape and two more were tried for "joint enterprise" for their role as onlookers. The Cable News Network broadcast the proceedings live.[4] Ultimately, the four men were convicted of aggravated assault; the other two were acquitted of joint enterprise.[5]

In an incident that received immense media attention in part because it involved a member of a famous political family, William Kennedy Smith was arrested and charged with the rape of Patricia Bowman in Palm Beach, Florida.[6] According to Bowman, Smith, son of the businessman and Democratic fund-raiser Stephen Smith and nephew of Senator Edward Kennedy (D-Mass.), raped her at the Kennedy compound after they had spent time together at a local bar. In the months before the trial, media coverage focused on Bowman's past, portraying her as leading a "fast" life and having emotional problems. Also before the trial, three other women came forward to allege similar acts of sexual abuse by Smith. In a key pretrial decision, the judge excluded any prosecution evidence of prior acts of sexual abuse by the defendant, supposedly in symmetry with the exclusion of Bowman's sexual past (Estrich 1992). Smith was acquitted.

Another celebrity case revolved around the charges brought against heavyweight boxing champion Mike Tyson by Desiree Washington in 1991. At the time of the rape, Washington was a contestant in the Miss Black America beauty pageant being held in Indianapolis, of which Tyson was a distinguished guest. The eighteen-year-old woman accompanied Tyson to his hotel room, where the rape took place. At his 1992 trial, the boxer was found guilty and subsequently served four years of a maximum eighteen-year sentence.

These trials, covered by newspapers, news services, and television stations and networks across the country, raised a number of issues significant to the problem of rape and to developments in the campaign against it. First, ethnicity and race played significant roles in the Big Dan's and Mike Tyson cases. In the former, the New Bedford community (largely Portuguese American) and the press made much of the ethnic backgrounds of the parties involved: while the victim was of Portuguese descent, the defendants were immigrants from Portugal. Allegations of being ethnically biased against the men who had been charged were directed toward the prosecution and the reporters covering the case. In the community, as much victim blaming as Portuguese blaming took place, and ethnic relations were highly strained from the date of the rape through the end of the trial (Benedict 1992, 97). Frequently, the press portrayed the matter as revolving around tension between feminists and the ethnic Portuguese community, a tension that reporters often exaggerated (Cuklanz 1996, 69–70).

In the Tyson case, the rape issue divided the black community. Women and men were pressed to take sides when the National Baptist Convention, the largest African American church group, of which both Tyson and Washington were members, announced its support of the boxer (Baker-Fletcher 1992). More significantly, the long-held belief among many African Americans that black women should not openly accuse black men of violence—a position that black feminists (Wallace 1979; Shange 1975; Giddings 1992) have criticized—was a major concern throughout the episode.[7] The reasoning behind this viewpoint is that black men are already oppressed enough, and accusations by black women would only expose them to further oppression by the predominantly white criminal justice system. Moreover, it was argued, such charges would hold the entire African American community up to excessive scrutiny by the white public, forcing black people to "air their dirty laundry" in front of all. With regard to the Tyson case, prominent black feminists saw these views as promoting silence about violence against black women and as placing an undue burden on them to endure rape (Kelly 1992). The tension over the Tyson case within the African American community, the complexity of the issues involved, and the response by black feminist activists are delineated by Aaronette White (1999) and Kevin Brown (1999).

Another issue, typical of rape trials, had to do with the lives of the victims themselves. This was an important element of the Big Dan's and Smith cases. (If anything, Desiree Washington's virginal reputation and age probably helped win a conviction of Mike Tyson, although many commentators openly wondered what she expected when she went to his hotel room.) The rape shield law in Massachusetts barred introducing the sexual history of the Big Dan's victim, but other information, such as an earlier rape allegation she had made and her questioning about alleged welfare fraud, were admitted at trial. Information on prior criminal convictions of the defendants was ruled inadmissible. New Bedford residents interviewed by the press openly speculated about what kind of woman would patronize a bar such as Big Dan's, suggesting that the victim was "asking for it."

Reporters made much of Patricia Bowman's lifestyle and past during the trial of William Kennedy Smith. While information on her sexual history was ruled inadmissible at trial, the press did acquire information about Bowman's psychiatric history, which the defense had attempted to use to call her credibility and mental stability into question (Estrich 1992). The implication—made explicit by the defense attorney following the verdict—was that a mentally unstable woman with a reputation as a social climber and a past drug user would fabricate a rape charge for her own advantage.

A final issue in the Big Dan's and Smith cases, one that is also frequently raised in other rape trials, is that of the press's role in revealing the identity of the victim. Although the constitutional right to report a rape victim's name has been upheld by the Supreme Court (*Cox Broadcasting Corporation v. Cohn,* 1975; *Florida Star v. B.J.F.,* 1989), the media are by no means required to do so. Many of the news organizations covering the events in New Bedford and Palm Beach chose to identify the victims by name before and during these trials, in spite of the women's wishes to remain anonymous.[8] Since the Big Dan's trial was televised live, moreover, stations could not help broadcasting the victim's name, used frequently in the courtroom as a matter of course. The devastation of being identified by the press was so severe that, once the trial had ended, the victim left New Bedford to escape the ongoing harassment that resulted from the common knowledge of her identity. The stations broadcasting the Smith trial had the advantage of technology that allowed them to televise Bowman's testimony while positioning a large blue dot over her image to conceal her face. This gesture aside, her identity was well-known because many news organizations had reported her name before the trial.

These cases provide a glimpse into what might happen to a woman who reports a rape—namely, harassment and threats from neighbors, and being forced into exile to protect herself and her children, as happened to the Big Dan's victim, or having one's painful life experiences (unrelated to the rape charges) scrutinized, as was the case for Patricia Bowman. As Lisa Cuklanz notes, "If anything, [the Big Dan's] case was an eloquent argument for victims *not* to tell their stories" (1996, 65; emphasis in original). The issue of identifying victims is part of the larger problem of how rape continues to be perceived in the press and in the wider society. These nationally prominent cases, as well as those that receive only local coverage, can serve as a warning of what might happen to a woman who reports rape.

The highly publicized trials point to the enormous strides made in the public understanding of rape and to the main issues that continue to affect victims in spite of the anti-rape movement's efforts. Some commentators (Estrich 1992; Benedict 1992; Cuklanz 1996) have observed that cases such as these might never have been prosecuted had the events taken place twenty years earlier. In the 1960s, for example, it is doubtful that Desiree Washington would have made a charge of rape after she had willingly accompanied Mike Tyson to his hotel room. But these cases also point to the tenacity of the traditional thinking on rape that the movement has tried to debunk. In spite of the passage of rape shield laws, the press and the public drew strong inferences about the sexual pasts of the Big Dan's victim and of Patricia

Bowman and the charges they brought, while Desiree Washington's reputation only helped her case (Estrich 1992). Thus, the message about rape conveyed by these three trials is that a woman with a reputation for virtue probably has a good case against a black man with a reputation for uncontrollable anger, while women with less than spotless pasts should be ready to defend their life histories if they proceed with charges.

Other Rape Cases

More recent reports have attracted national interest and renewed the attention paid to rape in the media. In late 1995, a rape accusation made by a twelve-year-old girl against three U.S. Marines on the Japanese island of Okinawa received substantial news coverage. This case ignited a controversy over whether the accused would be tried in local courts or under U.S. military law (*Los Angeles Times* 1995). The decision to let the case proceed through the Japanese legal system prompted some outrage in the military establishment and among the families of the men charged. The matter also proved to be the "last straw" for Okinawans who had long been displeased with the American military presence on their island. However, demands that the military base be shut down went unmet, despite Japanese women's organized protests against the widespread victimization and prostitution that accompanied the presence of U.S. forces (Sallot 1995). Admiral Richard Macke, commander of U.S. military operations in the Pacific, was forced to take early retirement after publicly stating that, instead of renting a car the night of the rape (as the accused men did), they should have hired a prostitute. On 6 March 1996, the three marines were convicted in an Okinawa court.[9]

In recent years, rape and sexual harassment charges have been brought against several U.S. Army commissioned and noncommissioned officers at the Aberdeen Proving Ground in Maryland and at other military bases. The allegations were widely treated as a "sex scandal" instead of a "rape scandal" by the news media (e.g., Spinner and Levine 1996); this highlights how easily charges involving sexual violence can be trivialized into titillating sex scandal (more closely associated with a public figure's marital infidelity, for example, than with a violent assault and abuse of rank). These cases demonstrate the public's continuing discomfort with the violence inherent in the act of rape and its failure to view incidents involving nonconsensual sex as acts of violence. Since the charges were first brought, several of the white women who made them have publicly admitted that the sexual relations in question were truly consensual, but have added that they were threatened by ranking army officers, who instructed them to make the rape allegations against the black officers. The NAACP called for an inquiry into the case and charged army officials with a racist frame-up.

These charges remained in the news for several years. In one case, Army Staff Sergeant Delmar G. Simpson was sentenced to twenty-five years in prison in May 1997 for the rape of six female trainees. The sentence was proclaimed to be too lenient by women's organizations and too stiff by African American groups (Richter 1997). And in the most visible case resulting from the scandal, Sergeant Major Gene Mc-Kinney, the army's top enlisted man, was charged in May 1997 with eighteen counts of adultery, maltreatment, and sexual misconduct with subordinates (Ruane 1997). In March 1998, McKinney was cleared of all sexual charges in a ruling that angered victims' rights organizations. McKinney's case also raised charges of racist bias in the military justice system, charges that have informed the framing of rape on the public agenda since it first became public in the early 1970s.

Anti-Rape Organizing on Campus

Colleges and universities provided a vital organizing space for the anti-rape movement in its formative years. Administrators' response across the country represented a first step toward addressing the issue of campus rape by devising new policies. But in recent years, as researchers and news organizations have paid more attention to date and acquaintance rape, student activism has grown in scope and in numbers. Media coverage of such efforts has bolstered the anti-rape campaign and has made the issue of campus rape an important focus of its activities.

The revitalization of the movement by students in the 1980s and 1990s represents a significant development in anti-rape organizing.

In the 1970s, university campaigners against rape focused on the problem of assaults by strangers—protecting women on campus from assault by dangerous outsiders. But as attention to date and acquaintance rape grew throughout the 1980s, feminists made logical connections between college life and the phenomenon of date rape. One of the first articles to draw attention to campus and university organizing appeared in *Ms.* in the early 1980s (Barrett 1982). It notes that while universities and their communities can fairly easily recognize the seriousness of stranger rape—especially when the strangers involved are black, poor, and fit the stereotypical profile of the rapist—it is far more difficult for young women to perceive being attacked by dates as rape and to report such crimes to campus authorities or law enforcement, and more difficult still to convince those in power that acquaintance rape is a problem. It was not until the early 1980s, then, that the problem of rape on campus became linked with the growing attention to sexual assaults by dates and acquaintances and led to a new wave of concern and a new form of organizing.

Throughout the 1980s and into the next decade, student anti-rape groups began to spring up in universities across the country. Among them were Students United for Rape Elimination (SURE) at Stanford University, Students Together Against Acquaintance Rape (STAAR) at the University of Pennsylvania, and Students Concerned About Rape (SCARE) at Syracuse University; there were similar organizations at Barnard College, Duke University, Evergreen State College, and Rutgers University. At some schools, women's groups have expanded their focus to include rape; Students for Women's Concerns at Vanderbilt University and Sisters in Solidarity to Eradicate Sexism (SISTERS) at Spelman College are but two examples. Likewise, campus men's groups, such as Tulane Men Against Rape (TMAR), Duke University's Men Acting for Change (MAC), and North Carolina State University's Rape Education and Active Leadership (REAL-Men), have concluded that men must become active in the fight to prevent rape.[10] Although they have organized in varied ways, the themes of upholding sexual autonomy and preventing acquaintance rape run through all of them.

The efforts of these students resemble those of the early anti-rape activists. Their first goal was to uncover the truth about hidden rape and encourage victims to step forward.[11] Speak-outs and take back the night marches were planned, attempting to reveal to women the reality of campus acquaintance rape, much as speak-outs and consciousness-raising groups functioned at the beginning of the movement to generate personal stories from survivors. On campus, marches have become the centerpiece among events designed to promote awareness.

The validation of date rape as a serious offense was a necessary component of this consciousness-raising. Research establishing the prevalence of attacks by acquaintances in young women's lives bolstered campus efforts (Koss 1988). Students organized escort programs and patrols, held rape education seminars for men and women, offered self-defense classes, and sponsored other awareness-raising events (Barrett 1982). On some campuses, activists began to use radical tactics: students at Brown University, for example, kept "rape lists" on bathroom walls, where women wrote the names of male students who had allegedly raped female students. This development led the administration to examine the school's sexual assault policy and make changes (Sanday 1996, 266–67). Elsewhere, particularly among men's groups, student-initiated peer education became the focal point of the anti-rape agenda. As media attention to such activities and to the problem of date rape increased, campus organizing against sexual assault likewise grew in numbers and political strength.

Intercollegiate coalitions of anti-rape projects have also formed. For example, in March 1992, at the University of Pennsylvania, STAAR hosted the First National Student Conference on Campus Sexual Violence, where more than three hundred women and men investigated the issue and shared resources. The success of this and subsequent conferences led organizers to establish the National Student Coalition Against Sexual Violence (NSCASV) in August 1994. The coalition holds two conferences yearly, one in the western United States and one in the East. This sort of cross-campus organizing strengthens the movement and contributes to its momentum.

In an attempt to spark the interest of college officials, students have sought to effect campus-wide policies to punish rapists and assist victims. This has proved significantly more difficult than efforts to raise consciousness. Administrators have preferred to focus on stranger rape—which can be treated as a criminal justice issue—with the goal of sealing the campus off from intruders. To recognize the reality of acquaintance rape would be to acknowledge that the problem of sexual attacks existed within the university and that campus life itself perhaps fostered and excused assaultive behavior. College officials, looking out for the reputations of their institutions, were slow to make such a recognition. Students continued to pursue their attention, however, and at times met with success. Some institutions set up programs such as the University of Florida's Sexual Assault Recovery Service (Foster 1987) or Princeton University's SHARE, the Sexual Harassment/Assault Advising Resources and Education office (Sanday 1996, 256–58). Many universities have incorporated rape-awareness education into first-year orientation programs, hoping to stop the problem as early as possible.

Students' search for policy responses from administrators in the matter of rape has been criticized. Unlike the protesters of the 1960s, whose goals were to eliminate the *in loco parentis* role of the university and to gain more autonomy for students, anti-rape activists pushing for the creation and enforcement of harsher rules have reinforced the university's paternalistic role. Adopting rules and regulations treats rape as an individual concern, critics charge, instead of as a social problem connected to larger structures of power and control (Kauffman 1988). Moreover, when universities opt to treat campus rape as a disciplinary matter, rather than as a law enforcement issue to be adjudicated by the criminal courts, the result is a differing standard of justice for attacks on and off campus. Victims reported dissatisfaction with how university judicial boards handled their rape cases to one researcher (Warshaw 1988, 147–50). This dual standard simply reinforces the trivialization of acquaintance rape and fails to hold rapists legally accountable.[12]

But making such demands of university administrations, however compromised the demands might be, affords student organizers a unique opportunity to effect change. College students are by definition a transient population in a university or community. Individuals are unlikely to be able to sustain their activism within a given university for more than a few years, and the potential for renewing the activist base from each incoming class is uncertain. Because of this, such organizations are frequently unable to maintain enough interest and energy to become a long-term presence on or off campus. Accordingly, student anti-rape activists recognize that influencing administrative policies represents their best chance at making effective change, change that will outlive their relatively short time at the university.

One of the most vigorously debated sexual assault codes in higher education is the Antioch College Sexual Offense Policy, in place since 1992. It is the result of feminist students' demands for an administrative response to the problem of date rape and of the local media's attention to demonstrations at the college in 1990 (Pfister 1994, 14). Designed by a committee of students, faculty, and administrators, the policy requires Antioch students to obtain affirmative consent from their partner at every stage of a sexual encounter: kissing, touching, undressing, and so on. It applies to all students, regardless of the gender of those involved. Unconscious, sleeping, or drunken persons are assumed incapable of consent. The purpose of the policy is to encourage sexual communication and to affirm the right of bodily integrity for all women and men. One writer observes that such an approach "includes the apparently controversial idea that potential lovers should *ask* before foisting sexual attention on their partners, and that partners should clearly answer 'yes' or 'no' " (Pfister 1994, 13; emphasis in original). The controversy revolves around ideas about sexuality and the role of the university. Proponents state that Antioch's policy discourages date rape and encourages sexual communication. But critics charge that it insults women by implying that they are unable to deal with sexuality and must rely on a paternalistic code to negotiate sexual encounters for them (Matalin 1993; Sanday 1996, 272–77), even though the language used is gender neutral. Others claim that the college's approach imposes a standard of "sexual correctness" that ignores the reality that sexuality necessarily involves ambiguity, danger, and risk (Crichton 1993). In spite of criticism, the policy remains in place. At its students' initiative, Stanford has adopted a similar sexual assault policy. What is clear from these examples is that student-led attempts to address the problem of date rape have resulted in university policies that have the potential to reduce its occurrence on campus, or at least to promote an understanding of nonconsensual sexual activity as rape. This represents an important development in the anti-rape movement, and suggests that campus organizing constitutes the latest wave of activity in the campaign against sexual assault.

Keeping Rape on the Institutional Agenda

After the initial flurry of policy activity across the country between 1973 and 1980, rape remained on the institutional agenda in various forms and contexts. Recent policy initiatives have been concentrated at the federal level, involving both Congress and the courts.

The House and the Senate on Rape, 1980s and 1990s

The 1980s and 1990s saw considerable action by the central government on the issue. Between 1979 and 1996, fifty-three rape-related bills were introduced in Congress. Most of them never emerged from committee, but several significant pieces of legislation have been passed.

Victims of Crime Act of 1984   Although it does not specifically focus on rape, the Victims of Crime Act of 1984 (VOCA) proved to be a major funding resource for rape crisis centers. Administered through the Department of Justice, VOCA establishes a fund made up of fines levied against violent offenders and allocates these monies to the states, which distribute them to victim-service providers. The act requires that priority be given to programs that provide services to victims of sexual assault, spousal abuse, and child abuse. All organizations receiving disbursements must be incorporated as nonprofits or must be operated by a public agency. In addition to its financial support of rape crisis centers, VOCA provides funds for state-based programs that compensate crime victims.

Sexual Abuse Act of 1986   Representative Steny Hoyer (D-Md.) introduced the Sexual Abuse Act in Congress in 1984 and again in 1985. Although the bill failed to pass in those years, it was revived in 1986; this time introduced in the House by Representative John Conyers, Jr. (D-Mich.), and in the Senate by Senator Charles E. Grassley (R-Iowa), it was signed by President Ronald Reagan in November of that year (P.L. 99-654). The act amended Title 18 of the U.S. Code pertaining to rape and essentially brought federal law into conformity with changes instituted in many states in previous years. Thus, in 1986, the United States caught up with several states in revising the rape law.

Like other elements of the federal code, this law applies only to crimes taking place in specific federal territorial and maritime jurisdictions, including federal prisons, post offices, military bases, and Indian reservations. This means that the federal law can be invoked only in a small percentage of all rape cases. The act divides the crime into the categories of aggravated sexual abuse, sexual abuse, sexual abuse of a minor or ward, and abusive sexual contact. Circumstances that distinguish aggravated sexual abuse from sexual abuse include the presence of force, serious bodily injury, threats of serious bodily injury or death, and kidnapping. Further aggravating circumstances include purposefully rendering a person unconscious—with drugs or by other means—before engaging in a sexual act. Penalties vary with the category of the crime. Significantly, the new code contains no spousal exemption for rape (see Appendix 5).

Violence Against Women Act of 1994   The capstone federal policy initiative to date on the issue of sexual assault is the Violence Against Women Act (VAWA), Title IV of the Violent Crime Control and Law Enforcement Act of 1994 (P.L. 103-322) (see Appendix 6). This law amended the Omnibus Crime Control and Safe Streets Act of 1968, the act that created the now defunct LEAA, and also stood as the national epitome of the tough-on-crime approach. Its passage in September 1994 was perhaps the most significant accomplishment of the anti-rape movement. Senator Joseph R. Biden (D-Del.) was the principal author and sponsor of the bill, which was introduced in every Congress from 1990 to 1994. Representative Jack Brooks (D-Tex.) sponsored the VAWA in the House. The bill addresses two forms of violence against women—rape and domestic battering—but it came close to ignoring rape altogether. According to Mary Beth Carter, president of the National Coalition Against Sexual Assault (NCASA) from 1989 to 1992,

> When I . . . became president, one of the issues that we found out about was the Violence Against Women Act. Senator Joe Biden's office was writing that. And we found out that, when they were writing it, it was only for domestic violence. And we questioned why you could call this "violence against women" and not include rape. The focus, they said, was on prevention, and shelters are prevention against domestic violence. . . . And we said that rape is as important an issue, and needs funding, and there are ways to prevent rape. (telephone interview, 13 January 1997)

NCASA's Legislative Committee began helping Biden's office amend the bill to include rape. Other women's organizations collaborated with the senator's staff in drafting the proposed law. Sally Goldfarb and Pat Reuss of the NOW Legal Defense and Education Fund—the latter once a lobbyist for WEAL (Costain 1988, 37)—both lent their expertise, and they joined Victoria Nourse, counsel of the Senate Judiciary Committee, in testifying in favor of the bill before Congress. The National Association of Women Judges publicly endorsed the measure (Frazee 1995, 42), and the rape researcher Mary Koss also testified in support.

The opposition was also imposing, however. The Judicial Conference of the United States took an official stance against the legislation in 1990 (with Chief Justice William Rehnquist supporting that position in public statements), but reversed itself in 1993 after there had been some rewording of the bill. The ACLU joined in the opposition as well. Both of these bodies opposed the act's inclusion of violence against women within the spectrum of civil rights legislation, taking the view that it would be impossible for the courts to establish whether a woman had been raped or battered because of her gender or for some other reason. They also feared that VAWA cases would clog the federal courts with issues of little national import (Frazee 1995, 43–44). The ACLU was among the groups testifying against the proposed legislation before Congress.

Biden's language in support of his bill reveals that a far more pro-victim, pro-woman approach to rape was being espoused by at least some members of Congress than had been the case when rape appeared on the institutional agenda in 1973. Biden (U.S. Congress, Senate 1993, iv) expressed concern at the lack of popular outrage about the reality of the crime of rape:

> Imagine the public outcry if we were to learn today that one-quarter of convicted kidnappers or bank robbers were sentenced to probation or that 54 percent of arrests for these crimes never led to conviction. We would consider such a system of justice inadequate to protect the Nation's property, yet we tolerate precisely such results when the rape of women is at issue. Where the victim knows the perpetrator, there is a tendency to consider the crime a product of a private relationship, not a matter of public injustice.

This represents a major advance over the protectionist rhetoric of "car[ing] for our women" that Senator Charles Mathias used in 1973, and it suggests a tremendous change in policy makers'—and the public's—perceptions of rape.

Long and detailed, the Violence Against Women Act covers a number of policy areas. It provides Department of Transportation grants for local parks and transportation systems to reduce crime; amends and updates the Federal Rules of Evidence for rape; authorizes Department of Health and Human Services (HHS) grants for rape prevention and education; authorizes Department of Justice grants to states and

Indian tribal governments to improve the handling of rape investigations; authorizes DOJ grants for the training and education of judges in state and federal courts; authorizes DOJ grants for studying the problem of rape on college campuses; and provides a civil rights remedy for civil suits against accused rapists (for those rapes that are determined to be "gender-motivated"). It was this final provision that sparked the greatest controversy. Altogether, the VAWA authorized $1.62 billion to fund programs dealing with violence against women over six years. In March 1995, the Violence Against Women Office was opened within the DOJ, with Bonnie J. Campbell, formerly attorney general of Iowa, as director; in July of that year, U.S. Attorney General Janet Reno and Secretary of Health and Human Services Donna Shalala announced the formation of the Advisory Council on Violence Against Women, with forty-six members (see Appendix 7).

As an instance of anti-rape policy making, the VAWA has the most far-reaching implications among all pieces of federal rape legislation. For example, the policy limitations of the rape shield amendment to the Federal Rules of Evidence remain the same as when Elizabeth Holtzman's bill first amended them in 1978—the law applies only to rapes taking place on federal property, such as national parks and military bases. But the VAWA's authorization of federal grants to states and Indian tribes contains much potential. These sorts of funds have been allocated to state agencies, which, in turn, have disbursed monies to rape crisis centers and other groups developing programs focusing on preventing the crime. Moreover, by making the receipt of funds contingent, not automatic, the federal law mandates state compliance with certain policies. An example is the act's denial of monies to states that do not pay for evidence collection kits ("rape kits") in public hospitals; imposing this requirement enforces a certain level of compliance with federal standards. With its provision for a civil rights remedy, the VAWA also reaches the state and federal courts in a way that no other federal rape policy has. As I will discuss below, the question of the constitutionality of the act—specifically, of its civil rights provision—has reached the federal courts and remains open.

Drug-Induced Rape Prevention and Control Act   In 1995, the use and availability of so-called date rape drugs began to make headlines. The illegal drug Rohypnol (flunitrazepam)—nicknamed "roofies" or "roaches" on the streets—first appeared in the popular press in a page-one article in the *Dallas Morning News* on 15 June 1995 (Howland 1995). Rohypnol is a potent, mind-altering sedative that can induce amnesia; its effects are intensified by alcohol. In 1995, law enforcement officials reported that the use of the drug in acquaintance rapes and gang initiations was increasing dramatically, particularly in Florida and Texas, where it can easily be smuggled in from Latin American countries that do not regulate flunitrazepam. Women have reported being raped after Rohypnol was slipped into their drinks in social settings. Such cases are difficult to prosecute, however, because victims cannot recall details to report to prosecutors; medical tests can now detect the presence of the drug. Similar drugs, such as gamma-hydroxybutyrate (GHB), pose similar problems. Not surprisingly, the expert advice directed at women is never to leave a drink unattended or accept a drink from a stranger (*Chicago Tribune* 1995).

As a partial remedy to this growing problem, the Drug-Induced Rape Prevention and Control bill was presented to Congress in 1996. Introduced in the House by Representative Gerald B. H. Solomon (R-N.Y.) and co-sponsored in the Senate by Orrin Hatch (R-Utah) and Kay Bailey Hutchison (R-Tex.), the measure was signed into law (P.L. 104-305) by President Bill Clinton. The Rohypnol Act amends the U.S. Code to provide stiffer penalties for violent crimes committed in conjunction with the distribution of an illegal drug to the victim without her or his knowledge. The act also adds flunitrazepam to the controlled substances listed in the code (see Appendix 8). Thus, new developments involving the issue of rape, including the availability of sophisticated new drugs, have restimulated the policy process and prompted changes that were certainly unanticipated when sexual assault first became part of the national institutional agenda in 1973.

Federal Courts

As in the 1970s, the federal bench has seen only moderate activity in rape policy throughout the 1980s and 1990s. In spite of the courts' potential to effect sweeping policy changes (O'Connor 1996), this branch of government has not been a significant arena for rape-related policies. Nevertheless, the judiciary has been important in interpreting the statutory and constitutional implications of rape legislation, and it may play such a role to a greater degree in coming years. The following are the significant Supreme Court cases of the 1980s and 1990s dealing with rape.[13]

Florida Star v. B.J.F. (1989). In *Cox Broadcasting Corporation v. Cohn* (1975), the Court ruled that information obtained at a public trial, such as the identity of a rape victim, was public information, so the media are justified in relating it to the public. In the *Florida Star* case, the newspaper reported a victim's name as obtained through a local police department, not through court records. The police department had released her name in violation of a state law protecting the identity of rape victims. The woman involved, B.J.F., brought suit against the paper and was awarded $75,000 in damages in the Florida court. The Supreme Court reversed the ruling, holding that information made public by an agency of the government remains public, in spite of that agency's violation of state law. Because it was reporting public information, the newspaper could not be held liable for damages. Together, *Cox Broadcasting Corporation v. Cohn* and *Florida Star v. B.J.F.* give the press First Amendment protection in deciding whether and how to report on rape trials and cases.

Michigan v. Lucas (1991). The Supreme Court has never handed down a decision on the constitutionality of rape shield legislation, but in this case it did rule on a narrow procedural requirement of the Michigan rape shield statute. That state's law, one of the strongest, most restrictive in the country, prohibits the admission of evidence about the victim's sexual past except as it involves the defendant; it further requires the defense to request judicial *in camera* hearing of such evidence within ten days of arraignment. Lucas, the defendant, argued that he was denied his Sixth Amendment guarantee of a fair trial when evidence of his prior relationship with the woman in the case was prohibited on the grounds that he failed to make such a request in compliance with the statute. The Michigan appeals court ruled in his favor, finding the provision in question to be overly restrictive and the ten-day time limit to be arbitrary. The Supreme Court, however, upheld the provision and, most importantly, did so in language that suggests support for the substantive issues in rape shield legislation.

United States v. Lanier (1997). This case is more specifically concerned with rape issues than either of the foregoing. Judge David Lanier of Tennessee was tried and convicted in federal court on seven counts—two felony and five misdemeanor—of willfully depriving another person of Fourteenth Amendment rights guaranteed by the Constitution while acting in the capacity of an official of the government, a violation of the federal code (18 U.S. Code § 242 [1994]). Among the acts for which Lanier was convicted was forced oral copulation with Vivian Forsythe-Archie, a woman over whose divorce and child custody cases he had just presided. He was fined and sentenced to twenty-five years in prison. A three-judge panel of the U.S. Court of Appeals for the Sixth Circuit confirmed the conviction; after rehearing the case *en banc,* however, the appeals court reversed the conviction, holding that, because the Supreme Court never stated that the statute covers sexual assault, this conduct is not prohibited by § 242. A unanimous Supreme Court vacated this decision and sent it back to the appeals court, saying that the judges were mistaken in limiting the application of the statute to violations delineated by the High Court. The nine justices did not address the conviction itself, nor whether § 242 applies to sexual assault.[14]

The Violence Against Women Act in Federal Courts

The Supreme Court has not yet decided any cases concerning the constitutionality of the VAWA. Federal courts have issued contradictory decisions involving this question. In one, a federal judge let a domestic violence lawsuit, brought under the VAWA's civil rights provision, go forward in June 1996. But in March 1999, the U.S. Court of Appeals for the Fourth Circuit threw out a case in which a female student charged two football players at the Virginia Polytechnic Institute and State University with rape under the civil rights provision of the VAWA.

In January 2000, the Supreme Court heard oral arguments in the Virginia Tech case (*United States v. Morrison et al.* and *Brzonkala v. Morrison et al.*) and, it is hoped, will settle the question of the VAWA's constitutionality.

The issue of rape, then, has been prominent on the institutional agenda ever since it arrived there in 1973. Public perception of the issue has evolved dramatically since that time. But at the dawn of the twenty-first century, it is clear that the public anti-rape agenda and the feminist anti-rape agenda diverge nearly as sharply as they did in the early 1970s, even as public attention to the problem remains strong. Given the distractions and distortions of recent years—the sex wars and the backlash against the anti-rape movement—the tension between these agendas promises not to diminish.

Feminism and the Sex Wars

During the feminist conflict that has been dubbed the "sex wars," issues of violence against women, pornography, and power—and their role in feminist politics—have come to the forefront of public discourse and have occasionally supplanted the rape discourse that feminists started in 1970. The question of whether an anti-violence political stance requires a concurrent opposition to verbal, pictorial, or other depictions that might encourage sexual violence, or to practices that appear inconsistent with anti-violence ideology, has become important to both sides in recent years. The sex wars can be loosely defined as the conflict between feminists who oppose pornography and sadomasochism (S&M) because both degrade women and promote violence against them, and "pro-sex" feminists who argue that feminism should be committed to opening up all sexual options for women rather than limiting their sexuality. The opposing sides of the debate have been dubbed the "radical feminists" and the "libertarian feminists" (Berger, Searles, and Cottle 1991).[15]

The conflict is far more complex than definitions can indicate. Carole S. Vance (1989, 1), a pro-sex theorist, summarizes the theoretical component of the debate:

For some, the dangers of sexuality—violence, brutality, and coercion, in the form of rape, forcible incest, and exploitation, as
well as everyday cruelty and humiliation—make the pleasures
pale by comparison. For others, the positive possibilities of sexuality—explorations of the body, curiosity, intimacy, sensuality,
adventure, excitement, human connection, basking in the infan-
tile and non-rational—are not only worthwhile but provide sus-
taining energy.

According to the writer Jackie Goldsby (1993, 115), the significant
themes of the sex wars pose these questions: "Where does the line
fall demarcating pornography from erotica? How does a viewer's gaze
enable or circumscribe the subjectivity of the object (s)he beholds?"

Because of a strong historical link between the anti-pornography
and anti-rape movements, the two are frequently conflated. For example, the sex historians John D'Emilio and Estelle Freedman (1988, 351)
explain that during the 1970s, when anti-rape efforts were well under
way, "the eruption of pornographic imagery into the public sphere
seemed like the last straw for activists who daily encountered the victims of violence. . . . But, before long, they telescoped the problem into
a singleminded preoccupation with pornography." Critics charge that
the anti-pornography feminists' attribution of the source of sexism
to pornography, commercial sex, and sexual minorities (such as trans-
sexuals and sadomasochists) has replaced the older focus on "family,
religion, education, child-rearing practices, the media, the state, psychiatry, job discrimination, and unequal pay," where it more rightly belongs (Rubin 1989, 302). This new focus, they claim, diverts feminist
energies away from the real causes of sexism.

The sex wars can be traced to early radical feminist theory and
practice that challenged violence against women in all its forms. As
such, they stem from the same source as the campaign against rape.
Very early in the women's movement, feminists made connections between pornography and violence against women. For example, the first
issue of the radical feminist tabloid *Woman's World* made the front-
page plea "Boycott All Newsstands Selling Pornography" (1971), and

condemned the increased availability of pornographic magazines for encouraging "sexual sadism and exploitation." The piece was accompanied by a graph tracing increases in rates of forcible rape as compiled by the FBI for the years 1960–69, implying a causal connection between the availability of pornography and rape rates. Andrea Dworkin's 1974 book, *Woman Hating,* elucidates this theme of causality more extensively from the radical feminist perspective. Thus, the idea of a connection between sexual violence and explicit depictions of violent sex is linked to the same feminist impulses that gave rise to the anti-rape movement.[16]

In the late 1970s feminists, including some anti-rape activists, began to pay more attention to the growing pornography industry, the role of violence against women in it, and the ways in which even the mainstream media were tending toward depictions of women that involved degradation and violence. For example, the newsletter of the Feminist Alliance Against Rape printed stories of feminist anti-pornography activism, such as the actions of Women Against Pornography (WAP), alongside rape crisis center news. In 1976, the group Women Against Violence in Pornography and Media (WAVPM) was founded by the rape researcher Diana Russell and others to protest a wide range of violent depictions of women. Beginning in the late 1970s, take back the night (TBN) marches, protesting both pornography and violence against women, flourished in cities across the country (present-day TBN protests, however, focus on sexual abuse and battering more than pornography). In Los Angeles, Women Against Violence Against Women (WAVAW) took a national role in protesting the recording industry's portrayal of women as persons who, in advertising and on album covers, enjoy their own victimization (WEA Boycott 1977). Finally, the publication of the anthology *Take Back the Night: Women on Pornography* (Lederer 1980) marked a turning point for the feminist movement, for by then the anti-violence and anti-pornography positions had become nearly synonymous.[17]

Opposition to the anti-pornography stance appeared in 1979, when Samois, a San Francisco lesbian S&M group, protested against the WAVPM's position that lesbian sadomasochism constitutes violence against women (Berger, Searles, and Cottle 1991, 33). Its members argued instead that, under certain consensual circumstances, pain and dominance/submission can be pleasurable and can even achieve feminist goals by freeing participants to confront their sexual repression and internalized fears. They further argued that radical feminists were dangerously close to promoting a single, politically correct sexual paradigm that would limit women's sexual options and ignore the range of sexual possibilities, including experimentation with pornography, pain, and power (Tong 1989, 121–22).

In the 1980s, the possible connection between images of explicit and violent sex and actual sexual violence, as advanced by anti-pornography feminists, was tested in practice by the radical feminist activists Catharine MacKinnon and Andrea Dworkin. In 1983 and 1984, they worked with the cities of Minneapolis and Indianapolis to draft and pass ordinances defining pornography as

> the graphic sexually explicit subordination of women, whether in pictures or in words, that also includes one or more of the following: (i) women are presented dehumanized as sexual objects, things, or commodities; or (ii) women are presented as sexual objects who enjoy pain or humiliation; or (iii) women are presented as sexual objects who experience sexual pleasure in being raped; or (iv) women are presented as sexual objects tied up or cut up or mutilated or bruised or physically hurt; or (v) women are presented in postures of sexual submission, servility or display; or (vi) women's body parts—including but not limited to vaginas, breasts, and buttocks—are exhibited, such that women are reduced to those parts; or (vii) women are presented as whores by nature; or (viii) women are presented being penetrated by objects or animals; or (ix) women are presented in scenarios of degradation, injury, torture, shown as filthy or inferior, bleeding, bruised, or hurt in a context that makes these conditions sexual. (MacKinnon 1987, 262)

These ordinances declared pornography a civil offense and a violation of women's civil rights. A cause of action was granted to any woman (or man, child, or transsexual person in a woman's place) who could establish that she was forced into a pornographic performance, that she was raped or otherwise assaulted because of a specific piece of pornography, or that she was compelled to perform sexual acts based on pornography (Tong 1989, 116). Unlike a criminal law, the ordinances would allow alleged victims (not prosecutors) legal action against pornographers and distributors. The regulations did not criminalize or regulate the production or distribution of pornography. The Indianapolis ordinance was held unconstitutional by the U.S. Court of Appeals for the Seventh Circuit in *American Booksellers Ass'n. Inc. v. Hudnut* and summarily affirmed by the U.S. Supreme Court in 1986. The Minneapolis ordinance was passed twice by the city council and vetoed twice by the mayor (MacKinnon 1987, 262). Attempts to pass similar ordinances in other parts of the country failed, although usually by only slim margins.

Anti-pornography activism in general, and the ordinance effort in particular, provoked significant opposition, notably among feminists. For example, much has been made of the issue of consent. On the one hand, MacKinnon (1989) has argued that the concept of women's consent is meaningless under conditions of male dominance. On the other hand, while anti-rape activists have fought to have a woman's "no" recognized as a sign of nonconsent by a potential rapist, and by law enforcement officers and juries,[18] liberal or libertarian feminists have argued that a woman's "yes" must be equally valued. It would be paternalistic, they argue, to expect the legal codes to enforce a policy that strips women of the right to exercise and enjoy all aspects of their sexuality, especially when those codes are enforced and interpreted by a male-biased legal system (Burstyn 1985; Berger, Searles, and Cottle 1991). Thus, women who use and enjoy pornography, who engage in nontraditional sex practices, or who choose to work in the sex industry as strippers, prostitutes, actors, or models must be considered free and consenting adults, say libertarian feminists.

There is no simple solution to the conflict contained in the sex wars. Although the popular conflation of anti-rape and anti-pornography organizing remains, it is uncertain what effect these debates will have on anti-rape organizing. Some feminists working against pornography assert that the anti-rape movement and the battered-women's movement are not taking enough of a role in the campaign against pornography. For example, Diana Russell (1990, xxiv) remarks that

> while rape crisis centers are often oppressively busy helping survivors, the multi-billion-dollar pornography industry continues to encourage increasing numbers of men to act out their rape desires. What are the rape crisis centers doing or saying about this? . . .
>
> . . . How often does NCADV [National Coalition Against Domestic Violence] or NCASA [National Coalition Against Sexual Assault] include a workshop on this subject [pornography] at their conferences or in their training?

It is clear that the sex wars have introduced a mounting tension into the women's movement and the anti-rape effort. While it is unlikely that this tension will paralyze the movement, whose strength lies in its diversity and accomplishments, it can have the effect of silencing dissent and diverting energy toward the debate and away from action against rape.

Anti–Anti-Rape Backlash

Feminist commentators, most notably the journalist Susan Faludi (1991), have tracked the rise of a right-wing reaction against the women's movement in recent years. Social-movement theorists have noted the significance of the "anti" position in the overall development of social movements (Mottl 1980; Lo 1982). Tahi Mottl (1980, 620) defines a countermovement as "a conscious, collective, organized attempt to resist or to reverse social change." Nancy McGlen and Karen O'Connor (1983, 32) remark:

> [A]ll social movements can expect to encounter resistance from those in power positions, but women's rights advocates have faced an additional source of conflict, resistance and sometimes organized opposition to woman suffrage, to the ERA, and to reproductive freedom.

> . . . [A] countermovement is most likely to form when the
> proposed change is perceived by some to be a pure public bad
> that necessitates changes that may adversely affect life-styles and
> in which all will be compelled to partake.

Groups of this sort, once organized and funded, have the potential to
disrupt the trajectory of a social movement, even without gaining support from the majority of the polity; such was the case with those
opposed to the passage of the equal rights amendment and with the
pro-life organizations that have managed to chip away at the reproductive freedoms gained in 1973. Opposition groups can indeed become
social movements in their own right, sharing characteristics with the
organizations they set out to oppose.[19] "Anti" movements, then, can
wield considerable power to halt or retard the efforts of social-
movement groups.

The anti-rape movement, by and large, has been spared the burden
of resisting the efforts of an organized, well-funded, politically savvy,
single-issue opposition. This is due, in large part, to the nature of the
issue involved: very few people would admit to holding "pro-rape"
beliefs. There is widespread agreement that rape is a heinous crime,
that rapists should be punished, and that services to support victims
should be available. By contrast, StopERA and pro-life organizations
have viewed the ultimate goals of the ERA and abortion-rights movements (respectively) as morally wrong and destructive of society. Public
policies dealing with rape—pro-victim criminal laws, rape shield laws,
and funding for research and services, for example—can be seen as
pure public goods that benefit all rape victims and even attempt to
reduce the incidence of sexual assault. But, as McGlen and O'Connor
mention above, when the changes sought can be perceived by some as
public bads, the potential for the rise of an opposition movement increases. In the case of anti-rape policy, the specter of wives pressing
charges against their husbands and of young women making formal
accusations against their male dates after a "bad night" has brought on
a backlash that has denounced this challenge to the sexual order as a
public bad.

In recent years, anti-rape organizing, theorizing, and discourse have been under fire from a cadre of pundits and scholars, and from self-described feminists such as Camille Paglia, Katie Roiphe, and Christina Hoff Sommers. These writers have not derided most of the substantive policy advances of the anti-rape movement as being undesirable for society. Rather, they have focused on the connection between feminist politics, feminist theory, and the anti-rape movement, locating the problem, as they see it, in overly broad feminist redefinitions of rape. As the efforts of the anti-rape movement gained renewed media coverage through the growing attention paid to date and acquaintance rape, these commentators became increasingly vocal in their opposition. Backlash writers have placed the greatest emphasis on the reliability of rape statistics put forth in the findings of researchers and on the rhetoric of date rape as played out on university campuses. The backlash can be characterized more as an ideological battle waged through the media than as a countermovement involving lobbyists and legislators.[20]

Paglia, Roiphe, and Sommers

The anthropologist Peggy Reeves Sanday (1996, 242) traces the reaction against the anti-rape movement to an article appearing in the magazine *Reason* in July 1990 and reprinted in the October 1990 issue of *Playboy*. It argues that feminists have gone too far in expanding the definition of rape to include situations in which a young woman's "no" might have been justifiably misread as "yes" (Gutmann 1990). Sanday links the rise of the backlash to the introduction of the Violence Against Women Act, and wonders whether it was purely coincidental that the *Reason* article appeared so quickly on the heels of the first submission of the VAWA to Congress in June 1990.[21]

Camille Paglia, a professor of art, is perhaps the most flamboyant and visible opponent of the feminist rape agenda. Before joining in the rape backlash, Paglia had received little public attention in her academic role. She entered the rape discourse with a series of editorials on date rape that appeared in the popular press and with a number of speeches in the early 1990s; these have been excerpted and reprinted in her book *Sex, Art, and American Culture* (1992). Paglia begins her first date rape editorial for New York's *Newsday* by proclaiming her opposition to sexual assault: "Rape is an outrage that cannot be tolerated in civilized society." She then launches into an attack on feminism's role in promoting panic about rape, particularly among young women (Paglia 1992, 49–50). The origins of rape, for Paglia, are quite simple (1992, 50–51):

> The sexes are at war. Men must struggle for identity against the overwhelming power of their mothers. Women have menstruation to tell them they are women. Men must do or risk something to be men. Men become masculine only when other men say they are. Having sex with a woman is one way a boy becomes a man. . . .
>
> . . . Aggression and eroticism are deeply intertwined. Hunt, pursuit, and capture are biologically programmed into male sexuality.

Rather than heeding feminists who are "lost in a fog of social constructionism," Paglia says, young women are better advised to accept the facts of human biology and learn to be tough, learn not to get raped, and accept "courtship [as] a dangerous game in which the signals are not verbal but subliminal" (1992, 52). The problem, for her, is not only that feminists are out of touch with the realities of human nature, but that young women who believe them are failing to protect themselves against rape.

Paglia (1992, 304) defends her approach to date rape as one informed by studies of history and literature:

> My position on date rape is partly based on my study of *The Faerie Queene* . . . : In 1590, the poet Edmund Spenser already sees that passive, drippy, naïve women constantly get themselves into rape scenarios, while talented, intelligent, alert women, his warrior heroines, spot trouble coming or boldly trounce their male assailants. My feminism stresses courage, independence, self-reliance, and pride.

Judging from this statement, its author would make an effective advocate of martial arts and assertiveness training for women. However, despite her emphasis on courage and self-reliance, she ignores the advances in self-defense and rape prevention that feminists have made (see Chapter 2).

Paglia demonstrates her anthropological acumen, as well as her ignorance of the historical connection between race and rape, with the statement, "Notice it's not black or Hispanic women who are making a fuss about this—they come from cultures that are fully sexual and they are fully realistic about sex" (1992, 57). This presents a remarkable contrast to Paula Giddings's (1992) assertion, from the point of view of a black woman, that frank discussion of sexuality and sexual violence within the black community constitutes the "last taboo," the ultimate silence, among African Americans. Paglia's statement also fails to account for research that establishes the prevalence of rape among black women at about one in four (Wyatt 1992). Nonetheless, she quickly became popular with the media for her reactionary positions and outspokenness on such issues as rape, AIDS, homosexuality, and mass culture.[22]

Katie Roiphe joined the backlash in 1991. She emerged as the experienced voice of a recent Harvard graduate, a current graduate student at Princeton, and a firsthand witness to the supposed date rape hysteria on university campuses. Roiphe's first entry into the debate was a 1991 opinion piece for the *New York Times,* followed by a 1993 article in the *New York Times Magazine* and then a book, *The Morning After* (1994). She begins the 1993 article (which later appeared in her book), not surprisingly, by using anecdotal evidence to challenge the researcher Mary Koss's statistics on the prevalence of rape: "One in four college women has been the victim of rape or attempted rape. One in four. . . . If I was really standing in the middle of an 'epidemic,' a 'crisis'—if 25 percent of my women friends were really being raped—wouldn't I know it?" (Roiphe 1993, 27). She borrows from Neil Gilbert's (1991) undocumented study to call into question the validity of the 25 percent figure and the expanded understanding of rape that informed Koss's study. Roiphe claims an ability to see through these numbers that instill in young women a great fear that limits their sexual choices and, even worse, hearkens back to a Victorian prudery that focused more on the dangers of sexuality than on its joys. Feminists promote hysteria about this "rape crisis" to the detriment of young women, she says.

Roiphe places the blame for this problem squarely on the "rape crisis feminists": Naomi Wolf "uses rape as a red flag" to "rally the feminist troops" (1993, 28); Susan Estrich communicates her own belief that "women are often unwilling [sexual] participants" (1993, 29); and Catharine MacKinnon adopts the neo-Victorian "language of virtue and violation" that "reinforces retrograde stereotypes" (1993, 29). In her view, such feminists have replaced the traditional rape myths with a new one: the myth of innocence lost, which makes young women dwell on their violation and resultant trauma, to no useful purpose (1993, 30, 40). And, echoing Paglia, Roiphe asserts (1993, 40): "With their expansive version of rape, rape-crisis feminists are inventing a kinder, gentler sexuality. Beneath the broad definition of rape, these feminists are endorsing their own utopian vision of sexual relations: sex without struggle, sex without power, sex without persuasion, sex without pursuit." Like Paglia, Roiphe views the feminist efforts to change the relationship between the sexes—even in ways that make male-female relations more communicative—as a destructive public bad.

Further contributing to this body of backlash literature, Christina Hoff Sommers's 1994 book *Who Stole Feminism?* challenges various elements of feminist theory and women's studies scholarship, including the rape studies by Koss and others. Because Sommers attempts to address academic issues in feminism, her chapter on rape focuses more on research than on the overall campaign against it, although she does link the two. Sommers (1994, 208) begins her discussion with a disclaimer similar to Paglia's, asserting rape's grievous nature: "I apologize to the reader for the clinical tone of this chapter. As a crime against the person, rape is uniquely horrible in its long-term effects. . . . Yet, it remains clear that to arrive at intelligent policies and strategies to decrease the occurrence of rape, we have no alternative but to gather and analyze data, and to do so does not make us callous." Thus,

Sommers sets up her presentation as one that favors "intelligent" rape policies and the use of accurate statistics in guiding them. But she offers little new analysis: Sommers restates Gilbert's (1991) criticisms of Koss's one-in-four statistic, and Roiphe's agreement with his analysis. She questions Koss's (and others') methodology and use of "advocacy numbers," and makes much of the finding that a large percentage of respondents did not label an experience as rape (1994, 214, 217).

As for the problem of campus rape, Sommers finds that, despite the feminist clamor over high rates, fewer than one thousand rapes were reported to campus police throughout the United States in 1990 (1994, 218). Again like Roiphe, she views socioeconomic class and privilege as a main source of the date rape problem, and reiterates the commonly held belief that rape by a stranger is far worse than rape by an acquaintance. Citing feminist statements that the victim in a typical date rape scenario is harmed as much as someone raped by a stranger in the street, Sommers responds that "by such a definition, privileged young women in our nation's colleges gain moral parity with the *real* victims in the community at large. . . . After all, it is much more pleasant to deal with rape from an office in Princeton than on the streets of downtown Trenton" (1994, 220; emphasis added). So, the attention to campus rape comes only at the expense of rape programs located in the inner city. She uses this assertion to chide the writers of the VAWA, stating that Biden's bill would allocate twenty million dollars to programs dealing with campus rape to the detriment of more deserving rape crisis services (1994, 221). This outlay would also come at the expense of men who have been raped; Sommers claims that the problem of rape of male prisoners by other male prisoners might outweigh the problem of rape as women experience it every day (1994, 225). Feminists, she says, are impeding effective research and policy development on rape: "We need the truth for policy to be fair and effective. If the feminist advocates would stop muddying the waters we could probably get at it" (1994, 222). For Paglia, Roiphe, and Sommers, feminist advocates are part of the problem, not part of the solution. Their thinking reinforces myths about rape and seeks to halt the progress of the movement against it.

Organized Backlash

Beyond this vocal opposition to the anti-rape movement, women's organizations have lent their voices to a chorus that disdains both feminism and the feminist anti-rape effort. Unlike the movement organized to prevent the passage of the Nineteenth Amendment, the StopERA group founded by Phyllis Schlafly specifically to derail the ratification of the equal rights amendment, and the pro-life organizations dedicated to ending legal abortion, no single-issue movement has attempted to reverse or stall the success of the anti-rape campaign. But countermovement groups that have formed in recent years have spoken and written on the issue of rape and have expressed their opposition to policy programs that address violence against women and to how feminists have framed the problem. As with the writings and speeches of Paglia, Roiphe, and Sommers, these organizations have publicly opposed the substantive policy advances of the anti-rape movement and have attempted to interfere with its success.

One such group, the Women's Freedom Network (WFN), formed in 1993 by Rita Simon, professor of law, justice, and society at American University, addresses the issue of rape in its general criticisms of feminist politics. The WFN was founded, according to Simon, to provide a middle ground, or alternative, to the "extremism" of the organizations she perceives as the poles of the groups addressing women's issues: NOW on one side, Concerned Women for America and Schlafly's Eagle Forum on the other. Even though they represent only the extremes, these organizations are frequently portrayed in the media as representing women's views, Simon explains.[23]

Despite its ostensible devotion to middle-ground politics, the WFN's agenda primarily targets feminism and works to reverse or modify the gains made by the women's movement, including the anti-rape campaign's achievements for rape victims. For example, the group's statement of principles, outlined in the undated first issue of the *Women's Freedom Network Newsletter* (1994), declares:

> We reject the creeping paternalism that, under a feminist guise, portrays women as victims who are not responsible for their

behavior. Special protections in areas such as employment, child care, the justice system and personal relations minimize our accomplishments and undermine our equal status. The rhetoric of victimization trivializes real abuse, demeans women, and promotes antagonism instead of real partnerships between the sexes.

The WFN charges that feminist organizations and writers have too often cast women in the role of victim and men in the role of enemy (Simon 1995, vii–viii). Simon claims that anti-rape writers and activists excuse young women from taking responsibility for their sexual actions by allowing too many situations to be labeled as rape. These charges are levied at such diverse groups and individuals as NOW, Susan Estrich, Catharine MacKinnon, Carolyn Heilbrun, and the American Association of University Women (Simon 1995). In effect, the WFN has revived the specter of a young woman who "asks for it" by going on a date with a man or entering his apartment.

Cathy Young, the group's vice president and a columnist for the *Detroit News,* has made numerous statements that challenge the major efforts of the anti-rape movement. In one column (1996), Young remarks that she will no longer support any Republican member of Congress who voted for the VAWA because of her (and the WFN's) opposition to its funding of violence against women programs. Statements of this kind highlight the potential political power that an organized countermovement can wield.

Concerned Women for America (CWA), one of the most active and visible women's organizations seeking to restore traditional values to a society disturbed by feminism, was founded by Beverly LaHaye in 1979. She was already well known in evangelical Christian circles for co-authoring with her husband an explicit sex manual for Christian couples (Faludi 1991, 251). The CWA poses no immediate organized challenge to the anti-rape movement, but its overall agenda—a return to the traditional roles of mother and wife for women, a reversal of gains made in reproductive freedom, and other conservative goals—does threaten the larger women's movement. Because the CWA seeks to undermine nearly all the successes of the women's movement, which it views as having devastated American womanhood, anti-rape efforts cannot be considered immune from the group's political targeting. So long as activists advocate freedom from rape as one element of women's sexual freedom, policy initiatives directed against the problem of rape remain vulnerable to attack by right-wing groups such as the Concerned Women for America.

Implications of the Backlash

Even though the media attention to Paglia, the Women's Freedom Network, and other individuals and groups calls into question the entire project of redefining and understanding rape, it has coincided with a number of significant victories by the anti-rape movement. The most important and comprehensive piece of legislation dealing specifically with the crime—the VAWA—was passed in 1994 in the face of fervent attacks from conservatives. The anti-rape movement's success in gaining public funding for studies such as those by Koss marks a significant step in uncovering the actual numbers behind this social problem and in describing the reality behind the numbers. The studies of rape have, in turn, led to further organizing and policy refinements. And, in a victory of sorts, the most strident of the anti–anti-rape writers, Paglia, Roiphe, and Sommers, make sure to stress the urgency with which all "real" rape should be treated; this indicates at least a degree of consensus about the seriousness of some kinds of rape, one that did not exist before the anti-rape movement began to mobilize.

None of those who advance this backlash seem able to offer alternatives to the anti-rape campaign's goals and tactics. Peggy Sanday asks (1996, 263), if one is prohibited from analyzing sexual violence and gender simultaneously, as anti-rape activists have done, how might one attempt to analyze rape? Paglia, Sommers, Roiphe, and the Women's Freedom Network offer a wealth of criticism and a dearth of solutions. Paglia hints that promoting strength and courage may be an effective rape-prevention strategy, but she will not enlarge this point to include such productive ends as anti-rape projects that stress self-defense and that work to undo women's socialized passivity. The inevitable conclusion is that those who have joined in the backlash are less interested in mitigating the problem of rape (even when it is narrowly defined) than in derailing a movement that has elevated public consciousness of sexual assault.

The backlash has met with varied reactions from anti-rape activists. Certainly the rise of a concerted reaction may be interpreted as a sign of the movement's immense impact. As Jodi Gold, a student activist at the University of Pennsylvania, notes, "You don't get a backlash unless you've ruffled some feathers. It means we've really pushed the envelope and things are happening" (quoted in Pfister 1994, 13). Like the opposition to the ERA, which was not organized until Congress had submitted the amendment to the states, the backlash can be taken as a sign of progress, a mark of the success of the anti-rape movement.

But this phenomenon is having a deleterious effect on the campaign against rape insofar as it reverses the trend of recognizing sexual violence as a social problem or it transforms this attention into a preoccupation with baseless charges against the anti-rape movement and rape research. The feminist activist Gloria Dialectic points out that Katie Roiphe's book—written in an "illogical, unscholarly, rambling, smug style"—found favor with a major publisher, Little, Brown, which was obviously willing to publish a title with such sensationalistic potential. If such a book was directed toward a scholarly audience who could see through its illogic and misrepresentation of social science research, its impact would be minimal. But, says Dialectic (1995, 4), "We know that books like Roiphe's are not intended for the scholarly audience but for the general reading public. In the popular market, they cause damage by legitimizing disregard for necessary legislation, adequate funding of programs, and appropriate institutional response to victims, much less for radical changes in consciousness and behavior." This damage is not extensive enough to derail the entire anti-rape movement, but it does cast doubt upon the movement's agenda among the citizenry.

The history and politics of rape on the public agenda have proven to be a confluence of shifting meanings and evolving awareness. The subject no longer carries the taboo that it did in the 1960s, and it has been confronted, necessarily, at every level of policy making. The FBI's

Uniform Crime Reports indicate that notifying law enforcement officers about rape has generally increased since 1981, although the problems that existed with the *UCR* in the 1970s remain today: the FBI narrowly defines rape as forced heterosexual intercourse, and rapes that are not reported cannot be counted. Still, the bureau's figures do indicate that women are probably more likely to bring rape cases to the authorities now than they were in the 1960s (see Table 4.2).

Despite its failure to shock Americans any longer, the issue of rape continues to capture attention, even outside the context of highly sensationalized charges and trials. In 1990 Clayton Williams, running for the governorship of Texas, publicly quipped that bad weather was like rape: if you can't do anything about it, just relax and enjoy it. Feminists

Table 4.2 *FBI* Uniform Crime Reports, *Incidence of Rape, 1981–1998*

Year	Total Number of Rapes Reported	Number of Rapes per 100,000 Females
1981	81,536	69
1982	77,763	65
1983	78,918	66
1984	84,233	69
1985	87,340	71
1986	90,434	73
1987	91,111	73
1988	92,486	73
1989	94,504	75
1990	102,555	80
1991	106,593	83
1992	109,062	84
1993	104,806	79
1994	102,096	77
1995	97,464	72
1996	95,769	71
1997	96,122	70
1998	93,103	67

were outraged, the people did not believe Williams's rationalization that his comment was not intended for publication, and his opponent Ann Richards won the race for governor by a close margin. How much these words harmed his candidacy cannot be measured, but such crassness surely did not help it. When California's Disneyland chose to change its popular "Pirates of the Caribbean" attraction in January 1997, the rape issue emerged in yet another form. In the exhibit, mechanized pirates pillage the settlement where their ship has run aground, chasing the local women with the intent of raping them. The Disney corporation decided to equip the fleeing women with platters of food to give the impression that the pirates want only to eat, not to rape. This decision raised the issue of whether the theme park was giving in to the demands of "political correctness" or making a public statement opposing assaultive behavior (*Buffalo News* 1997). Such incidents keep rape on the public agenda at the dawn of the millennium, albeit in the context of a backlash all too willing to portray the issue as overblown.

Like other feminist concerns such as abortion, rape is on the public agenda to stay. The move toward a more nuanced discussion of the different kinds of rape has prompted news coverage, advanced research, and stimulated public interest. There have been similar developments at the university level, even though such changes affect only a small segment of the population. Unlike abortion, which incites more controversy than consensus, anti-rape policy making still enjoys much support among lawmakers and the public, abetted by a political climate that purports to be tough on crime. Anti-rape policies will continue to marshal widespread support into the twenty-first century.

5
CONCLUSIONS AND IMPLICATIONS

THIS BOOK HAS FOCUSED on the accomplishments of and controversies surrounding the anti-rape movement in the United States, attempting to demonstrate that the movement has resulted in public goods for women. The accomplishments are evident in the historical record, but even the most casual observer can note the impact of this movement on everyday life. Rape is now a topic of discussion in numerous public forums, from the Centers for Disease Control to Oprah Winfrey's talk show. Telephone numbers for crisis lines are routinely posted in campus buildings, hotel rooms, phone booths, and other public places. Episodic and thematic news stories on sexual assault are commonplace on the evening news. Rape victims now claim a range of options for dealing with their trauma. The anti-rape movement's loftiest goal, putting an end to rape as we know it during our lifetimes, has not been realized, but this elevation of public consciousness and the availability of options have fundamentally changed both the perception and the experience of sexual assault in the United States. Effectiveness measures put forth by social-movement scholars add further depth to our understanding of the impact of the anti-rape campaign.

Theorists have commented in various ways on how a social movement's relative success can be determined. The sociologist William Gamson postulates that a social-movement group's success can be understood as a set of outcomes that cluster around (1) the level of acceptance of a social-movement group by its antagonists, and (2) whether the movement's beneficiaries gain new advantages from the group's challenge (1975, 28–29).[1] Critics charge that Gamson's measure oversimplifies the questions of effectiveness and acceptance by not accounting for those groups whose goal is the collapse of the status quo, not acceptance into it (Handler 1978).

In response, the sociologist Suzanne Staggenborg (1995) suggests that these concepts of acceptance and new advantages be expanded to account for movement success in broadening the public agenda to include movement demands and the policy changes achieved. Drawing on the work of Paul Schumaker (1975) and Steven Buechler (1990), she identifies three categories of movement outcomes stemming from Gamson's original model: "(1) political and policy outcomes; (2) mobilization outcomes; and (3) cultural outcomes" (1995, 341). She thus proposes a broader view of social-movement success than a strict application of Gamson's model would produce. Based on her research on the socialist feminist Chicago Women's Liberation Union (CWLU) of the late 1960s and 1970s, Staggenborg has found that movement organizations may have long-term effects that radiate well beyond a group's demise, beyond the achievement of (or failure to achieve) revolutionary goals, and beyond the attainment of tangible policy advances. For Staggenborg, these findings confirm Buechler's (1990, 61) concept of the social movement community, through which communications networks are maintained and ideology and mobilization are continuous (Staggenborg 1995, 348). Such communities can keep the ideas and strategies of social movement groups alive, even after particular organizations have disappeared.

Staggenborg's elaboration of effectiveness measures permits a complex assessment of the effectiveness of the anti-rape movement. Advances such as reforms in criminal law, gains in funding for rape research and service providers, institutional reform on the local level, and passage of the comprehensive Violence Against Women Act represent major political and policy outcomes. These have been the most visible and concrete changes the movement has effected. The anti-rape campaign's mobilization outcomes include the diversity of organizations (e.g., rape crisis centers and coalitions) and the actions (e.g., take back the night) and strategies (e.g., self-defense training) employed by activists and the substantial growth in numbers of movement organizations and members. Last, the movement's cultural outcomes have been immense. It has virtually transformed public perceptions of rape and its victims. This is evident in the enormous amount of sympathetic media attention paid to rape throughout the movement's largest growth period (the 1970s), the recent surges in campus organizing and media attention to acquaintance rape, and the widespread availability and use of rape crisis services throughout the country. The importance of this outcome cannot be overstated: the way we, as a culture, understand rape today marks a radical break from the public consciousness of the late 1960s. By any measure, the effectiveness of the anti-rape campaign cannot be denied.

Rape Policy Analysis

In addition to considering the effectiveness of the effort against rape as a social movement, one can use policy analysis to understand better the reasons for advances in anti-rape policy. An important question policy analysts pose is, why does a particular policy initiative succeed or fail? In "A Framework for Policy Analysis," Ellen Boneparth (1982, 1–14) suggests a number of lenses through which policies can be examined and assessed. Three broad factors provide the context in which a policy can succeed or fail: environmental variables, which include social, economic, and political climates; systemic variables, most importantly in the United States the decentralized government and the necessity for incremental policy making; and political variables, such as lobbying, political coalitions, and governmental leadership. The foregoing chapters have explored each of these. First, the social, political, and economic climate of the 1960s helped give rise to the women's movement, whose political agenda came to include rape. The law-and-order climate of this period created a number of unusual allies for movement women seeking more just, pro-victim statutes for rape. Next, although the federal system, and the incrementalism it necessitates, has proven to be a major stumbling block to a comprehensive, cohesive rape policy that would be binding on all states, it has also proven responsive to many feminist demands for change. Finally, anti-rape activists were able to tap into the relatively new women's lobby for expertise on legislative matters, even though leadership from the legislative and executive branches of government was inconsistent. The social-movement atmosphere of the early 1970s further improved chances that policy makers would adopt a number of anti-rape goals as their own.

Theodore Lowi (1960) has suggested a policy typology that has proven useful, if not definitive, in analyzing the implications of various policy choices.[2] According to Lowi, distributive policies allocate resources to groups or people; regulatory policies regulate the treatment of people or groups by private concerns (such as industry) or by institutions; and redistributive policies move resources from one group to another. The amount of conflict that results from any given policy, in his view, is determined by where it falls within this typology: distributive policies will cause the least conflict, redistributive policies will cause the most.

Lowi's typology and prediction help to explain the apparent success of the anti-rape movement and the relatively low level of conflict generated by its initiatives. Anti-rape policies have generally fallen into the distributive and regulatory categories. Distributive rape policies include those designed to fund and support research and victim services. But most rape legislation has sought to regulate private behavior, as do most criminal statutes passed by state legislatures. Reformed rape laws did not create a new category of regulated behavior, but simply modified existing criminal categories. In addition, local policies regulate the treatment of rape victims by institutions such as police, hospitals, and prosecutors. True to Lowi's prediction, the regulatory policy initiatives related to rape have stirred up greater amounts of conflict than the distributive initiatives. This is particularly true of those that would require the criminal justice system and other institutions to take stranger, acquaintance, and spousal rape equally seriously. It is in this area that the greatest amount of work remains.

Future Research

Future researchers on anti-rape politics have a field that continues to be ripe for investigation. First, while social movements in general, and the women's movement in particular, have been examined extensively over the years, little focused attention has been paid to the emergence of what Jo Freeman (1995) calls submovements (although many social-movement commentators mention the rise of submovements to some extent). In the case of the women's movement, lists of its successes frequently mention the gains made by the women's health, anti-rape, and battered-women's submovements (Boneparth and Stoper 1988; Echols 1989; Hartmann 1989; Davis 1991). The time has come for a more sophisticated understanding of these spin-off efforts, one that accounts for their origins in and relationships to the larger movements while treating them as the largely self-reliant, unique entities they have become. I have argued in these pages that the campaign against rape, in its emergence and development, has resembled other social movements, but, because the issue of rape was never divorced from the feminist agenda, that campaign should not be considered an entirely independent social movement. Whether the anti-rape effort is considered as just one part of the women's movement or as an entity of its own will have implications for assessing the degree to which it can be considered successful. Refining the understanding of spin-off movements will improve the understanding of feminist and anti-rape politics.

There can be little doubt that the anti-rape movement brought about significant changes for victims who face the aftermath of rape. Where women once reported feeling raped a second time by institutional representatives, today police, hospital, and court procedures are far more likely to treat them in a sensitive and humane way, even though the charge of a "second rape" persists (Madigan and Gamble 1991). Nearly all victims are likely to have access to a rape crisis center that can offer immediate assistance as well as counseling and other follow-up care. Centers offer preventive and educational programs in an attempt to keep rape from occurring in the first place. Colleges and universities routinely present date rape seminars as part of first-year-student orientation. Moreover, victims who report their rapes to law enforcement today can expect their rape charges to be taken more seriously than ever before. This is a far cry from the hostility of police officers and hospital personnel described in the rape testimonials that began appearing in 1970. Such advances, I have noted, have proven to be no small feat.

Even with these accomplishments, however, the anti-rape movement has not fulfilled the revolutionary hopes of its earliest members. The political climates of the 1970s, 1980s, and 1990s required activists to make compromises in their ideological stances and in their radical goals to achieve pro-victim legislation, funding for rape crisis services, and other policy advances. Scholars have noted with regret the co-optation of the anti-rape movement (e.g., Echols 1989; Collins and Whalen 1989).

The public policy accomplishments of the campaign against rape have gone hand in hand with a tough-on-crime political agenda that views rape as just one of many heinous crimes requiring a strict and severe legal response. The law-and-order agenda took hold in the 1960s and early 1970s, a time of widespread challenge to authority by the student and antiwar movements, and the civil rights and black power movements. Fears of black criminality and underclass insurgency informed this agenda. Policy makers, wanting to appear tough on crime, saw the opportunity to support legislation being advanced by anti-rape activists as politically advantageous. Thus, political compromises with tough-on-crime legislators, coupled with the formalization and co-optation of anti-rape projects, have dulled the radical potential of the movement.

The most fundamental challenge posed by the anti-rape campaign, and its greatest innovation, has been the challenge to the existing sexual order, which, feminist activists and theorists agree, overempowers men as it strips women of sexual agency. For three decades, the movement has been calling into question the sexual entitlement of American men. The code of masculinity that confers sexual privileges upon men is the same code that lends credence to the rape myths that activists have sought to dispel: women invite rape, and if they don't want it they can resist. It is also this code that rewards men for sexual behavior that is punished in women. At its core, the anti-rape movement is a threat to the male right of sexual dominance. This radical shift in U.S. culture will not be accomplished in legislatures or state houses, and it requires that men become as vocal and persistent in the campaign against rape as women have been for decades.

The role of women of color has proved another contested issue. While this study has unearthed information on black women's participation in the anti-rape movement—a finding that contradicts assertions that black women refused to become involved—the record suggests that women of color had reason to distrust both the campaign against rape and the larger women's movement. This phenomenon, to be sure, is based on the anti-rape campaign's inability to issue an analysis of sexual violence that confronted in a complex way the differences between black and white women's experiences. Activists and writers were quick to assert that all women are equally subject to the risks of rape and its aftermath, an assertion that assumed uniformity of women's experiences. Loretta Ross (1982), though, points out that black women have never expected fair treatment from the criminal justice system, which they perceived as not only racist but sexist. Furthermore, bell hooks (1984) notes that a failure to analyze violence as grounded in multiple systems of domination—racism, classism, and sexism, among others—represents a failure to engage the tangled roots of violence in all women's lives. Thus, significant shortcomings mar the movement's successes, especially as it claims to represent all women.

Jo Freeman (1975, 6) precisely describes the position of anti-rape campaigners in her discussion of social movements in general:

> It is here that we encounter a paradox. Movements that conform themselves to the norms of behavior in order to participate successfully in political institutions often find themselves forsaking their major goals for social change. Long-range ideals are warped for the sake of short-range gains. But movements that hold steadfast to their radical goals and disdain political participation of any kind in an "evil" system often find themselves isolated in a splendid ideological purity which gains nothing for any one. They are paralyzed by their own fear of cooptation; and such paralysis is in turn the ultimate cooptation as inactive revolutionaries are a good deal more innocuous than active "reformists."

The successes of the anti-rape movement—although falling short of the early goals of complete societal transformation, and with major shortcomings involving race and class—were achieved in a political reality that demands compromise even as it accepts incremental social change. Participants in the movement who seek an end to rape— myself among them—can take up this challenge of further progress by casting a mindful eye toward this history and a hopeful eye toward the future.

Appendix 1

Time Line of Anti-Rape Events

1892   Ida B. Wells's pamphlet *Southern Horrors* protests the lynching of black men in the name of protecting white womanhood from rape

1955   Rape section of the Model Penal Code (MPC) first presented to the American Law Institute (ALI)

1962   ALI passes final draft of MPC, including provisions for graded offenses in rape statutes

1970   Susan Brownmiller's consciousness-raising group (West Village 1) initiates discussion of rape as a women's issue; rape arrives on the feminist agenda

1971   New York Radical Feminists (NYRF) holds first speak-out on rape. Some three hundred women attend, and forty give rape testimonies

       NYRF hosts rape conference as follow-up to speak-out

       Resolution 115, taking a general position against rape, passes at annual National Organization for Women (NOW) conference

       Formation of Bay Area Women Against Rape (BAWAR)

       Formation of Women's Anti-Rape Group, forerunner to the rape crisis center New York Women Against Rape (NYWAR)

       Formation of Los Angeles Anti-Rape Squad

1972   Feminists in Washington, D.C., meet to discuss rape project. Group goes on to plan for and establish the D.C. Rape Crisis Center (D.C. RCC) in the same year, the first such center offering a package of services to rape victims

1973   New York City announces formation of police department's
        Rape Investigation Unit, led by Lieutenant Julia Tucker

        Resolution 148, establishing the Rape Task Force (NOWRTF),
        passes at annual NOW conference; Mary Ann Largen elected
        coordinator

        Formation of Michigan Women's Task Force on Rape
        (MWTFR) to pursue rape law reform

        Women's Anti-Rape Coalition (WARC) formed in New York
        to work on repealing the statutory corroboration requirement
        and to raise public awareness of rape issue; declares August
        "rape prevention month"; coalition is invited to join Mayor's
        Task Force on Rape, formed by Mayor John Lindsay of New
        York City

        Sen. Charles Mathias (R-Md.) introduces S. 2422 in Congress,
        a bill to establish the National Center for the Prevention and
        Control of Rape within the National Institute of Mental
        Health; introduced in House by Rep. H. John Heinz III
        (R-Pa.)

1974   New York state legislature unanimously passes—and Gover-
        nor Malcolm Wilson signs—bill to repeal statutory corrobora-
        tion requirement for rape cases

        Rape of Inez Garcia in Soledad, Calif.

        Resolution 20, proposing model rape law prepared by NOW-
        RTF, passes at NOW conference; conference sponsors two
        rape workshops

        Governor William Milliken of Michigan signs landmark crim-
        inal sexual conduct statute into law; first comprehensive state
        rape reform. Based on model law designed by MWTFR

        Joann Little kills rapist/jailer Clarence Alligood in self-defense
        in Beaufort County, N.C., jail

Formation of Feminist Alliance Against Rape in Washington, D.C., as a coalition of anti-rape projects

Rape of singer Connie Francis in room of New York Howard Johnson's Motor Lodge

1975   Supreme Court hands down decision in *Cox Broadcasting Corporation v. Cohn*

Passage of federal law creating National Center for the Prevention and Control of Rape, after presidential veto and congressional override

NOW holds nationwide events to reclaim the night and the public streets for women, a forerunner of take back the night

Publication of Susan Brownmiller's *Against Our Will*

1976   Rep. Elizabeth Holtzman (D-N.Y.) introduces Privacy Protection for Rape Victims bill in Congress; introduced by Sen. Lloyd Bentsen (D-Tex.) in Senate

Nebraska becomes first state to expand rape law to include spousal rape

1977   The Kitty Genovese Women's Project publishes list of all men indicted for sex offenses since 1960 in Dallas County, Tex.

Protesters in Madison, Wis., achieve a recall of Judge Archie Simonson, who opined from the bench that a fifteen-year-old boy convicted of raping a schoolmate was simply reacting "normally" to relaxed cultural attitudes about sex and revealing clothing for women. Judge Moria Krueger replaces Simonson

Supreme Court rules capital punishment for rape unconstitutional in *Coker v. Georgia*

Special one-hour episode of *All in the Family* depicts attempted rape of beloved Edith Bunker

Delegates to the first National Women's Conference in Houston adopt rape resolution

1978   Founding of National Coalition Against Sexual Assault (NCASA)

Passage of federal Privacy Protection for Rape Victims Act

John Rideout found not guilty of raping wife, Greta, in Oregon, a high-profile case prosecuted under new state law eliminating spousal exemption from rape charges

1979   First NCASA conference held in Lake Geneva, Wis.

1980   D.C. RCC sponsors National Conference on Third World Women and Violence, the first of its kind in the nation

1981   Supreme Court upholds California's statutory rape law, which applies only to male offenders, in *Michael M. v. Superior Court*

1982   The National Coalition Against Domestic Violence joins FAAR and the Alliance Against Sexual Coercion (one of the first anti–sexual harassment organizations) in producing *Aegis: Magazine on Ending Violence Against Women,* formerly the *Feminist Alliance Against Rape Newsletter*

1983   Nationally reported gang rape of twenty-one-year-old woman at Big Dan's Tavern in New Bedford, Mass.

1984   Rep. Steny Hoyer (D-Md.) introduces Sexual Assault bill in House

Four of six men prosecuted for gang rape at Big Dan's Tavern are convicted of aggravated rape

1986   Passage of federal Sexual Abuse Act (Hoyer's Sexual Assault bill)

1989   NOW's Expanded Bill of Rights for the Twenty-First Century endorses "the right to be free from violence"

Supreme Court upholds the press's right to print public information—including rape victims' names—in *Florida Star v. B.J.F.*

Central Park jogger rape case makes headlines

1990   Sen. Joseph Biden (D-Del.) introduces Violence Against Women Act (VAWA) as part of crime bill package in Congress

NYWAR, Manhattan's leading rape crisis center, closes its doors

Stephanie Gutmann's article " 'It Sounds Like I Raped You!' " appears in *Reason,* kicking off the anti–anti-rape backlash

1991   Judicial Conference of the United States and American Civil Liberties Union publicly express opposition to the VAWA

Formal charges of sexual battery (rape) brought against William Kennedy Smith in Palm Beach, Florida

Supreme Court supports state's rape shield law in *Michigan v. Lucas*

1992   Antioch College adopts sexual assault policy requiring students to obtain partner's consent at every stage of a sexual encounter

Conviction of Mike Tyson for rape of Desiree Washington in Indianapolis

Students Together Against Acquaintance Rape (STAAR) at the University of Pennsylvania hosts the First National Student Conference on Campus Sexual Violence

1993   Backlash article "Date Rape's Other Victim," by Katie Roiphe, appears in *New York Times Magazine*

1994   Passage of federal VAWA as part of Violent Crime Control and Law Enforcement Act

1995   Violence Against Women Office opens within U.S. Department of Justice. Bonnie Campbell, former attorney general of Iowa, appointed director

1996   U.S. District Court judge Janet Bond Arterton in Connecticut upholds constitutionality of VAWA

Jackson Kiser, Chief U.S. District Judge, rules VAWA unconstitutional

1997   Supreme Court defines rape by a governmental official as a violation of the Fourteenth Amendment's due process guarantee in *United States v. Lanier*

Sergeant Major Gene McKinney, the army's top enlisted man, is charged with sexual misconduct one day after Staff Sergeant Delmar Simpson is sentenced to twenty-five years in prison for raping female trainees

1998   In a trial of Rwandan authorities accused of war crimes, a United Nations tribunal declares rape a crime of genocide. This is the first time such a designation is made

Gene McKinney is cleared of sexual misconduct charges

1999   Supreme Court places on its docket a case challenging the constitutionality of the Violence Against Women Act. Oral arguments are held January 2000

Appendix 2

Bylaws of the Rape Crisis Center, Washington, D.C.

The Rape Crisis Center is a voluntary association of women to provide necessary assistance to rape victims and victims of sexual attacks, and to provide the community with information on rape.

Article 1: Membership. Membership in the Center is open to all women who have been involved in the Center's activities. All members are expected to share in the responsibilities pertaining to the Center's continuing activities.

Article 2: Meetings. The Center will hold weekly meetings which are open to all members. All policy decisions are to be made by the members present at the general meeting at which the decision is to be made. Minutes of the meetings will be taken at every meeting and distributed at the following meeting. This responsibility will rotate among members.

Article 3: Finances. Book-keeping responsibility will be shared by those women who are empowered to sign checks. Women in the Center who accept speaking engagements on rape are expected to contribute their speaking fees to the Center.

Article 4: Functions of the Center

    a. Emergency phone service: provides immediate contact and information to women who have been raped or attacked.

    b. Discussion groups: Groups of 5–10 women will be formed to discuss their reactions to the rape or the attack and how they feel they can resolve these feelings.

    d. [*sic*] Escort service to the police or hospital.

    e. Emergency housing.

    f. Publication and dissemination of information.

Article 5: Revision of Bylaws. Bylaws can be revised by a majority of the members present at the meeting following the proposed revision.

ADOPTED 24 MAY 1972

Appendix 3

Rape Prevention and Control Act of 1975

[Title Ii, Part D, Health Services Act]

Public Law 94-63
89 Stat. 328
94th Congress—1st Session
29 July 1975

SEC. 231. (a) The Secretary shall establish within the National Institute of Mental Health an identifiable administrative unit to be known as the National Center for the Prevention and Control of Rape (hereinafter in this section referred to as the "Center").

    (b) (1) The Secretary, acting through the Center, may, directly or by grant, carry out the following:

      (A) A continuing study of rape, including a study and investigation of—

        (i)   the effectiveness of existing Federal, State, and local laws dealing with rape;

        (ii) the relationship, if any, between traditional legal and social attitudes toward sexual roles, the act of rape, and the formulation of laws dealing with rape;

        (iii) the treatment of the victims of rape by law enforcement agencies, hospitals or other medical institutions, prosecutors, and the courts;

        (iv) the causes of rape, identifying to the degree possible—

           (I) social conditions which encourage sexual attacks, and

           (II) the motives of offenders, and

        (v) the impact of rape on the victim and the family of the victim;

(vi)   sexual assaults in correctional institutions;

(vii) the effectiveness of existing private and local and State government educational, counseling, and other programs designed to prevent and control rape.

(B)   The compilation, analysis, and publication of summaries of the continuing study conducted under subparagraph (A) and the research and demonstration projects conducted under subparagraph (E). The Secretary shall annually submit to the Congress a summary of such study and projects together with recommendations where appropriate.

(C)   The development and maintenance of an information clearinghouse with regard to—

(i)   the prevention and control of rape;

(ii)   the treatment and counseling of the victims of rape and their families; and

(iii) the rehabilitation of offenders.

(D)   The compilation and publication of training materials for personnel who are engaged or intend to engage in programs designed to prevent and control rape.

(E)   Assistance to community mental health centers and other qualified public and nonprofit private entities in conducting research and demonstration projects concerning the prevention and control of rape, including projects—

(i)   for the planning, developing, implementing, and evaluating of alternative methods used in the prevention and control of rape, the treatment and counseling of the victims of rape and their families, and the rehabilitation of offenders;

(ii)   for the application of such alternative methods; and

(iii) for the promotion of community awareness of the specific locations in which, and the specific social and other conditions under which, sexual attacks are most likely to occur.

(F) Assistance to community mental health centers in meeting
the costs of providing consultation and education services
respecting rape.

(2) For purposes of this subsection, the term "rape" includes statutory and attempted rape and any other criminal sexual assault (whether homosexual or heterosexual) which involves
force or the threat of force.

(c) The Secretary shall appoint an advisory committee to advise,
consult with, and make recommendations to him on the implementation of subsection (b). The Secretary shall appoint to such
committee persons who are particularly qualified to assist in carrying out the functions of the committee. Members of the advisory committee shall receive compensation at rates, not to exceed
the daily equivalent of the annual rate in effect for grade GS-18
of the General Sechedule, for each day (including traveltime)
they are engaged in the performance of their duties as members
of the advisory committee and, while so serving away from their
homes or regular places of business, each member shall be allowed travel expenses, including per diem in lieu of subsistence,
in the same manner as authorized by section 5703 of title 5,
United States Code, for persons in Government service employed intermittently.

(d) For the purposes of carrying out subsection (b), there are authorized to be appropriated $7,000,000 for fiscal year 1976, and
$10,000,000 for fiscal year 1977.

[. . .]

Appendix 4

Privacy Protection for Rape Victims Act of 1978

Public Law 95-540
92 Stat. 2046
95th Congress—2nd Session
28 October 1978

AN ACT

To amend the Federal Rules of Evidence to provide for the protection of the privacy of rape victims.

[. . .]

SEC. 2. (a) Article IV of the Federal Rules of Evidence is amended by adding at the end thereof the following new rule:

RULE 412. RAPE CASES; RELEVANCE OF VICTIM'S PAST BEHAVIOR

(a) Notwithstanding any other provision of law, in a criminal case in which a person is accused of rape or of assault with intent to commit rape, reputation or opinion evidence of the past sexual behavior of an alleged victim of such rape or assault is not admissible.

(b) Notwithstanding any other provision of law, in a criminal case in which a person is accused of rape or of assault with intent to commit rape, evidence of a victim's past sexual behavior other than reputation or opinion evidence is also not admissible, unless such evidence other than reputation or opinion evidence is—

   (1) admitted in accordance with subdivisions (c) (1) and (c) (2) and is constitutionally required to be admitted; or

(2) admitted in accordance with subdivision (c) and is evidence of—

  (A) past sexual behavior with persons other than the accused, offered by the accused upon the issue of whether the accused was or was not, with respect to the alleged victim, the source of semen or injury; or

  (B) past sexual behavior with the accused and is offered by the accused upon the issue of whether the alleged victim consented to the sexual behavior with respect to which rape or assault is alleged.

(c) (1) If the person accused of committing rape or assault with intent to commit rape intends to offer under subdivision (b) evidence of specific instances of the alleged victim's past sexual behavior, the accused shall make a written motion to offer such evidence not later than fifteen days before the date on which the trial in which such evidence is to be offered is scheduled to begin, except that the court may allow the motion to be made at a later date, including during trial, if the court determines either that the evidence is newly discovered and could not have been obtained earlier through the exercise of due diligence or that the issue to which such evidence relates has newly arisen in the case. Any motion made under this paragraph shall be served on all other parties and on the alleged victim.

(2) The motion described in paragraph (1) shall be accompanied by a written offer of proof. If the court determines that the offer of proof contains evidence described in subdivision (b), the court shall order a hearing in chambers to determine if such evidence is admissible. At such hearing the parties may call witnesses, including the alleged victim, and offer relevant evidence. Notwithstanding subdivision (b) of rule 104, if the relevancy of the evidence which the accused seeks to offer in trial depends upon the fulfillment of a condition of fact, the court, at the hearing in chambers or at a subsequent hearing in chambers scheduled for such

purpose, shall accept evidence on the issue of whether such condition of fact is fulfilled and shall determine such issue.

(3) If the court determines on the basis of the hearing described in paragraph (2) that the evidence which the accused seeks to offer is relevant and that the probative value of such evidence outweighs the danger of unfair prejudice, such evidence shall be admissible in the trial to the extent an order made by the court specifies evidence which may be offered and areas with respect to which the alleged victim may be examined or cross-examined.

(d) For purposes of this rule, the term "past sexual behavior" means sexual behavior other than the sexual behavior with respect to which rape or assault with intent to commit rape is alleged.

[. . .]

Appendix 5

Sexual Abuse Act of 1986

Public Law 99-654
100 Stat. 3660
99th Congress—2d Session
14 November 1986

AN ACT

To amend title 18, United States Code, with respect to sexual abuse.

[. . .]

Title 18, United States Code, is amended by inserting after chapter 109 the following new chapter:

CHAPTER 109A—SEXUAL ABUSE

[. . .]

§ 2241. Aggravated sexual abuse.
  (a) BY FORCE OR THREAT.—Whoever, in the special maritime and territorial jurisdiction of the United States or in a Federal prison, knowingly causes another person to engage in a sexual act—
    (1) by using force against that other person; or
    (2) by threatening or placing that other person in fear that any person will be subjected to death, serious bodily injury, or kidnapping;
    or attempts to do so, shall be fined under this title, imprisoned for any term of years or life, or both.

(b) BY OTHER MEANS.—Whoever, in the special maritime and territorial jurisdiction of the United States or in a Federal prison, knowingly—

    (1) renders another person unconscious and thereby engages in a sexual act with that other person; or

    (2) administers to another person by force or threat of force, or without the knowledge or permission of that person, a drug, intoxicant, or other similar substance and thereby—

        (A) substantially impairs the ability of that other person to appraise or control conduct; and

        (B) engages in a sexual act with that other person;

or attempts to do so, shall be fined under this title, imprisoned for any term of years or life, or both.

[. . .]

§ 2242. Sexual abuse.

Whoever, in the special maritime and territorial jurisdiction of the United States or in a Federal prison, knowingly—

    (1) causes another person to engage in a sexual act by threatening or placing that other person in fear (other than by threatening or placing that other person in fear that any person will be subjected to death, serious bodily injury, or kidnapping); or

    (2) engages in a sexual act with another person if that other person is—

        (A) incapable of appraising the nature of the conduct; or

        (B) physically incapable of declining participation in, or communicating unwillingness to engage in, that sexual act;

or attempts to do so, shall be fined under this title, imprisoned not more than 20 years, or both.

[. . .]

§ 2244. Abusive sexual contact.

(a) SEXUAL CONDUCT IN CIRCUMSTANCES WHERE SEXUAL ACTS ARE PUNISHED BY THIS CHAPTER.—Whoever, in the special maritime and territorial jurisdiction of the United States or in a Federal prison, knowingly engages in or causes sexual contact with or by another person, if so to do would violate—

(1) section 2241 of this title had the sexual contact been a sexual act, shall be fined under this title, imprisoned not more than five years, or both;

(2) section 2242 of this title had the sexual contact been a sexual act, shall be fined under this title, imprisoned not more than three years, or both;

[. . .]

(b) IN OTHER CIRCUMSTANCES.—Whoever, in the special maritime and territorial jurisdiction of the United States or in a Federal prison, knowingly engages in sexual contact with another person without that other person's permission shall be fined not more than $5,000, imprisoned not more than six months, or both.

§ 2245 Definitions for chapter.

As used in this chapter—

(1) the term "prison" means a correctional, detention, or penal facility;

(2) the term "sexual act" means—

(A) contact between the penis and the vulva or the penis and the anus, and for purposes of this subparagraph contact involving the penis occurs upon penetration, however slight;

(B) contact between the mouth and the penis, the mouth and the vulva, or the mouth and the anus; or

(C) the penetration, however slight, of the anal or genital opening of another by a hand or finger or by any object, with an intent to abuse, humiliate, harass, degrade, or arouse or gratify the sexual desire of any person; and

(3) the term "sexual contact" means the intentional touching, either directly or through the clothing, of the genitalia,

anus, groin, breast, inner thigh, or buttocks of any person with an intent to abuse, humiliate, harass, degrade, or arouse or gratify the sexual desire of any person;

(4) the term "serious bodily injury" means bodily injury that involves a substantial risk of death, unconsciousness, extreme physical pain, protracted and obvious disfigurement, or protracted loss or impairment of the function of a bodily member, organ, or mental faculty.

(5) the term "official detention" means—

(A) detention by a Federal officer or employee, or under the direction of a Federal officer or employee, following arrest for an offense; following surrender in lieu of arrest for an offense; following a charge or conviction of an offense, or an allegation or finding of juvenile delinquency; following commitment as a material witness; following civil commitment in lieu of criminal proceedings or pending resumption of criminal proceedings that are being held in abeyance, or pending extradition, deportation, or exclusion; or

(B) custody by a Federal officer or employee, or under the direction of a Federal officer or employee, for purposes incident to any detention described in subparagraph (A) of this paragraph, including transportation, medical diagnosis or treatment, court appearance, work, and recreation;

but does not include supervision or other control (other than custody during specified hours or days) after release following a finding of juvenile delinquency.

SEC. 3. CONFORMING AND RELATED AMENDMENTS

(a) OTHER TITLE 18 AMENDMENT.—Title 18, United States Code, is amended—

(1) by striking out chapter 99;

(2) in subsection (a) of section 113 by striking out "or rape";

in subsection (b) of section 113 by striking out "rape" and inserting in lieu thereof "a felony under chapter 109A";

(4) in subsection (a) of section 1111 by striking out "rape" and inserting in lieu thereof "aggravated sexual abuse or sexual abuse."

[. . .]

SEC. 4. EFFECTIVE DATE

This Act and the amendments made by this Act shall take effect 30 days after the date of the enactment of this Act.

Appendix 6

Violence Against Women Act of 1994, Summary

Congressional Information Service, Inc.
94 CIS PL 103322; 103 CIS Legis. Hist. P.L. 322
LEGISLATIVE HISTORY OF: P.L. 103-322
TITLE: Violent Crime Control and Law Enforcement Act of 1994
DATE: Sept. 13, 1994
LENGTH: 356 p.
ENACTED-BILL: 103 H.R. 3355 Retrieve Bill Tracking report
STAT: 108 Stat. 1796
CONG-SESS: 103-2
ITEM No: 575

"To control and prevent crime."

[...]

TITLE IV, THE VIOLENCE AGAINST WOMEN ACT OF 1994

Revises and expands protections for women against violent crime.

Directs the U.S. Sentencing Commission to promulgate revised sentencing guidelines for sex crime offenders, and mandates financial restitution to victims by offenders.

Authorizes Department of Justice grants to States and local governments for law enforcement, prosecution, and victim services in violent crimes against women.

Authorizes DOT [Department of Transportation] grants for capital improvements to prevent crimes in public transit systems and other grants to reduce crime in public parks.

Amends the Federal Rules of Evidence pertaining to sexual assault cases.

Amends the Public Health and Human Services Act to authorize State use of certain funds for rape prevention and education programs.

Amends the Runaway and Homeless Youth Act to authorize grants for runaway, homeless, and street youth who have been subjected to or are at risk of being subjected to sexual abuse.

Authorizes various programs under the Victims of Child Abuse Act of 1990.

Amends the Family Violence Prevention and Services Act to authorize an HHS [Department of Health and Human Services] national domestic violence telephone hotline.

Establishes criminal penalties for crossing State lines to commit domestic violence or violate protection orders.

Authorizes appropriations for grants for battered women's shelters, community programs on domestic violence, and rural domestic violence and child abuse enforcement.

Establishes a civil rights cause of action for civil suits against persons who commit sexual assault and other gender-motivated crimes.

Authorizes State Justice Institute grants for education and training of Federal and State judges and court personnel on topics pertaining to violent crimes against women.

Amends the Immigration and Nationality Act to authorize certain aliens suffering spousal abuse to petition for change of immigration status.

Title IV, subtitle A, is cited as the Safe Streets for Women Act of 1994; subtitle B, as the Safe Homes for Women Act of 1994; subtitle C, as the Civil Rights Remedies for Gender-Motivated Violence Act; and subtitle D, as the Equal Justice for Women in the Courts Act of 1994.

[...]

Appendix 7

Advisory Council on Violence Against Women

Co-Chairs

Hon. Janet Reno

Hon. Donna Shalala

Members

Gail Abarbanel

Michael P. Barnes

Larry A. Bedard, M.D.

Carl C. Bell, M.D.

Alana Bowman

Reginald K. Brack, Jr.

Sarah M. Buel

Lem Burnham, Ph.D.

Hon. Karen Burnstein

Hon. Jane Campbell (D-Ohio)

Carol A. Cartwright, Ph.D.

Jerome A. Chazen

Vicki Coffey

Ellen R. Cohen

Carl Cohn

Catherine O'Reilly Collette

Susan Dey

Linda A. Fairstein

Rev. Marie M. Fortune, Ph.D.

Linda Gordon, Ph.D.

Kathryn Walt Hall

Hon. Scott Harshbarger

Robin S. Hassler

Hon. Paul Helmke

Joan A. Kuriansky

Joyce Ladner, Ph.D.

Eppie Lederer (Ann Landers)

Hon. Cindy Lederman

Wilma P. Mankiller

Robert E. McAfee, M.D.

Helen R. Neuborne

Brian Kenji Ogawa, Ph.D.

Ruben B. Ortega

Hon. Vincent James Poppiti

Roberta Cooper Ramo

Judy Rex

Jerome R. Rossi

Susan Schechter

Esta Soler

Norm H. Stamper, Ph.D.

Diane Stuart

Louis W. Sullivan, M.D.

Susan L. Taylor

Sara Torres, R.N., Ph.D.

Marvin L. Van Haaften

Rosalyn Weinman, Ph.D.

Sheila Wellstone

Ex-Officio Members

Susan J. Blumenthal, M.D.

Joseph E. Brann
Hon. Bonnie J. Campbell
Peter B. Edelman

Appendix 8

Drug-Induced Rape Prevention and Control Act of 1996

Public Law 104-305
110 Stat. 3807
104th Congress—2nd Session
13 October 1996

Synopsis: An Act to combat drug-facilitated crimes of violence, including sexual assaults.

[. . .]

SEC. 2. PROVISION RELATING TO USE OF A CONTROLLED SUBSTANCE
WITH INTENT TO COMMIT A CRIME OF VIOLENCE

(a) PENALTIES FOR DISTRIBUTION—Section 401(b) of the Controlled Substances Act is amended by adding at the end the following:

. . . (A) IN GENERAL—Whoever, with intent to commit a crime of violence, as defined in section 16 of title 18, United States Code (including rape), against an individual, violates subsection (a) by distributing a controlled substance to that individual without that individual's knowledge, shall be imprisoned not more than 20 years and fined in accordance with title 18, United States Code.

(B) DEFINITION—For purposes of this paragraph, the term "without that individual's knowledge" means that the individual is unaware that a substance with the ability to alter that individual's ability to appraise conduct or to decline participation in or communicate unwillingness to participate in conduct is administered to the individual.

(b) ADDITIONAL PENALTIES RELATING TO FLUNITRAZEPAM—

(1) GENERAL PENALTIES—Section 401 of the Controlled Substances Act (21 U.S.C. 841) is amended. . . .

(3) SENTENCING GUIDELINES—

(A) AMENDMENT OF SENTENCING GUIDELINES—Pursuant to its authority under section 994 of title 28, United States Code, the United States Sentencing Commission shall review and amend, as appropriate, the sentencing guidelines for offenses involving flunitrazepam. . . .

(c) INCREASED PENALTIES FOR UNLAWFUL SIMPLE POSSESSION OF FLUNITRAZEPAM—Section 404(a) of the Controlled Substances Act (21 U.S.C. 844(a)) is amended by inserting "exceeds 1 gram" in the following: "Notwithstanding any penalty provided in this subsection, any person convicted under this subsection for the possession of fluni-trazepam shall be imprisoned for not more than 3 years, shall be fined as otherwise provided in this section, or both."

SEC. 3. STUDY ON RESCHEDULING FLUNITRAZEPAM

(a) STUDY—The Administrator of the Drug Enforcement Adminis-tration shall, in consultation with other Federal and State Agencies, as appropriate, conduct a study on the appropriateness and desirability of rescheduling flunitrazepam as a Schedule I controlled substance under the Controlled Substances Act (21 U.S.C. 801 et seq.).

(b) REPORT—Not later than 180 days after the date of the enactment of this Act, the Administrator shall submit to the Committees of the Judi-ciary of the House of Representatives and the Senate the results of the study conducted under subsection (a), together with any recommenda-tions regarding rescheduling of flunitrazepam as a Schedule I controlled substance under the Controlled Substances Act (21 U.S.C. 801 et seq.).

SEC. 4. EDUCATIONAL PROGRAM FOR POLICE DEPARTMENTS

The Attorney General may—

(1) Create educational material regarding the use of controlled substances (as that term is defined in section 102 of the Controlled Substances Act) in the furtherance of rapes and sexual assaults; and

(2) Disseminate those materials to police departments throughout the United States

[. . .]

Notes

Introduction

1. Despite the growing body of literature on rape (e.g., Burgess and Holmstrom 1974; Russell 1975; Brownmiller 1975; Russell 1984; MacKinnon 1987; Sanday 1990; Koss and Harvey 1991; Francis 1996; McCaughey 1997), a comprehensive historical exploration of its development as an issue within the women's movement has not yet been conducted. Even those studies that attempt to present the background of the anti-rape movement provide little comprehensive data on the movement in its entirety and tend to focus on a single trend, such as rape crisis center development, rape law reform, or developments in rape theory (Marsh, Geist, and Caplan 1982; Estrich 1987; MacKinnon 1989; Matthews 1994; Sanday 1996). Furthermore, in spite of excellent accounts of the growth and contributions of the women's movement and trends within it (Freeman 1975; Ruzek 1978; Evans 1979; Ferree and Hess 1985; Echols 1989; Davis 1991; Woliver 1993; McGlen and O'Connor 1995), the anti-rape movement is devoid of a research tradition that traces its development from the beginnings of contemporary feminism until the present.

2. *Incidence* refers to the number of new rapes occurring within a specified period, usually one year. *Prevalence* refers to the percentage of persons who have been raped at any time during their lives (Koss 1992, 62).

3. The methods of various national surveys for rape victimization, and their resultant estimates, are reviewed in Lynch (1996). The NCVS has been redesigned in an attempt to represent the incidence of rape more accurately. See U.S. Department of Justice (1994b).

4. Translated into an incidence rate for the twelve months (1978) before the survey, Russell's study found 2,688 attempted or completed rapes per 100,000 women.

5. Koss (1993) points out that other studies have revealed contrasting prevalence rates, and reviews the major methodological differences that account for the discrepancies.

6. The backlash introduced here, of which Roiphe's writings are just one element, is discussed at greater length in Chapter 4.

7. The law professor Susan Estrich (1987, 81) objects to the replacement of *rape* with words such as *assault* in law codes on the grounds that these other words "may obscure [rape's] unique indignity." The term *anti-rape movement* has been in circulation for quite some time. For example, the Feminist Alliance Against Rape, formed in 1974, viewed itself as a "movement" made up of anti-rape projects. Among others, the theorist Angela Y. Davis (1983, 172–202) uses the term "antirape movement," and the sociolo-

gist Nancy Matthews refers to the "anti-rape movement" in her book on this subject (1994). The term *survivor* is currently more popular in rape crisis centers than is *victim,* which has connotations that may be construed as excessively negative or disempowering to women. This book views the survivor as someone who goes through a lengthy, often difficult, process of transformation. As Koss and Harvey (1991, ix) remark, "The survivor is the victim who has not only endured, but who has prevailed and who has rebuilt the meaning shattered by rape." Finally, some observers have argued that the feminist movement of recent years is distinct from that of the 1970s, and thus merits consideration as a "third wave" of feminism. See Findlen (1995) and Walker (1995).

8. Nearly all of the activists I interviewed for this book expressed delight that a researcher was interested in the history of the movement and insisted that such a project would be useful to the anti-rape campaigners of today.

9. Feminist content analysis, oral history, and interviewing methods are reviewed in Reinharz (1992).

10. Brownmiller and Craft sent me papers they thought relevant to my research.

Chapter 1

1. This is not to suggest that nineteenth- and early-twentieth-century activists, including Wells, used or did not use the term *feminist* to describe themselves or their activism. Indeed, black feminist authors have claimed the work of Wells and other black women activists and writers of the earlier era as feminist in recent years (Guy-Sheftall 1995, xiv).

2. Early financial support for the *Revolution* was provided by George Francis Train, a controversial Democrat well known for his virulent racism.

3. I borrow the term *controlling image* from Patricia Hill Collins (1991). The ideological power of controlling images, loosely defined as negative stereotypes, joins with economic exploitation and political subordination to operate as a "highly effective system of social control designed to keep African-American women in an assigned, subordinate place" (Collins 1991, 7).

4. The statutes prohibiting miscegenation have been traced to the colonial period—the first such laws went into effect in Maryland in 1661 and Virginia in 1691. States continued to adopt them throughout the eighteenth century. By 1932, thirty states prohibited miscegenation (Brownfeld 1965, 52). The laws endured until the 1967 Supreme Court decision in *Loving v. Virginia.* Indeed, in that year sixteen states had still refused to repeal their miscegenation statutes (Porterfield 1978, 29). See also Washington (1993).

5. The historian Darlene Clark Hine theorizes that black women also coped through "a cult of secrecy, a culture of dissemblance" by which they hid the truth of their sexual exploitation from themselves and from the rest of society (Hine 1989, 915). She suggests that it was imperative that black women "collectively create alternative self-images and shield from scrutiny these private, empowering definitions of self" (Hine 1989, 916). The escape from

situations of sexual terror, in her view, was at least as important to black women's northward migration patterns around 1900 as was the opportunity for better jobs and pay (Hine 1989, 913). Hine characterizes her hypothesis of a culture of dissemblance as a "preliminary thought" awaiting further research and elaboration.

6. For more thorough coverage of the history and activities of the women's movement than this summary provides, see, among others, Hole and Levine (1971), Evans (1979), McGlen and O'Connor (1983), Giddings (1984), Klein (1984), Ferree and Hess (1985), Echols (1989), Buechler (1990), Davis (1991), Costain (1992), and Ryan (1992). Some observers argue that the branches described here have merged substantially since the emergence of the second wave (Carden 1977; Ferree and Hess 1985; Freeman 1995).

7. The view of women's place in the civil rights movement as a slight modification of the traditional feminine role is put forth by, among others, Sara Evans (1979). By contrast, in her book *Freedom Song* (1987), Mary King describes women's experiences as organizers for the Student Nonviolent Coordinating Committee (SNCC) quite differently. King, herself a SNCC organizer and the co-author of two famous position papers from 1964 and 1965 about the position of women in the radical civil rights group, asserts that "by and large, [SNCC] was peopled by women"; in her view, accounts such as Evans's that focus only on women's prescribed roles "bel[ie] the seriousness and earnestness with which women in SNCC were involved and den[y] the important debate within SNCC that gave rise to our two documents" (King 1987, 459). King offers a more complex view of the statements she wrote with Casey Hayden in response to discussions within SNCC about its future, the role of whites in the group, and the meaning of SNCC's embrace of democracy and decentralized leadership. But she acknowledges that many radical feminists trace their involvement in the women's movement directly to their exposure to the ideas presented by King and Hayden in their 1965 paper (King 1987, 466-67).

8. For thorough coverage of the divisiveness within the radical groups, see Freeman (1975), Willis (1984), and Echols (1989). They detail major differences within this branch of the movement, such as the split between "feminists" and "politicos," the gay/straight issue, and conflicts over strategy.

9. Resolution 115 reads: "*Whereas,* rape victims meet with disbelief and/or derision when attempting to report a rape to police, and *Whereas,* the conventional method of investigation is to pry into the private life of the rape victim in order to excuse the act committed, and *Whereas,* when the case is brought to court, the victim's personal life style is on trial with attendant [*sic*] publicity, and *Whereas,* the crime of rape as legally defined treats women as a separate class, *Therefore be it resolved:* That NOW take a strong position that the crime of rape be redefined as felonious assault, *Further:* That we work against humiliating treatment of rape victims by police officers,

judges, District Attorneys, probation officers and other legal personnel as well as, by society generally, and, *Further:* We recommend that the investigation of these cases be done by women. (Submitted by the Misogyny and Criminal Law Workshop)" (NOW records).

10. NOW did not hold a national conference in 1972.

11. *The Black Woman,* edited by Toni Cade (1970), is the first attempt to gather under one cover the writings of black women who "have been forming work-study groups, discussion clubs, . . . women's workshops on the campuses," etc. (1970, 9). The contributors primarily address the men in the black liberation movement over their sexist attitudes and behavior, but they also call into question the relevance of the predominantly white feminist movement to the lives of black women.

12. Denise Snyder, director of the D.C. RCC in 1995, notes that the center's staff in recent years has resembled the majority—African American population of Washington, D.C. (personal interview, 9 August 1995).

13. The term *co-optation* is used elsewhere in this book to signify the appropriation of a movement for institutional ends, or "a structural process of placing movement personnel into elite-sponsored positions" (Garner 1977, 14). Rape crisis centers are frequently described as having been "co-opted" by mainstream professionals and institutions.

14. In focusing on the connection between rape and the "little rapes," feminists did, of course, run the risk of conflating all sexual abuse into one problem and ignoring the unique trauma that accompanies rape. Andra Medea and Kathleen Thompson (1974, 50) argue, for example, that "rape, as we have defined it, is any sexual intimacy, whether by direct physical contact or not, that is forced on one person by another." Such a definition, in addition to bearing no resemblance to the legal understanding of rape, elevates street harassment to the same level as a violent sexual assault and runs the risk of trivializing the rape victim's experience. As demonstrated in the Medea and Thompson book, such overconnections did take place.

15. Other, less well known public events on rape include the 1970 packing of a meeting of the Berkeley City Council by Bay Area women's liberationists. The 150 members of Women for a Free Future presented demands for more protection for Berkeley women, such as free public transportation at night and self-defense training (*San Francisco Chronicle* 1970).

16. Brownmiller corrects one error in Sheehy's coverage: while Sheehy reports that even handicapped women attended the event, in reality the wheelchair in which one woman sat was simply a prop for a play in production at St. Clement's Church. The room was so crowded that people seated themselves anywhere they could (telephone interview, 2 September 1996). Although the crowd was diverse, to the organizers' knowledge no physically disabled women attended.

17. For example, the MPC maintains both gender specificity and the spousal

exemption for rape charges: "[a] male who has sexual intercourse with a female not his wife is guilty of rape if . . ." Further, the code explicitly provides "sexual promiscuous complainant" as a defense. Finally, the MPC states, "No person shall be convicted . . . upon the uncorroborated testimony of the alleged victim" (Model Penal Code, Art. 213, Final Draft 1962 [in Bienen 1976]).

18. A study of jurors' attitudes toward rape, rape victims, and rapists (Field and Bienen 1980) finds that, by the late 1970s, a number of the rape myths had lost some currency, but factors such as the racial composition of the victim-defendant dyad and the victim's appearance continued to affect jurors' decisions.

19. The most notable criticism of this position is by Catharine MacKinnon (1989, 134): "Aside from failing to answer the rather obvious question, if it is violence not sex, why didn't he just hit her? this approach made it impossible to see that violence is sex when it is practiced as sex."

20. Although by no means a feminist periodical, *Ramparts* was well known in women's liberation circles, and the article instantly became a classic of the anti-rape literature.

21. Brownmiller's thesis is grounded in radical feminist theory that views gender as the primary contradiction (see also Firestone 1970; Millett 1970). Alison Edwards ([1976?], 3) remarks that "Susan Brownmiller shares with other feminists the view that men as a group are the primary enemy of women as a group. . . . What these views have in common is a strategy for women's liberation isolated from the fight against all other forms of oppression." Edwards also criticizes Brownmiller's biologistic reasoning and her defense of all white women, among other aspects of the book ([1976?], 4–5). Griffin herself (1971, 29) points out that rape should not be viewed as simply either violence or sex, but that the two become inseparable when the act is committed.

22. This conceptualization of rapists has been traced to writings by Sigmund Freud early in the twentieth century and to the expansion of the psychological field of sexology (Donat and D'Emilio 1992, 11). Researchers have found that the myth of rapists as deranged persists even today (Scully 1990).

Chapter 2

1. Bateman describes her own experience of fighting off an attacker, thirteen years after starting the FKU, in Caignon and Groves (1987, 162–65).

2. The group chose its name in memory of a woman who, in 1964, was violently attacked and killed outside her home in Queens, New York, while dozens of witnesses failed to respond to her pleas for help.

3. Nikki Craft, now an anti-pornography activist in California, has since revealed that she was one of the five members of the KGWP.

4. Santa Cruz Women Against Rape (SCWAR) engaged in "unruly tactics" such as arranging confrontations between victims and their rapists. This strategy is described in Scott (1993).

5. By 1980, the concept of TBN had been taken up by anti-pornography protesters, who planned marches through red-light districts in cities such as
San Francisco to denounce pornography as violence against women. This
appropriation represents one of the ways in which the anti-rape and anti-
pornography efforts became conflated. The 1980 publication of *Take Back
the Night: Women on Pornography,* edited by Laura Lederer, further contributed to the confusion over TBN's origins. Anti-pornography strategies and
ideology are discussed in Chapter 4.

6. Among the organizations that antedated the D.C. RCC was Bay Area
Women Against Rape (BAWAR). Founded in Berkeley in the early 1970s,
it performed a number of services to promote rape awareness, distributed
information to victims and their advocates, worked to improve the treatment of rape victims by police and hospital personnel, and generally acted
as advocates for victims (Matthews 1994, 9–11). It appears that BAWAR did
not offer a full range of services for several years into its existence; the most
pervasive feature of the rape crisis center—the crisis line—did not begin
operating until later (Csida and Csida 1974, 148–50). Information on the
group's birth varies from one source to the next. The year of its founding,
for instance, has been variously stated in the literature as 1970 (Gornick,
Burt, and Pittman 1985, 249), 1971 (Csida and Csida 1974, 148), and 1972
(Schwendinger and Schwendinger 1983, 9; Matthews 1994, 9). In 1973,
BAWAR requested $25,000 from the city of Berkeley to establish a center,
complete with twenty-four-hour hotline (*Los Angeles Times* 1973). The request was denied. Thus, BAWAR did not function as a rape crisis center, as
they currently do, before 1973.

7. Although O'Sullivan researched and wrote the pamphlet (Rape Crisis Center 1977, iv), it was attributed to the entire collective.

8. The collective adopted the term *self-help* to describe the center's philosophy
before the term took on its current, more pejorative meanings. See Simonds
(1992) for a discussion of self-help books and self-help culture.

9. The Women's Crisis Center of Ann Arbor opened in April 1972, but its
focus was not on rape; that center set out to serve women with various
needs, such as referral for abortion (then illegal) and job discrimination
advice. The organization's Rape Education Committee was established in
January 1973 to respond to victims in crisis (Women's Crisis Center 1974).
Note that the decision to expand into the area of rape was concurrent with
the relegalization of abortion by the Supreme Court.

10. As a committed pro-defendant organization, the New York Legal Aid Society was a major opponent of several rape law reform efforts in that state in
the 1970s.

11. A well-known and oft-quoted (e.g., Ross 1973, 182) statistic is New York's
conviction rate for 1971: "out of 1085 arrests for rape, the state secured only
eighteen convictions."

12. The Feminists were criticized by others on the Left for focusing on a Puerto Rican teenager's trial; as they saw it, the rape charges were a tool for whites to oppress the members of Third World communities, even though feminist protesters who were arrested at the trial received harsher sentences than the defendant (Price 1971).

13. An unlikely advocate of repeal was Judge Millard L. Midonick of the New York Family Court, who revealed in a ruling that the corroboration require-ment had forced him to dismiss rape charges against two youths accused of raping and robbing a New York City woman, despite his belief that the evidence proved them true. He urged the state legislature to ease the restric-tive requirement, declaring that the rule results in the "denigration of the testimony of women who claim they have been victimized sexually" (Wag-goner 1972).

14. The group was also referred to as the Women's Rape Coalition in the press (Maitland 1974a, 1974b).

15. Estrich (1987) demonstrates that most rape laws are not neutral in their application. For example, although most such statutes make no explicit dis-tinction between aggravated and simple rape, agents of the criminal justice system routinely make judgments on the validity of a victim's claim with such distinctions in mind, resulting in the infrequent prosecution and con-viction of simple, or acquaintance, rape cases. Kalven and Zeisel define the distinction between aggravated and simple rape in *The American Jury* (1966).

Chapter 3

1. See Boneparth and Stoper (1988), Conway, Ahern, and Steuernagel (1999), and Gelb and Palley (1996) for more comprehensive coverage of the wide range of policy issues pursued by women activists.

2. The political scientist Mark Nadel (1975) disputes "the equation of public policy with government policy," arguing that the distinction between gov-ernmental and nongovernmental organizations is nebulous.

3. All policy issues, including those that the women's movement has raised, evolve in a similar way. O'Connor (1996, 5–7) and Anderson (1994, 37–38) delineate a multistage policy process, and I borrow their model here. At stage one, problem recognition and definition, an identified issue is put on the governmental agenda and becomes a matter of public attention. This step accounts for public definitions of the important issues on which the polity will demand governmental action. Making this an explicit stage ex-pands the array of individuals involved in policy making and accounts for the potentially tremendous amount of work needed to place an issue on the public agenda. At stage two, the agenda-setting phase, participants in the policy process identify or create possible options for addressing the problem. In formulating the policy, stage three, participants consider those courses of action that may be used to resolve the issue. At stage four, the policy is

adopted. Stage five is the budgeting phase. At stage six, the policy is implemented or carried out by some part of the government. Finally, policies must undergo evaluation (stage seven) to determine their effectiveness. This formula can be subject to substantial variation, involving such factors as repetition, overlap, and conflation of stages.

4. For a review of the history of psychiatry's medicalization of rape and rapists, see Scully (1990, 35–41). Also see Amir (1971). For a summary of Freudian theories of rape, see Brownmiller (1975, chapter 6).

5. The late 1960s and the 1970s saw the dawn of this punitive law-and-order approach; one can argue that the trend only intensified in subsequent decades. I am indebted to Elizabethann O'Sullivan for this insight.

6. See Estrich (1987) and Koss (1992) for criticisms of the NCVS methodology.

7. Wilson was never elected governor in the first place. Instead, as lieutenant governor, he assumed the office when Governor Nelson Rockefeller vacated it in 1973 to head the National Commission on Critical Choices for Americans (he became vice president under Gerald Ford in 1974).

8. The *New York Times Index* categorizes rape under the subject heading "sex crimes." To get an accurate number of rape-related stories, only those mentioning adult rape or sexual assault, or attempted rape or sexual assault, were counted. Stories on consensual sodomy, child sexual abuse, illegal abortion, and other non-rape subjects listed as sex crimes were not counted.

9. Another article in the same issue of *Intellect* is decidedly less pro-victim than the one by Hartwig and Sandler. See Sagarin (1975).

10. Television network news coverage of rape was far less uniform than that of newspapers and magazines. There appears to be no relationship between the levels of print and electronic coverage of such stories, although the late 1970s saw increased coverage.

Network (ABC, CBS, NBC) News Coverage of Rape, 1969–1980

Year	Number of Stories Indexed as "Rape"
1969	3
1970	12
1971	5
1972	8
1973	7
1974	7
1975	29
1976	18
1977	30
1978	40
1979	16
1980	3

11. Jordan is the co-author, with Elizabeth M. Schneider, of "Representation of Women Who Defend Themselves in Response to Physical or Sexual Assault," which appeared in *Women's Rights Law Reporter* (1978).

12. Little's first name is alternately spelled Joan, JoAnne, and JoAnn in various print sources.

13. The role of the ABA in political issues is by no means uncontested. Questions have arisen about the appropriateness of the organization's custom of taking stances on issues over which its membership may be divided. See Grossman (1965) for an exploration of this and related topics.

14. Schafran (1993) explores judges' attitudes toward rape. On the courts and the news media, see "Shall We Dance?" (1996).

15. The case reportedly sparked some racial tension in Madison. The accused boy was black and the victim was white. Some members of the black community claimed that this was the real source of the protesters' outrage, but the races of the parties involved had not been made public until after the actions against the judge began, according to protesters (Delaney 1977). Laura Woliver (1993) analyzes the Simonson case in depth.

16. Although the court actually reversed the decision on the legal technicality of incorrect jury instruction, language was included that suggested that the victim was to blame for the crime (Blake 1977).

17. Likewise, Representative Patricia Schroeder (D-Colo.) took a visible role as a sponsor of the Violence Against Women Act of 1994.

18. This contrasts with the Court's involvement in the abortion issue, for example; the justices set much of that policy process in motion with the 1973 *Roe v. Wade* decision. See O'Connor (1996).

19. According to a news item in the *Women's Rights Law Reporter* (Announcements 1974), the CWPS was actually a project "launched" by LEAA to conduct the rape study. The CWPS is one of the premier policy institutes for women's interests. Its first director was Margaret Gates, an early member of WEAL (Fraser 1983, 123). Persons involved in grassroots projects dealing with violence against women were critical of the CWPS. For example, the Boston-area activist Betsy Warrior, who compiled a directory of battered-women's projects starting in 1975, remarked: "In my opinion, groups like CWPS tend to take over issues that have been developed at the grass roots level after the need has been established and the hardest work done by others. Their . . . involvement arises at a point when an issue has become 'credible', 'fashionable', and even more importantly, 'fundable'. Because of this, perspectives and goals are often different from those of the initiating groups—to the detriment of the target population" (Warrior 1977, 6). The CWPS had offered to take over Warrior's directory, a project that she had been working on with little outside support or funding.

20. The related question of whether the anti-rape movement can be considered "successful" in terms of social-movement analysis is discussed in Chapter 5.

Chapter 4

1. In *Rape on Trial* (1996), Lisa Cuklanz explores news coverage of several sensationalized rape trials, including that of John Rideout, and how such attention constructs the public's understanding of the issues involved. Rideout was not the first man to be tried for raping his non-estranged wife. In 1974, for example, a Missouri court convicted James Edward Drope for his involvement in the gang rape of his wife (see *Washington Post* 1974). The *Drope* case received little publicity as compared to *Rideout*.

2. But as late as 1979, a California state senator, Bob Wilson, is reported to have said (to a group of women lobbyists), "But if you can't rape your wife, who can you rape?" (quoted in Russell 1990, 18).

3. A number of other highly publicized rape trials could also be included in this discussion. The famous Rideout case of 1978 was the most visible trial in which a man was prosecuted for raping his non-estranged wife. Rideout was acquitted (see Cuklanz 1996). Another significant event came in 1985, when Cathleen Crowell Webb publicly admitted that in 1979 she had falsely accused Gary Dotson of rape. He was eventually freed from prison by Governor James Thompson of Illinois (see Cuklanz 1996). The case of the Central Park jogger—a white professional woman raped and beaten by a group of nonwhite boys engaging in what came to be known as "wilding"— received more media attention in 1989 and 1990 for the racial tension it sparked than for the rape itself (see Benedict 1992). Finally, the gang rape of a first-year student at St. John's University in 1990 was covered in a variety of media and raised important issues about acquaintance rape and white male privilege (see Sanday 1996).

4. See Helen Benedict (1992, 89–146) for a thorough analysis of news coverage of the rape at Big Dan's.

5. The 1988 movie *The Accused,* starring Jodie Foster, was based on the Big Dan's case.

6. I mention Bowman by name here because, after the Smith trial, she came out publicly as the complaining witness. This is also true of the victim in the Tyson case, Desiree Washington, who was openly interviewed by Barbara Walters on the television news magazine *20/20* following the verdict. I do not use the name of the Big Dan's victim here because she never consented to be identified in connection with the trials in her case, even though she was named in the press.

7. Similar views were aired when, in 1991, Anita Hill accused Supreme Court nominee Clarence Thomas of sexual harassment on the job at the Equal Employment Opportunity Commission (see, e.g., Morrison 1992).

8. Susan Brownmiller, who has frequently expressed her belief that victims should be named in the press in order to alleviate the stigma of rape, explains that, during the Smith investigation and trial, she spoke to a prominent newspaper editor who told her that it was because of her position on

the issue that he decided to reveal Bowman's name. But Brownmiller notes that Bowman's identity was only made public in an effort to smear her, which was never the purpose of her own advocacy of naming victims (telephone interview, 2 September 1996).

9. The publicity surrounding the rape of the twelve-year-old prompted the establishment of the island's first rape crisis center (Sallot 1995).

10. Many of these student groups are discussed in Pfister (1994).

11. Mary Koss coined the term *hidden rape* in her study (1988) to refer to date and acquaintance rape.

12. Many of these observations originated in personal communication with Jim Lynch.

13. Some would argue that the 1981 case *Michael M. v. Superior Court* belongs to this discussion. There, the Court upheld the constitutionality of a gender-specific California statutory rape law that criminalized male sexual activity with a minor female, but not vice versa. Since the case involves statutory rape, it is outside my focus in this book. For more information on *Michael M.,* see Williams (1982).

14. Amicus curiae briefs were filed in support of the United States by the following groups: the ACLU, Southern Poverty Law Center, National Association of Human Rights Workers, California Women's Law Center, NOW Legal Defense and Education Fund, Anti-Defamation League, Ayuda (a legal-services organization serving the Latino community), Center for Women Policy Studies, Connecticut Women's Education and Legal Fund, D.C. Rape Crisis Center, People for the American Way, Virginians Aligned Against Sexual Assault, Women's Law Project, and Women's Legal Defense Fund. In addition, NCASA submitted a brief for Vivian Forsythe-Archie written by Catharine MacKinnon.

15. For a more complete delineation of the terms of the anti-pornography and anti-S&M argument, see Dworkin (1974), various contributions to Lederer (1980), Dworkin (1981), MacKinnon (1989, 1993), and the various contributions to Russell (1993), among others. For criticisms of the anti-pornography argument, see Read (1989), Tong (1989, 112–23), Thompson (1994), and Strossen (1995).

16. Many social science researchers have conducted correlational and experimental studies attempting to prove or disprove the possible link between pornography and violence against women. The methods and the findings of the research have been quite diverse. See, for example, Donnerstein (1980); Zillmann and Bryant (1982); Malamuth and Check (1980, 1984); Malamuth (1985); Donnerstein, Linz, and Penrod (1987); and Baron and Straus (1989). Such investigations, the experimental studies in particular, have received much criticism (see, among others, Ashley and Ashley 1984; McCormack 1985). Reviews of the research on pornography and violence against women (e.g., Berger, Searles, and Cottle 1991) find that conclusions on the possible connection between the two are difficult to draw.

17. As I have noted, take back the night started in the 1970s as an anti-rape protest, through which women sought to reclaim the streets as their rightful place. By 1980, the phrase had come to refer to nighttime protests against pornography, often held in large cities' red-light districts.
18. This position is expressed in the popular slogans "What part of 'no' don't you understand?" and "If she says 'no' it's rape."
19. Jane Mansbridge (1986, chapter 13) cites many of the similarities between the movement to pass the ERA and the countermovement led by Phyllis Schlafly.
20. Other books that belong to the group I label "backlash" include Denfeld (1995), Fox-Genovese (1996), and Shalit (1999).
21. According to Mary Beth Carter of the NCASA, when Senator Joseph Biden's office was first planning the VAWA it was not even intended to address rape, only domestic violence.
22. For a range of topics on which Paglia has claimed authority and stirred controversy, see David Sheff's (1995) *Playboy* interview.
23. Christina Hoff Sommers sits on the WFN's board of trustees, as do other figures well known for their conservatism on women's issues: Mona Charen, Elizabeth Fox-Genovese, Jeane Kirkpatrick, Mary Ann Glendon, and Jean Bethke Elshtain, among others. For more information on the WFN, see the organization's self-published book, *Neither Victim nor Enemy,* edited by Rita J. Simon (1995).

Chapter 5

1. Gamson's model is intended for use in measuring the success of individual groups, as he employs it to analyze fifty-three "challenging groups" in existence between 1800 and 1945. But its application elides strict distinctions between social movements and social-movement groups; Staggenborg (1995, 342) observes: "In assessing movement success[es] and their determinants, we have to live with the fact that we cannot stay solely within the bounds of that convenient unit of analysis, the SMO [social-movement organization]. Not only are some outcomes the product of less organized aspects of a movement, but some movement organizations have less distinct boundaries than others."
2. Ellen Boneparth (1982, 12) points out that the distinctions between the types of policies is more blurred than Lowi acknowledges, and that persons affected by a policy alternative might perceive it differently from the persons who drafted it.

References

Works Consulted

Abbot, Sidney, and Barbara Love. 1971. Is women's liberation a lesbian plot? In *Woman in sexist society: Studies in power and powerlessness,* ed. Vivian Gornick and Barbara K. Moran, 601–21. New York: New American Library, Mentor.

Ahrens, Lois. 1980. Battered women's refuges: Feminist cooperatives vs. social service institutions. *Radical America* 14, no. 3: 41–47.

American Law Institute. 1980. *Model Penal Code and commentaries.* Part 2, article 213. Philadelphia: American Law Institute.

Amir, Menachem. 1971. *Patterns in forcible rape.* Chicago: University of Chicago Press.

Anderson, James E. 1994. *Public policymaking: An introduction.* 2d ed. Boston: Houghton Mifflin.

Announcements. 1974. *Women's Rights Law Reporter* 2, no. 2 (December): 1.

Anonymous. 1972. Rape: The experience. *Women: A Journal of Liberation* 3, no. 1: 18–19.

Armstrong, Louise. 1994. *Rocking the cradle of sexual politics: What happened when women said incest.* Reading, Mass.: Addison-Wesley.

Ashley, Barbara Renchkovsky, and David Ashley. 1984. Sex as violence: The body against intimacy. *International Journal of Women's Studies* 7: 352–71.

Babcock, Barbara Allen, Anne E. Freedman, Eleanor Holmes Norton, and Susan C. Ross. 1973. *Sex discrimination and the law: Causes and remedies.* Boston: Little, Brown.

Babcox, Deborah, and Madeline Belkin, eds. 1971. *Liberation now!* New York: Dell.

Baker, Erwin. 1974. City council proposals would change rape case policies. *Los Angeles Times,* 13 November, pt. 2, 1.

Baker-Fletcher, Karen. 1992. Tyson's defenders and the church of exclusion. *New York Times,* 29 March, sec. 4, 17.

Barker, Karlyn. 1972. D.C. women hold conference on coping with rape problem. *Washington Post,* 9 April, C1, C11.

Barnett, Bernice McNair. 1995. Black women's collectivist movement organizations: Their struggles during the "doldrums." In *Feminist organizations: Harvest of the new women's movement,* ed. Myra Marx Ferree and Patricia Yancey Martin, 199–219. Philadelphia: Temple University Press.

Baron, Larry, and Murray A. Straus. 1989. *Four theories of rape in American society: A state-level analysis.* New Haven: Yale University Press.

Barrett, Karen. 1982. Date rape: A campus epidemic? *Ms.,* September, 48–51 and 130.

Barrett, William P. 1974. Coeds act to aid rape victims. *New York Times,* 7 April, 68.

Bart, Pauline B., and Patricia H. O'Brien. 1985. *Stopping rape: Successful survival strategies.* New York: Pergamon.

Bart, Pauline B., and Eileen Geil Moran, eds. 1993. *Violence against women: The bloody footprints.* Newbury Park, Calif.: Sage.

Baughman, Laurence Alan. 1966. *Southern rape complex: Hundred year psychosis.* Atlanta: Pendulum Books.

BenDor, Jan. 1975. Ending rape: A concept essay on strategies. *Feminist Alliance Against Rape Newsletter,* January/February/March, 4–6.

———. 1976. Justice after rape: Legal reform in Michigan. In *Sexual assault: The victim and the rapist,* ed. Marcia J. Walker and Stanley L. Brodsky, 149–60. Lexington, Mass.: Lexington Books.

Benedict, Helen. 1992. *Virgin or vamp: How the press covers sex crimes.* New York: Oxford University Press.

Beneke, Timothy. 1982. *Men on rape.* New York: St. Martin's.

Ben-Horin, Daniel. 1975. Is rape a sex crime? *Nation,* 16 August, 112–15.

Bergen, Raquel Kennedy. 1996. *Wife rape: Understanding the response of survivors and service providers.* Thousand Oaks, Calif.: Sage.

Berger, Ronald J., Patricia Searles, and Charles E. Cottle. 1991. *Feminism and pornography.* New York: Praeger.

Bernard, Jessie. 1971. *Women and the public interest: An essay on policy and protest.* Chicago: Aldine, Atherton.

Bessmer, Sue. 1984. *The laws of rape.* New York: Praeger.

Bienen, Leigh. 1976. Rape I. *Women's Rights Law Reporter* 3, no. 2: 45–57.

———. 1977. Rape II. *Women's Rights Law Reporter* 3, no. 3: 90–137.

———. 1980. Rape III—National developments in rape reform legislation. *Women's Rights Law Reporter* 6, no. 3: 170–213.

Blackwell, Alice Stone. 1930. *Lucy Stone: Pioneer of women's rights.* Boston: Little, Brown.

Blake, Gene. 1977. Conviction voided in rape of hitchhiker. *Washington Post,* 21 July, A2.

Blank, Robert, and Janna C. Merrick. 1995. *Human reproduction, emerging technologies, and conflicting rights.* Washington: Congressional Quarterly.

Blassingame, John W. 1972. *The slave community: Plantation life in the antebellum South.* New York: Oxford University Press.

Blitman, Nan, and Robin Green. 1975. Inez Garcia on trial. *Ms.,* May, 49–54, 84–88.

Boneparth, Ellen, ed. 1982. *Women, power, and policy.* With a foreword by Patricia Schroeder. New York: Pergamon Press.

Boneparth, Ellen, and Emily Stoper, eds. 1988. *Women, power, and policy:*

Toward the year 2000. 2d ed. With a foreword by Margarita Papandreou. New York: Pergamon Press.

Bonsor, Charles F., Eugene B. McGregor, Jr., and Clinton V. Oster, Jr. 1996. *Policy choices and public action.* Upper Saddle River, N.J.: Prentice-Hall.

Boston Women's Health Book Collective. 1973. *Our bodies, ourselves: A book by and for women.* New York: Simon and Schuster.

Bourque, Linda Brookover. 1989. *Defining rape.* Durham, N.C.: Duke University Press.

Boycott all newsstands selling pornography. 1971. *Woman's World,* 15 April, 1.

Breasted, Mary. 1977. Borough crisis units to aid abuse cases: 4 centers will attend women and children who are victimized. *New York Times,* 13 July, B3.

Brent, Linda [Harriet Jacobs]. 1973 [1861]. *Incidents in the life of a slave girl.* Edited by L. Maria Child. New introduction by Walter Teller. San Diego: Harcourt Brace Jovanovich.

Briere, John, and Neil Malamuth. 1983. Self-reported likelihood of sexually aggressive behavior: Attitudinal versus sexual explanations. *Journal of Research in Personality* 17: 315–23.

Bright-Sagnier, Barbara. 1974. 50 turn out to protest Calif. sentence. *Washington Post,* 22 October, B11.

Brown, Kevin. 1999. The social construction of a rape victim: Stories of African-American males about the rape of Desirée Washington. In *Black men on race, gender, and sexuality: A critical reader,* ed. Devon W. Carbado, 147–58. New York: New York University Press.

Brown, Les. 1974. Dembo replacing Townsend on C.B.S. *New York Times,* 1 March, 61.

Brownfeld, Allan C. 1965. Mixed marriage and the Supreme Court. In *Marriage across the color line,* ed. Clotye M. Larsson, 51–57. Chicago: Johnson Publishing.

Brownmiller, Susan. 1975. *Against our will: Men, women and rape.* New York: Simon and Schuster.

Buchwald, Emilie, Pamela R. Fletcher, and Martha Roth, eds. 1993. *Transforming a rape culture.* Minneapolis: Milkweed.

Buechler, Steven M. 1990. *Women's movements in the United States: Woman suffrage, equal rights, and beyond.* New Brunswick, N.J.: Rutgers University Press.

Buffalo News. 1997. Shiver me timbers, Walt Disney is forced to walk the plank for political correctness. 15 January, 9D.

Bunch, Charlotte. 1987. The reform tool kit. In *Passionate politics: Feminist theory in action,* ed. Charlotte Bunch, 103–17. New York: St. Martin's Press.

Bunch, Charlotte, and Sandra Pollack, eds. 1983. *Learning our way: Essays in feminist education.* Trumansburg, N.Y.: Crossing Press.

Burgess, Ann Wolbert, and Lynda Lytle Holmstrom. 1974. *Rape: Victims of crisis.* Bowie, Md.: Robert J. Brady.

Burgess, Ann Wolbert, ed. 1985. *Rape and sexual assault: A research handbook.* New York: Garland.

Burstyn, Varda, ed. 1985. *Women against censorship.* Vancouver, Can.: Douglas and McIntyre.

Cade, Toni, ed. 1970. *The black woman: An anthology.* New York: Penguin, Mentor.

Carabillo, Toni, Judith Meuli, and June Bundy Csida. 1993. *Feminist chronicles, 1953–1993.* Los Angeles: Women's Graphics.

Carden, Maren Lockwood. 1974. *The new feminist movement.* New York: Russell Sage.

———. 1977. *Feminism in the mid-1970s: The non-establishment, the establishment, and the future.* New York: Ford Foundation.

Caignon, Denise, and Gail Groves, eds. 1987. *Her wits about her: Self-defense success stories by women.* New York: Harper and Row, Perennial Library.

Carmody, John. 1972a. The tough TV subject of rape. *Washington Post,* 11 November, E2.

———. 1972b. Rape: The lonely crime. *Washington Post,* 18 November, C7.

Carroll, Susan J. 1984. Woman candidates and support for feminist concerns: The closet feminist syndrome. *Western Political Quarterly* 37 (June): 307–23.

Castro, Ginette. 1990. *American feminism: A contemporary history.* Translated by Elizabeth Loverde-Bagwell. New York: New York University Press.

Chicago Tribune. 1975. Foes of rape set major goals. 25 April, sec. 1A, 4.

———. 1995. New drug finds way into date-rape scenario. 27 November, 2C.

Cimons, Marlene. 1974. Rape concern reaches the federal level. *Los Angeles Times,* 9 May, pt. 4, 1, 8.

Clark, Anna. 1987. *Women's silence, men's violence: Sexual assault in England, 1770–1845.* New York and London: Pandora.

Clark, Lorenne, and Debra Lewis. 1977. *Rape: The price of coercive sexuality.* Toronto: Women's Press.

Cleaver, Eldridge. 1968. *Soul on ice.* New York: Dell.

Clines, Francis X. 1974. Wilson ad draws women's protest: NOW calls TV commercial on rape law "deceptive." *New York Times,* 17 September, 70.

Cobb, Roger W., and Charles D. Elder. 1972. *Participation in American politics: The dynamics of agenda-building.* Boston: Allyn and Bacon.

Cohn, Barbara N. 1972. Succumbing to rape? *Second Wave* 2, no. 2: 24–27.

Cohn, Victor. 1974. Five rape treatment centers urged by D.C. medical group. *Washington Post,* 8 March, C8.

Collins, Barbara G., and Mary B. Whalen. 1989. The rape crisis movement: Radical or reformist? *Social Work* 34: 61–63.

Collins, Patricia Hill. 1991. *Black feminist thought: Knowledge, consciousness, and the politics of empowerment.* New York: Routledge, Chapman, and Hall.

Conference on rape. 1971. *Everywoman,* 18 June, 2.

Connell, Noreen, and Cassandra Wilson. 1974. *Rape: The first sourcebook for women.* New York: New American Library.

Conroy, Mary. 1975. *The rational woman's guide to self-defense.* New York: Grosset and Dunlap.

Conway, M. Margaret, David W. Ahern, and Gertrude A. Steuernagel. 1999. *Women and public policy: A revolution in progress.* 2d ed. Washington: Congressional Quarterly.

Cook, Elizabeth Adell. 1989. Measuring feminist consciousness. *Women and Politics* 9, no. 3: 71–88.

Cooper, Anna Julia. 1988. *A voice from the South.* Xenia, Ohio: Aldine Printing House, 1892; reprint, New York: Oxford University Press (page references are to the reprint edition).

Costain, Anne N. 1988. Representing women: The transformation from social movement to interest group. In *Women, power, and policy: Toward the year 2000,* ed. Ellen Boneparth and Emily Stoper, 26–47. 2d ed. New York: Pergamon Press.

———. 1992. *Inviting women's rebellion: A political process interpretation of the women's movement.* Baltimore: Johns Hopkins University Press.

Crawford, Vicki L., Jacqueline Anne Rouse, and Barbara Woods, eds. 1993. *Women in the civil rights movement: Trailblazers and torchbearers, 1941–1965.* Bloomington: Indiana University Press.

Crichton, Sarah. 1993. Sexual correctness: Has it gone too far? *Newsweek,* 25 October, 52–56.

Csida, June Bundy, and Joseph Csida. 1974. *Rape: How to avoid it and what to do about it if you can't.* Chatsworth, Calif.: Books for Better Living.

Cuklanz, Lisa M. 1996. *Rape on trial: How the mass media construct legal reform and social change.* Philadelphia: University of Pennsylvania Press.

Davidson, Kenneth M., Ruth Bader Ginsburg, and Herma Hill Kay. 1974. *Sex-based discrimination: Text, cases, and materials.* St. Paul, Minn.: West.

Davis, Angela. 1975. JoAnne Little: The dialectics of rape. *Ms.,* June, 74–77, 106–8.

Davis, Angela Y. 1983. *Women, race and class.* New York: Random House, Vintage.

———. 1990. *Women, culture, and politics.* New York: Random House, Vintage.

Davis, Flora. 1991. *Moving the mountain: The women's movement in America since 1960.* New York: Simon and Schuster.

D.C. Rape Crisis Center. 1972. *How to start a rape crisis center.* Pamphlet. Manuscript, Elizabethann O'Sullivan collection.

——— [Rape Crisis Center of Washington, D.C.]. 1977. *How to start a rape crisis center.* Pamphlet, 2d ed.

Delaney, Paul. 1977. Judge's remarks in rape case create tension in blacks and feminists in Madison, Wis. *New York Times,* 15 June, A17.

D'Emilio, John, and Estelle B. Freedman. 1988. *Intimate matters: A history of sexuality in America.* New York: Harper and Row.

Denfeld, Rene. 1995. *The new Victorians: A young woman's challenge to the old feminist order.* New York: Warner.

Densmore, Dana. 1973. On rape. *No More Fun and Games* 6: 57–84.

Densmore, Dana, and Roxanne Dunbar. 1969. More slain girls. *No More Fun and Games* 3: 109–10.

[Detroit] Women Against Rape. 1971. *Stop rape.* Pamphlet.

Dialectic, Gloria. 1995. The truth will out: Affirming the anti–sexual assault movement. Paper presented at the annual conference of the National Women's Studies Association, Norman, Oklahoma, 12–15 June.

Disarm rapists. 1970. *It ain't me, babe,* 23 July–5 August, 13.

Dobash, R. Emerson, and Russell P. Dobash. 1992. *Women, violence, and social change.* London: Routledge.

Dodson, Debra L., and Susan J. Carroll. 1991. *Reshaping the agenda: Women in the state legislatures.* New Brunswick, N.J.: Center for the American Woman and Politics.

Donat, Patricia L. N., and John D'Emilio. 1992. A feminist redefinition of rape and sexual assault: Historical foundations and change. *Journal of Social Issues* 48, no. 1: 9–22.

Donnerstein, Edward. 1980. Aggressive erotica and violence against women. *Journal of Personality and Social Psychology* 39: 269–77.

Donnerstein, Edward, Daniel G. Linz, and Steven Penrod. 1987. *The question of pornography: Research findings and policy implications.* New York: Free Press.

Donovan, John C. 1970. *The policy makers.* New York: Pegasus.

DuBois, Ellen Carol. 1978. *Feminism and suffrage: The emergence of an independent women's movement in America, 1848–1869.* Ithaca, N.Y.: Cornell University Press.

Dubrow, Gail Lee, Carolyn Flynn, Renee Martinez, Jane Peterson, Seemin Qayam, Barbara Segal, and Mary Beth Welch. 1986. Planning to end violence against women. *Women and Environments* 8 (Spring): 4–27.

Durham, Alexis M., III. 1986. Pornography, social harm, and legal control: Observations on Bart. *Justice Quarterly* 3: 95–102.

Dworkin, Andrea. 1974. *Woman hating.* New York: E.P. Dutton.

———. 1981. *Pornography: Men possessing women.* New York: G.P. Putnam's Sons, Perigee Books.

Echols, Alice. 1989. *Daring to be bad: Radical feminism in America, 1967–1975.* Minneapolis: University of Minnesota Press.

Edwards, Alison. [1976?]. *Rape, racism, and the white women's movement: An answer to Susan Brownmiller.* 3d ed. Chicago: Sojourner Truth Organization.

Epstein, Cynthia Fuchs. 1993. *Women in law.* 2d ed. Urbana: University of Illinois Press.

Erin. 1970. Fight! *It ain't me, babe,* 23 July–5 August, 14, 17.

Estrich, Susan. 1987. *Real rape.* Cambridge: Harvard University Press.

———. 1992. Palm Beach stories. *Law and Philosophy* 11: 5–33.

Evans, Sara. 1979. *Personal politics: The roots of women's liberation in the civil rights movement and the New Left.* New York: Random House, Vintage.

―――. 1989. *Born for liberty: A history of women in America.* New York: Free Press.

Faludi, Susan. 1991. *Backlash: The undeclared war against American women.* New York: Crown.

Farr, William. DA announces new approach to rape cases. *Los Angeles Times,* 29 January, pt. 2, 1.

Feminist Alliance Against Rape Newsletter. 1974. [Introduction], 1.

―――. 1976. Interview: Black women and rape. November/December, 10–14.

Feminist Alliance Against Rape Staff. 1974. Mathias Bill. *Feminist Alliance Against Rape Newsletter,* July/August, 10–11.

―――. 1975. Feminism and professionalism: A discussion. *Feminist Alliance Against Rape Newsletter,* Fall, 13–17.

―――. 1976. National news notes: Baton Rouge, Louisiana. *Feminist Alliance Against Rape Newsletter,* September/October, 11–12.

Ferree, Myra Marx, and Beth B. Hess. 1985. *Controversy and coalition: The new feminist movement.* Boston: Twayne.

Ferree, Myra Marx, and Patricia Yancey Martin, eds. 1995. *Feminist organizations: Harvest of the new women's movement.* Philadelphia: Temple University Press.

Ferrell, Claudine. 1986. *Nightmare and dream: Antilynching in Congress, 1917–1922.* New York: Garland.

Field, Hubert S., and Leigh B. Bienen. 1980. *Jurors and rape: A study in psychology and law.* Lexington, Mass.: Lexington Books.

Findlen, Barbara, ed. 1995. *Listen up: Voices from the next feminist generation.* Seattle: Seal.

Firestone, Shulamith. 1970. *The dialectic of sex: The case for feminist revolution.* New York: William Morrow.

Flammang, Janet A. 1997. *Women's political voice: How women are transforming the practice and study of politics.* Philadelphia: Temple University Press.

Foster, Catherine. 1987. America's colleges are facing up to the problem of gang rape. *Christian Science Monitor,* 17 September, 3.

Fox-Genovese, Elizabeth. 1996. *"Feminism is not the story of my life": How today's feminist elite has lost touch with the real concerns of women.* New York: Doubleday.

Francis, Leslie. 1996. *Date rape: Feminism, philosophy, and the law.* University Park: Pennsylvania State University Press.

Fraser, Arvonne S. 1983. Insiders and outsiders: Women in the political arena. In *Women in Washington: Advocates for public policy,* ed. Irene Tinker, 120–39. Beverly Hills, Calif.: Sage.

Frazee, David. 1995. Gender-justice breakthrough: A plain-English guide to the new civil-rights law against violence against women: How it works . . .

what it means . . . how to use it . . . and who tried to kill it. *On the Issues,* Fall, 42–46.

Free Inez! 1974. *Feminist Alliance Against Rape Newsletter,* September/October, 9.

Freeman, Jo. 1973. The origins of the women's liberation movement. *American Journal of Sociology* 78: 792–811.

———. 1975. *The politics of women's liberation.* New York: David McKay.

———. 1979. Resource mobilization and strategy: A model for analyzing social movement organization actions. In *The dynamics of social movements: Resource mobilization, social control, and tactics,* ed. Mayer N. Zald and John D. McCarthy, 167–89. Cambridge, Mass.: Winthrop Publishers.

———. 1995. From suffrage to women's liberation: Feminism in twentieth-century America. In *Women: A feminist perspective,* ed. Jo Freeman, 509–28. Mountain View, Calif.: Mayfield Publishing.

Friedan, Betty. 1963. *The feminine mystique.* New York: Dell.

———. 1981. *The second stage.* New York: Summit Books.

Friedman, Deb. 1975. Professionalism. *Feminist Alliance Against Rape Newsletter,* Fall, 1–3.

———. 1976. Where has all the $$ gone? *Feminist Alliance Against Rape Newsletter,* September/October, 5–6.

———. 1978a. KGWP—Another view. *Feminist Alliance Against Rape Newsletter,* January/February, 9–10.

———. 1978b. Coalition takes on NY bureaucracy. *Feminist Alliance Against Rape Newsletter,* January/February, 18–21.

Fulenwider, Claire Knoche. 1980. *Feminism in American politics: A study of ideological influence.* New York: Praeger.

Funk, Rus Ervin. 1993. *Stopping rape: A challenge for men.* Philadelphia: New Society Publishers.

Gager, Nancy, and Cathleen Schurr. 1976. *Sexual assault: Confronting rape in America.* New York: Grosset and Dunlap.

Galligan, Pat, and Delpfine Welch. 1969. Females and self-defense. *No More Fun and Games* 3: 111–12.

Galvin, Harriet. 1986. Shielding rape victims in the state and federal courts: A proposal for the second decade. *Minnesota Law Review* 70: 763–905.

Gamson, William. 1975. *The strategy of social protest.* Homewood, Ill.: Dorsey.

Garner, Roberta Ash. 1977. *Social movements in America.* 2d ed. Chicago: Rand McNally.

Gelb, Joyce, and Marian Lief Palley. 1996. *Women and public policies.* 3d ed., rev. and exp. Princeton, N.J.: Princeton University Press.

Gelles, Richard J., and Donileen R. Loseke, eds. 1993. *Current controversies on family violence.* Newbury Park, Calif.: Sage.

Giddings, Paula. 1984. *When and where I enter: The impact of black women on race and sex in America.* New York: Bantam.

———. 1992. The last taboo. In *Race-ing justice, en-gendering power: Essays on Anita Hill, Clarence Thomas, and the construction of social reality,* ed. Toni Morrison, 441–63. New York: Random House, Pantheon.

Gilbert, Neil. 1991. The phantom epidemic of sexual assault. *Public Interest,* no. 103 (Spring): 54–65.

Goldsby, Jackie. 1993. Queen for 307 days: Looking b(l)ack at Vanessa Williams and the sex wars. In *Sisters, sexperts, queers: Beyond the lesbian nation,* ed. Arlene Stein, 110–28. New York: Penguin Books, Plume.

Goodyear, Sara Jane. 1973. A friendly voice to calm the rape victim. *Chicago Tribune,* 8 April, sec. 5, 4.

Gordon, Margaret T., and Stephanie Riger. 1989. *The female fear.* New York: Free Press.

Gornick, Janet, Martha R. Burt, and Karen J. Pittman. 1985. Structure and activities of rape crisis centers in the early 1980s. *Crime and Delinquency* 31: 247–68.

Gornick, Vivian, and Barbara K. Moran, eds. 1971. *Woman in sexist society: Studies in power and powerlessness.* New York: New American Library, Mentor.

Grant, Donald L. 1975. *The anti-lynching movement: 1883–1932.* San Francisco: R and E Research Associates.

Greenhouse, Linda. 1974. In Albany, the women show their strength. *New York Times,* 29 January.

Greenwald, Sue. 1977. Women's Transit Authority. *Feminist Alliance Against Rape Newsletter,* March/April, 15–16.

Griffin, Susan. 1971. Rape: The all-American crime. *Ramparts* 10: 26–35.

———. 1986. *Rape: The politics of consciousness.* Rev. ed. San Francisco: Harper and Row.

Grimstad, Kirsten, and Susan Rennie. 1973. *The new woman's survival catalog.* New York: Coward, McCann and Geoghegan/Berkley.

Grossman, Joel B. 1965. *Lawyers and judges: The ABA and the politics of judicial selection.* New York: J. Wiley.

Guillory, Ferrel. 1975. Rights groups back woman held in killing. *Washington Post,* 22 January, A6.

Gurr, Ted Robert. 1970. *Why men rebel.* Princeton, N.J.: Princeton University Press.

Gutmann, Stephanie. 1990. "It sounds like I raped you!" How date rape "education" fosters confusion, undermines personal responsibility, and trivializes sexual violence. *Reason* 22, no. 3 (July): 22–27.

Guy-Sheftall, Beverly, ed. 1995. *Words of fire: An anthology of African-American feminist thought.* New York: New Press.

Hall, Jacqueline Dowd. 1983. "The mind that burns in each body": Women, rape, and racial violence. In *Powers of desire: The politics of sexuality,* ed. Ann Snitow, Christine Stansell, and Christine Thompson, 328–49. New York: Monthly Review Press.

Halpern, Susan. 1978. *Rape, helping the victim: A treatment manual.* Oradell, N.J.: Medical Economics Company Book Division.

Handler, Joel F. 1978. *Social movements and the legal system: A theory of law reform and social change.* New York: Academic.

Harris, Angela P. 1990. Race and essentialism in feminist legal theory. *Stanford Law Review* 42: 581–616.

Hartmann, Susan M. 1989. *From margin to mainstream: American women and politics since 1960.* Philadelphia: Temple University Press.

Hartwig, Patricia A., and Georgette Bennett Sandler. 1975. Rape victims: Reasons, responses, and reforms. *Intellect* 103 (May/June): 507–11.

Henderson, Lynn. 1992. Rape and responsibility. *Law and Philosophy* 11: 127–78.

Herschberger, Ruth. 1948. *Adam's rib.* New York: Pellegrini and Cudahy.

———. 1969. Is rape a myth? In *Masculine/feminine: Readings in sexual mythology and the liberation of women,* ed. Betty Roszak and Theodore Roszak, 122–30. New York: Harper and Row.

Hine, Darlene Clark. 1989. Rape and the inner lives of black women in the Middle West: Preliminary thoughts on the culture of dissemblance. *Signs: Journal of Women in Culture and Society* 14: 912–20.

Hole, Judith, and Ellen Levine. 1971. *Rebirth of feminism.* New York: Quadrangle, New York Times.

hooks, bell. 1981. *Ain't I a woman: Black women and feminism.* Boston: South End.

———. 1984. *Feminist theory: From margin to center.* Boston: South End.

Horos, Carol V. 1974. *Rape.* New Canaan, Conn.: Tobey.

House of Delegates redefines death, urges redefinition of rape, and undoes the Houston Amendments. 1975. *ABA Journal* 61: 463–70.

Howland, Rebecca. 1995. Dangerous sedative being smuggled across border: Mind-altering drug reduces inhibitions, can cause amnesia. *Dallas Morning News,* 15 June, 1A.

Iyengar, Shanto. 1991. *Is anyone responsible? How television frames political issues.* Chicago: University of Chicago Press.

Iyengar, Shanto, and Donald R. Kinder. 1987. *News that matters: Television and American opinion.* Chicago: University of Chicago Press.

Jones, Jacqueline. 1985. *Labor of love, labor of sorrow: Black women and the family, from slavery to the present.* New York: Random House, Vintage.

Joreen [Jo Freeman]. 1973. The tyranny of structurelessness. In *Radical feminism,* ed. Anne Koedt, Ellen Levine, and Anita Rapone, 285–99. New York: Quadrangle, New York Times.

Kalven, Harry, Jr., and Hans Zeisel. 1966. *The American jury.* Boston: Little, Brown.

Katopoulos, Helen. 1971. Women speak out. *Woman's World,* 15 April, 4.

Katz, Lee Michael. 1981. Campuses increase anti-rape programs. *Washington Post,* 19 November, DC3.

Kauffman, L. A. 1988. Sexual harassment: How political is the personal? *Nation,* 26 March, 419.

Kellogg, Polly. 1971. Planning a rape conference. *Rat,* 2–20 March, 10.

Kelly, Suzanne P. 1992. Black women wrestle with abuse issue: Many say choosing racial over gender loyalty is too great a sacrifice. *Minneapolis Star Tribune,* 18 February, 1A.

Kick-ass for women. 1970. *Old Mole,* 7–27 August, 6–7.

Kiernan, Laura A. 1972. Rape crisis center described. *Washington Post,* 12 October, C4.

Killian, Lewis. 1964. Social movements. In *Handbook of modern sociology,* ed. Robert E. L. Faris, 426–55. Chicago: Rand McNally.

King, Mary. 1987. *Freedom song: A personal story of the 1960s civil rights movement.* New York: William Morrow.

Kingdon, John W. 1989. *Congressmen's voting decisions.* 3d ed. Ann Arbor: University of Michigan Press.

Kitty Genovese Women's Project. 1977. Newspaper.

Klein, Ethel. 1984. *Gender politics: From consciousness to mass politics.* Cambridge: Harvard University Press.

Klein, Freada. 1982. Violence against women. In *The women's annual, 1981: The year in review,* ed. Barbara Haber, 270–302. Boston: G. K. Hall.

———. 1983. Violence against women. In *The women's annual, 1982–1983,* ed. Barbara Haber, 230–62. Boston: G.K. Hall.

Knight, Michael. 1973. Police give rape victims a special phone number. *New York Times,* 22 March, 47.

Koedt, Anne. 1973. The myth of the vaginal orgasm. In *Radical feminism,* ed. Anne Koedt, Ellen Levine, and Anita Rapone, 198–207. New York: Quadrangle, New York Times.

Koss, Mary P. 1988. Hidden rape: Sexual aggression and victimization in a national sample of students in higher education. In *Rape and sexual assault II,* ed. Ann Wolbert Burgess, 3–25. New York: Garland.

———. 1992. The underdetection of rape: Methodological choices influence incidence estimates. *Journal of Social Issues* 48, no. 1: 61–75.

———. 1993. Rape: Scope, impact, interventions, and public policy responses. *American Psychologist* 48 (October): 1062–69.

Koss, Mary P., and Sarah Cook. 1993. Facing the facts: Date and acquaintance rape are significant problems for women. In *Current controversies on family violence,* ed. Richard J. Gelles and Donileen R. Loseke, 104–19. Newbury Park, Calif.: Sage.

Koss, Mary P., and Mary R. Harvey. 1991. *The rape victim: Clinical and community interventions.* 2d ed. Newbury Park, Calif.: Sage.

LaFree, Gary D. 1989. *Rape and criminal justice: The social construction of sexual assault.* Belmont, Calif.: Wadsworth.

Largen, Mary Ann. 1974. L.E.A.A. rape funding review. *Feminist Alliance Against Rape Newsletter,* September/October, 10–11.

————. 1976. History of women's movement in changing attitudes, laws, and treatment toward rape victims. In *Sexual assault: The victim and the rapist,* ed. Marcia J. Walker and Stanley L. Brodsky, 69–73. Lexington, Mass.: Lexington Books.

————. 1981. Grassroots centers and national task forces: A herstory of the anti-rape movement. *Aegis,* Autumn, 46–52.

————. 1985. The anti-rape movement: Past and present. In *Rape and sexual assault: A research handbook,* ed. Ann Wolbert Burgess, 1–13. New York: Garland.

————. 1988. Rape-law reform: An analysis. In *Rape and sexual assault II,* ed. Ann Wolbert Burgess, 271–90. New York: Garland.

Lear, Martha Weinman. 1972. Q: If you rape a woman and steal her TV, what can they get you for in New York: A: Stealing her TV. *New York Times Magazine,* 30 January, 10, 55–56, 60, 62–63.

Ledbetter, Les. 1971. Corroboration held vital to protection of rape suspects. *New York Times,* 28 October, 56.

Lederer, Laura, ed. 1980. *Take back the night: Women on pornography.* With an afterword by Adrienne Rich. New York: Morrow.

Leo, John. 1990. Wit is the opiate of politics. *U.S. News and World Report,* 26 November, 24.

Lerner, Gerda, ed. 1972. *Black women in white America: A documentary history.* New York: Random House, Pantheon.

Lewis, Nancy. 1974. The behind-the-scenes story of the unanimous repeal bill victory. *Majority Report,* March, 6–7.

Lichtenstein, Grace. 1971. Feminists hold rape-defense workshop. *New York Times,* 18 April, 68.

————. 1974. Rape squad. *New York Times Magazine,* 3 March, 4–5, 24–26.

Lincoln, Abbey. 1970. Who will revere the black woman? In *The black woman: An anthology,* ed. Toni Cade, 80–84. New York: Penguin, Mentor.

Lindemann, Barbara S. 1984. "To ravish and carnally know": Rape in eighteenth-century Massachusetts. *Signs: Journal of Women in Culture and Society* 10: 63–83.

Lindgren, J. Ralph, and Nadine Taub. 1993. *The law of sex discrimination.* 2d ed. Boulder, Colo.: Westview Press.

Lindsey, Karen, Holly Newman, and Fran Taylor. 1972. Aspects of rape. *Second Wave* 2, no. 2: 28–29.

Linsky, Martin. 1986. *Impact: How the press affects federal policymaking.* New York: W.W. Norton.

Lo, Clarence Y. H. 1982. Countermovements and conservative movements in the contemporary United States. *Annual Review of Sociology* 8: 107–34.

Loh, Wallace D. 1981. Q: What has reform of rape legislation wrought? A: Truth in criminal labelling. *Journal of Social Issues* 37, no. 4: 28–52.

Lorde, Audre. 1984. *Sister outsider.* Trumansburg, N.Y.: Crossing Press.

Los Angeles Times. 1972. Rape crisis center assists victims. 6 July, pt. 4, 12.

———. 1973. Rape crisis center set in Berkeley. 1 March, pt. 4, 13.

———. 1975. Women to use whistles in attempt to curb rapes. 9 August, pt. 1, 19.

———. 1977. Women protest decision voiding rape conviction. 26 July, pt. 2, 1.

———. 1995. Request made to move Japanese trial. 29 December, pt. A, 4.

———. 1997. Woman recants rape tale. 11 January, pt. C, 1.

Lowi, Theodore J. 1960. Distribution, regulation, redistribution: The functions of government. In *Public policies and their politics,* ed. Randall B. Ripley, 27–40. New York: W. W. Norton.

———. 1971. *The politics of disorder.* New York: Basic Books.

Lynch, James P. 1996. Clarifying divergent estimates of rape from two national surveys. *Public Opinion Quarterly* 60: 410–30.

Lyons, Richard L. 1975. Ford's veto of health bill is overridden. *Washington Post,* 30 July, A1.

Lystad, Mary Hanemann. 1985. The National Center for the Prevention and Control of Rape: A federal research agenda. In *Rape and sexual assault: A research handbook,* ed. Ann Wolbert Burgess, 14–34. New York: Garland.

MacKellar, Jean. 1975. *Rape: The bait and the trap.* New York: Crown.

MacKinnon, Catharine A. 1987. *Feminism unmodified: Discourses on life and law.* Cambridge: Harvard University Press.

———. 1989. *Toward a feminist theory of the state.* Cambridge: Harvard University Press.

———. 1993. *Only words.* Cambridge: Harvard University Press.

MacMillan, Jackie, 1975. LEAA research—East. *Feminist Alliance Against Rape Newsletter,* Fall 3–5.

MacMillan, Jackie, and Freada Klein. 1974. F.A.A.R. editorial. *Feminist Alliance Against Rape Newsletter,* September/October, 1–3.

MacMinn, Aleene. 1976. Griffin will host rape special. *Los Angeles Times,* 6 April, pt. 4, 16.

Madigan, Lee, and Nancy C. Gamble. 1991. *The second rape: Society's continued betrayal of the victim.* New York: Lexington Books.

Madriz, Esther. 1997. *Nothing bad happens to good girls: Fear of crime in women's lives.* Berkeley and Los Angeles: University of California Press.

Maitland, Leslie. 1974a. Defenses against rape outlined as women rally near City Hall. *New York Times,* 1 August, 34.

———. 1974b. Beame and Codd promise new efforts to prevent rape, but women's group assails "lack of funding." *New York Times,* 2 August, 5.

———. 1975. Colleges acting to protect students against rape. *New York Times,* 11 January, 18.

Malamuth, Neil M. 1985. The mass media and aggression against women: Research findings and prevention. In *Rape and sexual assault: A research handbook,* ed. Ann Wolbert Burgess, 392–412. New York: Garland.

Malamuth, Neil M., and James V. P. Check. 1980. Sexual arousal to rape and consenting depictions: The importance of the woman's arousal. *Journal of Abnormal Psychology* 89: 763–66.

———. 1984. Debriefing effectiveness following exposure to pornographic rape depictions. *Journal of Sex Research* 20: 1–13.

Mansbridge, Jane J. 1986. *Why we lost the ERA.* Chicago: University of Chicago Press.

Mansfield, Stephanie. 1979. Rape center warning: Most victims know assailants; center stresses "acquaintance rape." *Washington Post,* 13 October, C1.

Marcus, Sharon. 1992. Fighting bodies, fighting words: A theory and politics of rape prevention. In *Feminists theorize the political,* ed. Judith Butler and Joan W. Scott, 383–403. New York: Routledge.

Margolin, Debbie. 1972. Rape: The facts. *Women: A Journal of Liberation* 3, no. 1: 19–22.

Marsh, Jeanne C., Alison Geist, and Nathan Caplan. 1982. *Rape and the limits of law reform.* Boston: Auburn House.

Martin, Patricia Yancey. 1990. Rethinking feminist organizations. *Gender and Society* 4: 182–206.

Martin, Patricia Yancey, Diana DiNitto, Diane Byington, and M. Sharon Maxwell. 1992. Organizational and community transformation: The case of a rape crisis center. *Administration in Social Work* 16: 123–45.

Martin, Patricia Yancey, and Robert A. Hummer. 1989. Fraternities and rape on campus. *Gender and Society* 3: 457–73.

Matalin, Mary. 1993. Stop whining! The feminist fringe frets about oppression, but mainstream women want equality. *Newsweek,* 25 October, 62.

Mather, Anne. 1974. A history of feminist periodicals, part I. *Journalism History* 1, no. 3: 82–85.

Matthews, Nancy A. 1989. Surmounting a legacy: The expansion of racial diversity in a local anti-rape movement. *Gender and Society* 3: 518–32.

———. 1994. *Confronting rape: The feminist anti-rape movement and the state.* New York: Routledge.

———. 1995. Feminist clashes with the state: Tactical choices by state-funded rape crisis centers. In *Feminist organizations: Harvest of the new women's movement,* ed. Myra Marx Ferree and Patricia Yancey Martin, 291–305. Philadelphia: Temple University Press.

McAdam, Doug. 1982. *Political process and the development of black insurgency.* Chicago: University of Chicago Press.

McAllister, Bill. 1978. Publisher draws angry response: *Northern Virginia Sun* to publish names of rape victims. *Washington Post,* 9 February, C1, C12.

McCarrick, Earlean. 1995. Women and the criminal justice system. In *Women in public policy: A revolution in progress,* ed. M. Margaret Conway, David W. Ahern, and Gertrude A. Steuernagel. Washington: Congressional Quarterly.

McCarthy, John D., and Mayer N. Zald. 1987. Resource mobilization and social movements: A partial theory. In *Social movements in an organizational society: Collected essays*, ed. Mayer N. Zald and John D. McCarthy, 15–42. New Brunswick, N.J.: Transaction.

McCaughey, Martha. 1997. *Real knockouts: The physical feminism of women's self-defense*. New York: New York University Press.

McCormack, Thelma. 1985. Making sense of the research on pornography. In *Women against censorship*, ed. Varda Burstyn, 183–205. Vancouver, Can.: Douglas and McIntyre.

McDonald, Nancy. 1977. *All in the family* reviewed. *Feminist Alliance Against Rape Newsletter*, September/October, 11–12.

McDuff, Robin, Deanne Pernell, and Karen Saunders. 1977. Feminists critique anti-rape movement. *Feminist Alliance Against Rape Newsletter*, January/February, 2–5.

McFadden, Robert D. 1975. Rapes at Hunter spark student protest. *New York Times*, 30 September, 34.

McGinniss, Joe, 1969. *The selling of the president, 1968*. New York: Simon and Schuster, Trident.

McGlen, Nancy E., and Karen O'Connor. 1983. *Women's rights: The struggle for equality in the 19th and 20th centuries*. New York: Praeger.

————. 1995. *Women, politics, and American society*. Englewood Cliffs, N.J.: Prentice-Hall.

Medea, Andra, and Kathleen Thompson. 1974. *Against rape*. New York: Farrar, Straus and Giroux.

Mehrhof, Barbara, and Pamela Kearon. 1971. Rape: An act of terror. *Notes from the Third Year. Women's Liberation*: 79–81.

Mezey, Susan Gluck. 1978. Does sex make a difference? A case study of women in politics. *Western Political Quarterly* 31 (December): 492–501.

Millett, Kate. 1970. *Sexual politics*. New York: Doubleday.

[————]. 1974. Revolt against rape. *Time*, 24 July, 85.

Mills, Elizabeth Anne. 1982. One hundred years of fear: Rape and the medical profession. In *Judge, lawyer, victim, thief: Women, gender roles, and criminal justice*, ed. Nicole Hahn Rafter and Elizabeth Anne Stanko, 29–62. Boston: Northeastern University Press.

Minneapolis Tribune. 1974. Plans for rape-victim aid program announced by St. Paul committee. 28 August, 8B.

Minow, Martha. 1990. *Making all the difference: Inclusion, exclusion, and American law*. Ithaca, N.Y.: Cornell University Press.

Mitchell, Grayson. 1973. Rape-victim study sought. *Washington Post*, 21 March, A16.

Moe, Terry M. 1981. Toward a broader view of interest groups. *Journal of Politics* 43: 531–43.

Molotch, Harvey, 1979. Media and movements. In *The dynamics of social move-*

ments: Resource mobilization, social control, and tactics, ed. Mayer N. Zald and John D. McCarthy, 71–93. Cambridge, Mass.: Winthrop Publishers.

Montgomery, Paul L. 1973a. New drive on to make rape convictions easier. *New York Times,* 13 November, 47, 90.

———. 1973b. Legislators say changes in rape law are likely. *New York Times,* 16 November, 45.

Moraga, Cherríe, and Gloria Anzaldúa, eds. 1981. *This bridge called my back: Writings by radical women of color.* New York: Kitchen Table.

Morgan, Patricia. 1981. From battered wife to program client: The state's shaping of social problems. *Kapitalistate* 9: 17–39.

Morgan, Robin, ed. 1970. *Sisterhood is powerful: An anthology of writings from the women's liberation movement.* New York: Random House, Vintage.

Morrison, Toni, ed. 1992. *Race-ing justice, en-gendering power: Essays on Anita Hill, Clarence Thomas, and the construction of social reality.* New York: Random House, Pantheon.

Morton, Patricia. 1991. *Disfigured images: The historical assault on Afro-American women.* New York: Praeger.

Mottl, Tahi L. 1980. The analysis of countermovements. *Social Problems* 27 (June): 620–35.

Ms. 1972a. Mary self-worth. September, 79–82.

———. 1972b. I never set out to rape anybody. December, 22–23.

———. 1973. In the case of rape: The prosecution of the victims. September, 22.

———. 1980. *The decade of women: A* Ms. *history of the seventies in words and pictures.* With an introduction by Gloria Steinem. New York: G. P. Putnam's Sons, Paragon.

Murphy, Irene. 1973. *Public policy on the status of women: Agenda and strategy for the 70s.* With a foreword by Bernice Sandler. Lexington, Mass.: Lexington Books.

Murphy, Mary. 1972. Myths of rape focus of special. *Los Angeles Times,* 2 December, pt. 2, 8.

Nadel, Mark V. 1975. The hidden dimension of public policy: Private governments and the policy-making process. *Journal of Politics* 37: 2–34.

National Organization for Women. 1975a. August 26th alert: Stop violence against women. *Do It NOW,* July/August, 1, 10.

———. 1975b. August 26: Equality day around the nation. *Do It NOW,* September/October, 10–12.

Nelson, Barbara J. 1984. *Making an issue of child abuse: Political agenda setting for social problems.* Chicago: University of Chicago Press.

New York Times. 1971a. Court censures judge on coast for comments to a rape victim. 24 January, 49.

———. 1971b. Learning the law from women's view. 28 October, 34.

———. 1972. Iowa women join in drive on rape: Attacks in college city spur the formation of group. 6 August, 50.

————. 1973. City forms a task force to find "more compassionate" ways for handling rape cases. 9 August, 25.

————. 1974a. Editorial. 22 January.

————. 1974b. Nassau prosecutor forms rape squad headed by women. 8 March, 35.

————. 1975. Feminists ask role in establishment of rape crisis unit. 24 August, 38.

————. 1976a. New security plan is adopted by Yale after two rapes. 15 January, 27.

————. 1976b. Central Park night walk protests rapes. 5 August, 35.

————. 1979. Rape-case comment leads to censure. 29 March, B4.

Oberschall, Anthony. 1973. *Social conflicts and social movements.* Englewood Cliffs, N.J.: Prentice-Hall.

O'Connor, John J. 1977. TV: Rape, alcohol explored. *New York Times,* 26 May, C24.

O'Connor, Karen. 1980. *Women's organizations' use of the courts.* Lexington, Mass.: Lexington Books.

————. 1996. *No neutral ground? Abortion politics in an age of absolutes.* Boulder, Colo.: Westview Press.

Oelsner, Lesley. 1972. Law of rape: Because ladies lie. *New York Times,* 14 May, sec. 4, 5.

Olson, Mancur. 1971. *The logic of collective action: Public goods and the theory of groups.* Cambridge: Harvard University Press.

Omolade, Barbara. 1995. Hearts of darkness. In *Words of fire: An anthology of African-American feminist thought,* ed. Beverly Guy-Sheftall, 362–78. New York: New Press.

Orehek, Fred. 1974. Increased privacy: Plan aids rape victim. *Chicago Tribune,* 20 December, sec. 2, 1.

O'Sullivan, Elizabethann. 1978. What has happened to rape crisis centers? A look at their structures, members, and funding. *Victimology: An International Journal* 3: 45–62.

Paglia, Camille. 1992. *Sex, art, and American culture.* New York: Random House, Vintage.

Papachristou, Judith. 1976. *Women together: A history in documents of the women's movement in the United States.* New York: Alfred A. Knopf.

Parrot, Andrea, and Laurie Bechhofer, eds. 1991. *Acquaintance rape: The hidden crime.* New York: John Wiley.

Payne, Carol Williams. 1973. Consciousness raising: A dead end? In *Radical feminism,* ed. Anne Koedt, Ellen Levine, and Anita Rapone, 282–84. New York: Quadrangle, New York Times.

Peck, Abe. 1991. *Uncovering the sixties: The life and times of the underground press.* With an introduction by Martin A. Lee. New York: Citadel, Carol Publishing.

Pekkanen, John. 1976. *Victims: An account of rape.* New York: Dial Press.

Pfister, Bonnie. 1994. Swept awake! Negotiating passion on campus. *On the Issues,* Spring, 13–16.

Pittsburgh Action Against Rape. 1975. *Every woman's guide to rape prevention.* Pamphlet.

Piven, Frances Fox, and Richard A. Cloward. 1977. *Poor people's movements.* New York: Pantheon.

Pleck, Elizabeth. 1987. *Domestic tyranny: The making of social policy against family violence from colonial times to the present.* New York: Oxford University Press.

Porterfield, Ernest. 1978. *Black and white mixed marriages.* Chicago: Nelson-Hall.

Price, Colette. 1971. Bringing rapists to trial: A group effort. *Woman's World,* November/December, 6–7, 9.

———. 1972. Developing feminist theory: Consciousness-raising. *Woman's World* 2, no. 1, 10–12.

Pride, Anne. 1977. Women take back the night. *Feminist Alliance Against Rape Newsletter,* November/December 18–19.

Radford, Jill, and Diana E. H. Russell, eds. 1992. *Femicide: The politics of woman killing.* New York: Twayne.

Rape. 1971. *Everywoman,* 5 February, 8.

Rape Crisis Center of Washington, D.C. 1977. *How to start a rape crisis center.* Pamphlet, 2d ed.

Read, Daphne. 1989. (De)Constructing pornography: Feminisms in conflict. In *Passion and power: Sexuality in history,* ed. Kathy Peiss and Christina Simmons, with Robert A. Padgug, 277–92. Philadelphia: Temple University Press.

Reinharz, Shulamit. 1992. *Feminist methods in social research.* New York: Oxford University Press.

Revolution. 1868. The case of Hester Vaughan. 10 December, 357–58.

Rhode, Deborah. 1989. *Justice and gender.* Cambridge: Harvard University Press.

Rich, Adrienne. 1986. Compulsory heterosexuality and lesbian existence. In *Blood, Bread, and Poetry.* New York: W. W. Norton.

Rich, B. Ruby. 1983. Anti-porn: Soft issue, hard world. *Feminist Review* 13: 56–67.

Richardson, Laurel, and Verta Taylor. 1993. *Feminist frontiers III.* New York: McGraw-Hill.

Richter, Paul. 1997. Army sergeant gets 25-year term for rapes. *Los Angeles Times,* 7 May, A1.

Riger, Stephanie. 1994. Challenges of success: Stages of growth in feminist organizations. *Feminist Studies* 20: 275–300.

Robinson, Timothy S. 1976. CU ordered to pay student $20,000 in campus rape. *Washington Post,* 29 July, C1.

Roiphe, Katie. 1993. Date rape's other victim: In their claims of a date-rape epidemic, feminists subvert their own claims. *New York Times Magazine,* 13 June, 26–30, 40, 68.

———. 1994. *The morning after: Sex, fear, and feminism.* Boston: Little, Brown.

Ronan, Thomas P. 1971. Legislature approves expansion of board of elections in city. *New York Times,* 26 March, 44.

Rose, Vicki McNickle. 1977. Rape as a social problem: A byproduct of the feminist movement. *Social Problems* 25 (October): 75–89.

Rosenberg, Bernard. 1972. Crime on and off the streets. In *The seventies: Problems and proposals,* ed. Irving Howe and Michael Harrington, 386–404. New York: Harper and Row.

Rosenberg, Gerald. 1991. *The hollow hope: Can courts bring about social change?* Chicago: University of Chicago Press.

Ross, Loretta J. 1982. Rape and Third World women. *Aegis,* Summer, 39–48.

Ross, Susan C. 1973. *The rights of women: The basic ACLU guide to a woman's rights.* New York: Avon.

Roszak, Betty, and Theodore Roszak, eds. 1969. *Masculine/feminine: Readings in sexual mythology and the liberation of women.* New York: Harper and Row.

Rowan, Carl T., and David M. Mazie. 1974. The terrible trauma of rape. *Reader's Digest,* March, 198–204.

Ruane, Michael. 1997. Top enlisted man in Army accused of sex misconduct. *Houston Chronicle,* 8 May, A2.

Rubin, Gayle. 1989. Thinking sex: Notes for a radical theory of the politics of sexuality. In *Pleasure and danger: Exploring female sexuality,* ed. Carole S. Vance, 267–319. London: Pandora.

Rush, Florence. 1980. *The best kept secret: Sexual abuse of children.* Englewood Cliffs, N.J.: Prentice-Hall.

Russell, Diana E. H. 1975. *The politics of rape: The victim's perspective.* New York: Stein and Day.

———. 1984. *Sexual exploitation: Rape, child sexual abuse, and workplace harassment.* Beverly Hills, Calif.: Sage.

———. 1990. *Rape in marriage.* Exp. and rev. ed. Bloomington: Indiana University Press.

———. 1992. Femicidal lynching in the United States. In *Femicide: The politics of woman killing,* ed. Jill Radford and Diana E. H. Russell, 53–61. New York: Twayne.

———, ed. 1993. *Making violence sexy: Feminist views on pornography.* New York: Teachers College Press.

Ruzek, Sheryl Burt. 1978. *The women's health movement: Feminist alternatives to medical control.* New York: Praeger.

Ryan, Barbara. 1992. *Feminism and the women's movement.* New York: Routledge.

Sagarin, Edward. 1975. Forcible rape and the problem of the rights of the accused. *Intellect* 103 (May/June): 515–20.

Salaam, Kalamu ya. 1980. Rape: A radical analysis from an African-American Perspective. *Black Books Bulletin* 6, no. 4: 38–46.

Sallot, Jeff. 1995. Okinawa rape galvanizes women to protest U.S. military. *Atlanta Constitution,* 23 November, 3C.

Sanday, Peggy Reeves. 1981a. The socio-cultural context of rape: A cross-cultural study. *Journal of Social Issues* 37, no. 4: 5–27.

———. 1981b. *Female power and male dominance: On the origins of sexual inequality.* Cambridge: Cambridge University Press.

———. 1990. *Fraternity gang rape: Sex, brotherhood, and privilege on campus.* New York: New York University Press.

———. 1996. *A woman scorned: Acquaintance rape on trial.* New York: Doubleday.

San Francisco Chronicle. 1970. Women's lib "rape issue" in Berkeley. 11 November, 3.

San Francisco Women Against Rape. 1974. Letter to the editor. *Feminist Alliance Against Rape Newsletter,* November/December, 6–7.

———. 1975. LEAA research—West. *Feminist Alliance Against Rape Newsletter,* Fall, 6–7.

———. 1977. *Not a fleeting rage: A handbook on rape.* Pamphlet.

Sapiro, Virginia. 1994. *Women in American society: An introduction to women's studies.* 3d ed. Mountain View, Calif.: Mayfield.

Sarachild, Kathie. 1970. Feminist consciousness raising and "organizing." In *Voices from women's liberation,* ed. Leslie B. Tanner, 154–57. New York: New American Library, Signet.

Schafran, Lynn Hecht. 1993. Maiming the soul: Judges, sentencing, and the myth of the nonviolent rapist. *Fordham Urban Law Journal* 20: 439–53.

Scharfenberg, Kirk. 1973a. Changes in rape laws urged by council study. *Washington Post,* 10 July, A1 and A11.

———. 1973b. D.C. law on rape scored: More evidence needed than in murders. *Washington Post,* 21 September, C1 and C4.

Schechter, Susan. 1982. *Women and male violence.* Boston: South End.

Schmidt, Peggy. 1973. How to make trouble: Rape crisis centers. *Ms.,* September, 14–18.

Schneider, Elizabeth M., and Susan B. Jordan. 1978. Representation of women who defend themselves in response to physical or sexual assault. *Women's Rights Law Reporter* 4, no. 3 (Spring): 149–63.

Schreiber, Edward. 1973. Policewomen's unit is urged for rape cases. *Chicago Tribune,* 14 September, sec. 2, 10.

———. 1974. In city council meeting: Rape case units proposed. *Chicago Tribune,* 18 April, sec. 1, 5.

Schultz, Leroy G., ed. 1975. *Rape victimology.* Springfield, Ill.: Charles C. Thomas.

Schumaker, Paul D. 1975. Policy responsiveness to protest group demands. *Journal of Politics* 37: 488–521.

Schwendinger, Julia R., and Herman Schwendinger. 1983. *Rape and inequality.* Beverly Hills, Calif.: Sage.

Scott, Ellen Kaye. 1993. How to stop the rapists? A question of strategy in two rape crisis centers. *Social Problems* 40: 343–61.

Scully, Diana. 1990. *Understanding sexual violence: A study of convicted rapists.* Boston: Unwin Hyman.

Searles, Patricia, and Ronald J. Berger. 1987. The current status of rape reform legislation: An examination of state statutes. *Women's Rights Law Reporter* 10, no. 1 (Spring): 25–43.

———, eds. 1995. *Rape and society: Readings on the problem of sexual assault.* Boulder, Colo.: Westview Press.

Shales, Tom. 1977. Tonight: Edith Bunker's ordeal. *Washington Post,* 16 October, G1 and G2.

Shalit, Wendy. 1999. *A return to modesty: Discovering the lost virtue.* New York: Free Press.

Shall we dance? The courts, the community, and the news media. 1996. *Judicature* 80 (July–August): 30–42.

Shanahan, Eileen. 1973. Women's group vows poverty fight. *New York Times,* 20 February, 38.

Shange, Ntozake. 1975. *for colored girls who have considered suicide/when the rainbow is enuf.* New York: Macmillan.

Sheehy, Gail. 1971. Nice girls don't get into trouble. *New York,* 15 February, 26–30.

Sheff, David. 1995. *Playboy* interview: Camille Paglia. *Playboy,* May, 51–64.

Sheldon, Ann. 1972. Rape: A solution. *Women: A Journal of Liberation* 3, no. 1: 22–23.

Shulman, Alix. 1971. Organs and orgasms. In *Woman in sexist society: Studies in power and powerlessness,* ed. Vivian Gornick and Barbara K. Moran, 292–303. New York: New American Library, Mentor.

Sigal, Wendy. 1973. D.C. police official backs rape study. *Washington Post,* 12 July, B3.

Simon, Rita J. 1995. *Neither victim nor enemy: Women's Freedom Network looks at gender in America.* Lanham, Md.: Women's Freedom Network and University Press of America.

Simonds, Wendy. 1992. *Women and self-help culture: Reading between the lines.* New Brunswick, N.J.: Rutgers University Press.

Sisters pick up sisters. 1971. *Everywoman,* 5 February, 8.

Smelser, Neil J. 1963. *Theory of collective behavior.* Glencoe, Ill.: Free Press.

Sommers, Christina Hoff. 1994. *Who stole feminism? How women have betrayed women.* New York: Simon and Schuster.

Spinner, Jackie, and Susan Levine. 1996. Sex scandal derails three army careers. *Washington Post,* 17 November, B1.

Spohn, Cassia, and Julie Horney. 1992. *Rape law reform: A grassroots revolution and its impact.* New York: Plenum.

Springer, Kimberly. 1999. *Still lifting, still climbing: African American women's contemporary activism.* New York: New York University Press.

Staggenborg, Suzanne. 1988. The consequences of professionalization and formalization in the pro-choice movement. *American Sociological Review* 53: 585–606.

———. 1989. Stability and innovation in the women's movement: A comparison of two movement organizations. *Social Problems* 36: 75–92.

———. 1995. Can feminist organizations be effective? In *Feminist organizations: Harvest of the new women's movement,* ed. Myra Marx Ferree and Patricia Yancey Martin, 339–55. Philadelphia: Temple University Press.

Stanton, Elizabeth Cady. 1868. Hester Vaughan. *Revolution,* 19 November, 312.

Strong, Ellen. 1970. The hooker. In *Sisterhood is powerful: An anthology of writings from the women's liberation movement,* ed. Robin Morgan, 323–33. New York: Random House, Vintage.

Strossen, Nadine. 1995. *Defending pornography: Free speech, sex, and the fight for women's rights.* New York: Scribner.

Stumbo, Bella. 1972. Rape: Does justice turn its head? *Los Angeles Times,* 12 March, sec. E, 1, 8, 10–12.

Tanner, Leslie, ed. 1970. *Voices from women's liberation.* New York: New American Library, Signet.

Tarrow, Sidney. 1989. *Democracy and disorder: Protest and politics in Italy, 1965–1975.* New York: Oxford University Press.

Taylor, Stacy R. 1978. Rape victims: A right to anonymity? *Washington Post,* 9 February, A25.

Taylor, Verta. 1989. Social movement continuity: The women's movement in abeyance. *American Sociological Review* 54: 761–75.

Taylor, Verta, and Nancy Whittier. 1997. The new feminist movement. In *Feminist frontiers IV,* ed. Laurel Richardson, Verta Taylor, and Nancy Whittier, 533–48. New York: McGraw-Hill.

Thomas, Sue. 1994. *How women legislate.* New York: Oxford University Press.

Thompson, Bill. 1994. *Soft core: Moral crusades against pornography in Britain and America.* London: Cassell.

Tomaselli, Sylvana, and Roy Porter, eds. 1986. *Rape.* Oxford: Basil Blackwell.

Tong, Rosemarie. 1989. *Feminist thought: A comprehensive introduction.* Boulder, Colo.: Westview Press.

Toure, I. Nkenge. 1978. District attorney's guide to dealing with sexual assault victims. *Feminist Alliance Against Rape Newsletter,* January/February, 16–17.

Truman, David. 1971. *The governmental process: Political interests and public opinion.* 2d ed. New York: Alfred A. Knopf.

Turner, Ralph H. 1964. Collective behavior. In *Handbook of modern sociology,* ed. Robert E. L. Faris, 382–425. Chicago: Rand McNally.

Ulmschneider, Loret. 1977. Dallas rapists see their names printed. *Feminist Alliance Against Rape Newsletter,* July/August, 2–5.

Vance, Carole S., ed. 1989. *Pleasure and danger: Exploring female sexuality.* London: Routledge and Kegan Paul, 1984; reprint, London: Pandora (page references are to the reprint edition).

Waggoner, Walter H. 1972. Judge calls law on rape lenient: Midonick bids state end "corroboration" rule. *New York Times,* 1 January, 37.

Walker, Alice. 1982. *The color purple.* New York: Washington Square Press.

Walker, Rebecca, ed. 1995. *To be real: Telling the truth and changing the face of feminism.* New York: Anchor.

Wallace, Michele. 1971. Black and white women. *Woman's World,* November–December, 3, 9.

———. 1979. *Black macho and the myth of the superwoman.* New York: Dial Press.

Ware, Cellestine. 1970. *Woman power: The movement for women's liberation.* New York: Tower.

Warrior, Betsy. 1977. *National Directory*—a rip off? *National Communication Network for the Elimination of Violence Against Women,* December, 6–7.

Warshaw, Robin. 1988. *I never called it rape: The* Ms. *report on recognizing, fighting, and surviving date and acquaintance rape.* With an afterword by Mary P. Koss. New York: Harper and Row.

Washington, Joseph R., Jr. 1993. *Marriage in black and white.* New York: Lanham.

Washington Post. 1972a. Rape victims now can get telephone aid. 6 June, A28.

———. 1972b. Editorial. 12 June.

———. 1974. High court studies case of wife rape. 14 May, A15.

———. 1977. Feminist leaders heartened by acquittal of Inez Garcia. 6 March, A22.

Wasserman, Michelle. 1973. Rape: Breaking the silence. *Progressive* 37 (November): 19–23.

WEA boycott. 1977. *Women Against Violence Against Women Newsletter,* May, 1.

[Welch, M. S.]. 1973. Women against rape. *Time,* 23 April, 104.

Welch, Susan. 1985. Are women more liberal than men in the U.S. Congress? *Legislative Studies Quarterly* 10: 125–34.

Wells-Barnett, Ida B. 1969 [1892]. *On lynchings: Southern horrors; A red record; Mob rule in New Orleans.* New York: Arno Press.

———. 1995 [1900]. Lynch law in America. In *Words of fire: An anthology of African-American feminist thought,* ed. Beverly Guy-Sheftall, 70–76. New York: New Press.

West, Robin. 1988. Jurisprudence and gender. *University of Chicago Law Review* 55: 1–72.

White, Aaronette M. 1999. Talking black, talking feminist: Gendered micro-mobilization processes in a collective protest against rape. In *Still lifting, still climbing: African American women's contemporary activism,* ed. Kimberly Springer, 189–218. New York: New York University Press.

White, Deborah Gray. 1985. *Ar'n't I a woman? Female slaves in the plantation South.* New York: W. W. Norton.

Wicktom, Cynthia Ann. 1988. Focusing on the offender's forceful conduct: A proposal for the redefinition of rape laws. *George Washington Law Review* 56: 399–430.

Williams, Patricia J. 1991. *The alchemy of race and rights.* Cambridge: Harvard University Press.

Williams, Wendy W. 1982. The equality crisis: Some reflections on culture, courts, and feminism. *Women's Rights Law Reporter* 7: 175–200.

Willis, Ellen. 1984. Radical feminism and feminist radicalism. In *The 60s without apology,* ed. Sohnya Sayres, Anders Stephanson, Stanley Aronowitz, and Fredric Jameson, 91–118. Minneapolis: University of Minnesota Press.

Wilson, Carolyn F., with Barbara Haber. 1981. Violence against women. In *The Women's Annual, 1980: The Year in Review,* ed. Barbara Haber, 261–83. Boston: G. K. Hall.

Woliver, Laura R. 1993. *From outrage to action: The politics of grass-roots dissent.* Urbana and Chicago: University of Illinois Press.

Wolper, Andrea. 1994. Exporting healing: American rape crisis counselors in Bosnia. *On the Issues,* Spring, 27–31.

Women's Crisis Center [of Ann Arbor, Mich.]. 1974. *How to organize a women's crisis-service center.* Pamphlet.

Women's Freedom Network Newsletter. 1994. Statement of purpose, 1.

Wood, Jim. 1976. *The rape of Inez García.* New York: G.P. Putnam's Sons.

Wood, Pamela Lakes. 1975. The victim in a forcible rape case: A feminist view. In *Rape Victimology,* ed. Leroy G. Schultz, 194–217. Springfield, Ill.: Charles C. Thomas.

Woodhull and Claflin's Weekly. 1874. The great crime. 1 August, 8.

Wyatt, Gail Elizabeth. 1992. The sociocultural context of African American and white American women's rape. *Journal of Social Issues* 48, no. 1: 77–91.

Young, Cathy. 1996. One-and-a-half cheers for Susan Molinari. *Detroit News,* 13 August, A9.

Zald, Mayer N., and Roberta Ash. 1966. Social movement organizations: Growth, decline, and change. *Social Forces* 44: 327–40.

Zillmann, Dolf, and Bryant Jennings. 1982. Pornography, sexual callousness, and the trivialization of rape. *Journal of Communication* 32, no. 4 (Autumn): 10–21.

Government Documents

Privacy Protection for Rape Victims Act. *Statutes at large.* 1978. Vol. 92, 2046–47.

Rape Prevention and Control Act. *Statutes at large.* 1975. Vol. 89, sec. 231, 328–29.

Sexual Abuse Act. *Statutes at large.* 1986. Vol. 100, 3660–64.

U.S. Congress. Senate. 1973. *Rape prevention and control act.* 93rd Cong., 1st sess., S. 2422. *Congressional Record.* Vol. 119, pt. 23 (17 September), S29829–33.

U.S. Congress. House. 1976a. *Privacy protection for rape victims act of 1976.* 94th Cong., 2d sess., H.R. 12684. *Congressional Record.* Vol. 122, pt. 4 (19 February), H3925–26.

U.S. Congress. House. 1976b. Representative Elizabeth Holtzman introduces the text of the American Bar Association's resolution and recommendation concerning the revision of rape laws to the House of Representatives in support of the Rape Victims Privacy Act. 94th Cong., 2d sess. *Congressional Record.* Vol. 122, pt. 6. Daily ed. (23 March), H7691–93.

U.S. Congress. Senate. Committee on the Judiciary. 1993. *The response to rape: Detours on the road to equal justice.* 103rd Cong., 1st sess. Committee print 147.

U.S. Department of Health, Education, and Welfare. 1976. Rape prevention center established at NIMH. *Public Health Reports* 91, no. 4 (July/August): 385.

U.S. Department of Justice. Law Enforcement Assistance Administration. 1969. *First annual report of the Law Enforcement Assistance Administration.* Washington: U.S. Government Printing Office.

U.S. Department of Justice. 1972. *Attorney general's first annual report: Federal law enforcement and criminal justice assistance activities.* Washington: U.S. Department of Justice.

U.S. Department of Justice. Federal Bureau of Investigation. 1973. *Uniform Crime Reports.* Washington: U.S. Government Printing Office.

U.S. Department of Justice. Law Enforcement Assistance Administration. 1974a. *Sixth annual report of the Law Enforcement Assistance Administration.* Washington: U.S. Government Printing Office.

U.S. Department of Justice. Law Enforcement Assistance Administration. National Institute for Law Enforcement and Criminal Justice. 1974b. *First annual report of the National Institute for Law Enforcement and Criminal Justice.* Washington: U.S. Government Printing Office.

U.S. Department of Justice. Law Enforcement Assistance Administration. National Institute for Law Enforcement and Criminal Justice. 1975. *National Institute for Law Enforcement and Criminal Justice annual report, fiscal year 1975.* Washington: U.S. Government Printing Office.

U.S. Department of Justice. Law Enforcement Assistance Administration. National Institute for Law Enforcement and Criminal Justice. 1976. *National Institute for Law Enforcement and Criminal Justice annual report, fiscal year 1976.* Washington: U.S. Government Printing Office.

U.S. Department of Justice. Law Enforcement Assistance Administration. National Institute for Law Enforcement and Criminal Justice. 1977. *National Institute for Law Enforcement and Criminal Justice annual report, fiscal year 1977.* Washington: U.S. Government Printing Office.

U.S. Department of Justice. 1980. Crisis center increased rape convictions 90 percent. *Justice Assistance News,* August, 6–7.

U.S. Department of Justice. 1981. *First annual report of the Justice System Improvement Act Agencies: Bureau of Justice Statistics, Law Enforcement Assistance Administration, National Institute of Justice, Office of Justice Assistance, Research, and Statistics.* Washington: U.S. Government Printing Office.

U.S. Department of Justice. Bureau of Justice Statistics. 1994a. *Technical background on the redesigned National Crime Victimization Survey.* Washington: U.S. Department of Justice.

U.S. Department of Justice. Bureau of Justice Statistics. 1994b. *Bureau of Justice Statistics fact sheet: National Crime Victimization Survey redesign.* Washington: U.S. Department of Justice.

Victims of Crime Act. *Statutes at large.* 1984. Vol. 98, sec. 1401, 2170–75.

Violence Against Women Act. *Statutes at large.* 1994. Vol. 108, 1902–55.

Manuscript Collections

Atlanta Lesbian Feminist Alliance (ALFA) Records. Rare Book, Manuscript, and Special Collections Library, Duke University.

Gene Bishop Papers. Schlesinger Library, Radcliffe College.

Wini Breines Papers. Schlesinger Library, Radcliffe College.

Susan Brownmiller Papers, New York City. Private collection.

Lucy Candib Papers. Schlesinger Library, Radcliffe College.

Nikki Craft Papers. Rancho Cordova, California. Private collection.

Betty Friedan Papers. Schlesinger Library, Radcliffe College.

Kitty Genovese Women's Project Papers. Dallas, Tex. Private collection of Nikki Craft.

Elizabeth Holtzman Papers. Schlesinger Library, Radcliffe College.

National Organization for Women (NOW) Records. Schlesinger Library, Radcliffe College.

New York Women Against Rape (NYWAR) Records. Schlesinger Library, Radcliffe College.

Mary Orvan Papers. Schlesinger Library, Radcliffe College.

Nancy Osterud Papers. Schlesinger Library, Radcliffe College.

Elizabethann O'Sullivan Papers. D.C. Rape Crisis Center Papers. Raleigh, North Carolina. Private collection.

Annie Popkin Papers. Schlesinger Library, Radcliffe College.

Pennsylvania Coalition Against Rape Records. Enola, Penn.

Redstockings Women's Liberation Archive. New York City.

Women's Anti-Rape Group Records. Schlesinger Library, Radcliffe College.

Interviews

Libby Bouvier, 17 June 1996
Susan Brownmiller, 2 September 1996

Mary Beth Carter, 13 January 1997
Gloria Dialectic, 1 March 1997
Beverly Harris Elliott, 2 August 1996
Pat Groot, 20 August 1996
Laurie McLaughlin, 13 and 16 January 1997
Elizabethann O'Sullivan, 8 June 1995 and 15 March 1996
Loretta Ross, 16 October 1995
Susan Schechter, 20 August 1996
Denise Snyder, 9 August 1995
Nkenge Toure, 9 January 1997
Betsy Warrior, 26 and 28 June 1996

Table of Cases

Brown v. Board of Education, 347 U.S. 483 (1954)
Loving v. Virginia, 388 U.S. 1 (1967)
Roe v. Wade, 410 U.S. 113 (1973)
Cox Broadcasting Corporation v. Cohn, 420 U.S. 469 (1975)
Coker v. Georgia, 433 U.S. 584 (1977)
American Booksellers Ass'n v. Hudnut, 771 F.2d 323 (1985)
Meritor Savings Bank v. Vinson, 477 U.S. 57 (1986)
Michael M. v. Superior Court, 450 U.S. 464 (1981)
Florida Star v. B.J.F., 491 U.S. 524 (1989)
Michigan v. Lucas, 500 U.S. 145 (1991)
United States v. Lanier, 520 U.S. 259 (1997)

Index

Rape and Sexual Assault Center (Edwardsville, Ill.), 86

rape consciousness, 4, 144; and consciousness-raising sessions, 50–54; defined, 8; historical roots of, 19–26; in the women's movement, 3–4, 11, 32–33, 35, 57, 114, 126, 229n1

rape crisis centers, 4, 16, 49, 52, 66, 73–80; in 1980s, 153; as backbone of anti-rape movement, 73, 87–88, 195, 196; contradictory position of, 74, 82–83; co-optation of, 73, 82, 232n13; criticism of, 7–8; distrust of establishment by, 83, 84, 109; early, 81; early views of rape held by, 79, 234n9; founding of first, 74–75, 234n6; funding for, 147–48, 168–69, 172; policy toward rape reporting of, 83, 84–85; and rape law reform, 102–9; at Rutgers University, 48; service-provision model of, 102–3; treatment of victims by, 78, 84, 102, 107, 108–9, 229–30n7

rape culture: defined, 9

Rape: How to Avoid It and What to Do About It if You Can't (Csida and Csida), 47

rape law: common-law approach to, 88–89, 90; and rape crisis centers, 102–9; rape defined under, 88, 89, 98, 99, 100, 129, 142, 235n15; reform of, 56–57, 66, 88–102, 129, 142, 169, 232–33n17; and treatment of victims, 90, 92, 93, 99, 100, 102

rape policy, 112, 132, 197–98; analysis of, 196–97; budgetary, 147–49; and crime, 193, 199; evolution of issues, 113, 235–36n3; at federal level, 142, 143–47, 168–75; formation of, 138–39; local developments in, 139–42; measuring effectiveness of, 149–51; organizations opposing, 188–90

Rape Prevention and Control Act, 123, 125, 143, 211–13

rape shield, 106, 145, 160, 161, 172, 182; defined, 96; in Michigan, 96, 101, 174–75

rape testimonials, 52–53, 64

"Rape: The All-American Crime" (Griffin), 46, 58

Rape: The First Sourcebook for Women (Connell and Wilson), 47, 50, 56

rape trials, 127–29, 146, 157, 237n12, 238n3, 238n6; celebrity, 129, 146, 157, 158–61, 238–39n8; involving date rape, 154; involving marital rape, 155, 238n1; sensationalized, 127–29, 157–62, 238n3

Rape Victims Privacy Act, 144–45

rapists. *See* perpetrators

Rat, 43, 55

Reagan, Ronald, 153, 169; administration of, 149

Redstockings, 13, 56

Rehnquist, William, 170

Reinharz, Shulamit, 13

Reno, Janet, 172

Reuss, Pat, 170

Revolution, 20, 230n2

Richards, Ann, 193

Rideout, Greta, 155, 238n3

Rideout, John, 155, 238n1, 238n3

Riger, Stephanie, 6

Robins, Joan, 131

Rockefeller, Nelson, 236n7

Rodino, Peter, 126

Roe v. Wade, 36–37, 92, 157, 237n18

Rohypnol Act. *See* Drug-Induced Rape Prevention and Control Act

Roiphe, Katie: and anti-rape backlash, 7, 183, 185–86, 187, 188, 190; criticism of, 188, 190, 191

Ross, Loretta, 40–41, 78–79, 120–21, 200

Russell, Diana, 5, 7, 149; and pornography, 178, 181; rape studied by, 5, 52, 229n4

Russell, Pat, 139

Ryan, Barbara, 27

sadomasochism, 176, 177, 178–79

Saint Paul, Minn., 141

San Francisco Women Against Rape (SFWAR), 61, 68, 84, 107

Sanday, Peggy Reeves, 149, 183, 190

Santa Cruz Women Against Rape (SCWAR), 85, 233n3

Sarachild, Kathie, 37, 51

Saunders, Karen, 85

Sawyer, Marion, 33